Latin American
Spanish
phrase book

120th
anniversary
Berlitz

Berlitz Publishing Company, Inc.

Princeton   Mexico City   Dublin   Eschborn   Singapore

Contents

Pronunciation

This section is designed to make you familiar with the sounds of Spanish using our simplified phonetic transcription. You'll find the pronunciation of the Spanish letters and sounds explained below, together with their "imitated" equivalents. This system is used throughout the phrase book: simply read the pronunciation as if it were English, noting any special rules below.

The Spanish language

There are almost 350 million speakers of Spanish worldwide – it is the third most widely spoken language after Chinese and English.

These are the countries where you can expect to hear Spanish spoken (figures are approximate):

México Mexico
Spanish is spoken by most of the 98 m. population. Other languages: 6 m. speak Indian languages, esp. *Nahuatl* (1.5 m.), *Maya* (1 m.) in Yucatán.

América del Sur South America
Spanish is spoken by the great majority in **Argentina** (34 m.); **Bolivia** (less than half the 7.5 m. population), other languages: *Quechua* (2 m.), *Aymara* (1.5 m.); **Colombia** (35 m.), other: *Arawak*, *Carib*; **Ecuador** (11 m.), other: *Quechua* (0.5 m.); **Paraguay** – three quarters the 5.5 m. population, other: *Guarani* (3 m.); **Peru** (24 m.), other: *Quechua* (5 m.), *Aymara* (0.5 m.); **Uruguay** (3.5 m.); **Venezuela** (22 m.), other: *Arawak*, *Carib*.

América Central Central America
Spanish is spoken in **Costa Rica** (3.5 m.); **Cuba** (11 m.); **Dominican Republic** (8 m.); **Puerto Rico** (4 m.); **El Salvador** (6 m.); **Guatemala** (10 m.), other: *Quiché* (1 m.), *Cakchiquel* (0.5 m.); **Honduras** (5.5 m.), other: *Lenca*, *Carib*; **Nicaragua** (4 m.); **Panama** (3 m.).

Estados Unidos United States
Spanish is spoken by approx. 18 m. people, especially in Texas, New Mexico, Arizona, California, southern Florida, and New York City.

España Spain
Spanish is spoken by almost the entire population (40 m.). Other languages: *Catalan* in northeastern Spain (6 m.), *Galician* – a dialect of Portuguese – in northwestern Spain (3 m.) and *Basque* (almost 1 m.).

África Africa
Spanish is the official language of **Equatorial Guinea** (4.5 m.), other: *Fang*. Spanish is also spoken in the Spanish zone of **Morocco**.

The Spanish alphabet is the same as English, with the addition of the tilde on the letter ñ. The acute accent (´) indicates stress, not a change in sound.

Some Spanish words have been incorporated into English, for example **bonanza, canyon, patio, plaza, siesta**.

Until recently in Spanish, **ch** and **ll** were treated as separate letters, alphabetically ordered after **c** and **l** respectively. Look out for this when looking up old telephone directories or dictionaries.

There are some differences in vocabulary and pronunciation between the Spanish spoken in Spain and that in the Americas – although each is easily understood by the other. The *Berlitz Latin-American Spanish Phrase Book and Dictionary* is specifically geared to travelers in Spanish-speaking Americas.

Consonants

Letter	Approximate pronunciation	Symbol	Example	Pronunciation
ch, f, k, l, m, n, p, t, w, y	as in English			
b	1. as in English	*b*	**bueno**	*bweno*
	2. between vowels as in English, but softer	*b*	**bebida**	*bebeeda*
c	1. before **e** and **i**, like s in sit	*s*	**centro**	*sentro*
	2. otherwise like *k* in kit	*k*	**como**	*komo*
ch	as in English	*ch*	**mucho**	*moocho*
d	1. as in English *dog*, but less decisive	*d*	**donde**	*dondeh*
	2. at the end of a word, like *th* in *this*	*th*	**usted**	*oosteth*
g	1. before **e** and **i**, like *ch* in Scottish lo*ch* (except in Caribbean and Central America where pronounced like *h* in *h*at)	*kh*	**urgente**	*oorkhenteh*
	2. otherwise, like *g* in get	*g*	**ninguno**	*neengoono*
h	always silent		**hombre**	*ombreh*
j	like *ch* in Scottish lo*ch*	*kh*	**bajo**	*bakho*
ll	like *lli* in mi*lli*on; in some parts like *y* in yet or *s* in pleasure	*l-y*	**lleno**	*l-yeno*
ñ	like *ni* in o*ni*on	*ñ*	**señor**	*señor*
qu	like *k* in kick	*k*	**quince**	*keenseh*

7

Consonants (cont.)

r	more strongly trilled (like a Scottish *r*), especially at the beginning of a word	r	**río**	_ree_o
rr	strongly trilled	rr	**arriba**	ar_ree_ba
s	like *s* in sit often with a slight lisp	s	**vista**	_bee_sta
v	like *b* in bad, but softer	b	**viejo**	bee_ye_kho
x	1. usually like *x* in taxi	ks	**examen**	ek_sa_men
	2. before a consonant, like *s* in sit	s	**extraño**	es_tra_ño
	3. in several Indian words in Mexico, Central and South America, like *ch* in Scottish lo*ch*	kh	**México**	me_khee_ko
z	like *s* in sit	s	**zumo**	_soo_mo

Vowels

Letter	Approximate pronunciation	Symbol	Example	Pronunciation
a	in length, between *a* in English p*a*t, and *a* in English b*a*r	a	**gracias**	_gra_seeas
e	1. like *e* in g*e*t	e	**puedo**	_pwe_do
	2. in a syllable ending in a vowel like *e* in th*e*y	eh	**me**	meh
i	1. like *ee* in f*ee*t	ee	**sí**	see
	2. shorter, like *i* in sit		**gracias**	_gra_seeas
o	like *o* in g*o*t	o	**dos**	dos
u	1. like *oo* in f*oo*d	oo	**una**	_oo_na
	2. like *w* in well	w	**cuanto**	_kwan_to
	3. silent after **g** in words like **guerra**, except where marked **ü** as in antig**ü**edad			
y	only a vowel when alone or at the end of a word, like *ee* in f*ee*t	ee	**y**	ee

Note: to aid pronunciation the phonetic transcription uses *y* where applicable between groups of vowels to indicate the sound value of *y* in *yes*.

Stress

Stress has been indicated in the phonetic transcription: <u>underlined</u> letters should be pronounced with more stress (i.e. louder) than the others.

In words ending with a vowel, **-n** or **-s**, the next to last syllable is stressed, e.g. **mañana** (*ma<u>ña</u>na*); in words ending in a consonant, the last syllable is stressed, e.g. **señor** (*se<u>ñor</u>*); the acute accent (´) is used in Spanish to indicate that a syllable is stressed, e.g. **río** (*<u>ree</u>o*).

Some Spanish words have more than one meaning; the accent mark is employed to distinguish between them, e.g.: **él** (he) and **el** (the); **sí** (yes) and **si** (if); **tú** (you) and **tu** (your).

Pronunciation of the Spanish alphabet

A	*ah*	**Ñ**	*<u>en</u>yeh*
B	*beh*	**O**	*oh*
C	*seh*	**P**	*peh*
D	*deh*	**Q**	*koo*
E	*eh*	**R**	*<u>erreh</u>*
F	*<u>ehf</u>eh*	**S**	*<u>ehs</u>eh*
G	*kheh*	**T**	*teh*
H	*<u>ach</u>eh*	**U**	*oo*
I	*ee*	**V**	*beh*
J	*<u>khota</u>*	**W**	*<u>dobleh</u> beh*
K	*ka*	**X**	*<u>ek</u>ees*
L	*<u>ehl</u>eh*	**Y**	*ee gree<u>yeg</u>a*
M	*<u>em</u>eh*	**Z**	*<u>set</u>a*
N	*<u>aynn</u>eh*		

9

Basic Expressions

ESSENTIAL

Yes./No.	**Sí.** *see* / **No.** *no*
Okay.	**De acuerdo [Bueno].** *deh akwerdo [bweno]*
Please.	**Por favor.** *por fabor*
Thank you (very much).	**(Muchas) gracias.** *(moochas) graseeas*

Greetings/Apologies Saludos y disculpas

Hello./Hi!	**Hola./¡Qué tal!** *ola/keh tal*
Good morning./Good afternoon.	**Buenos días./Buenas tardes.** *bwenos deeyas/bwenas tardes*
Good evening.	**Buenas noches.** *bwenas noches*
Good night.	**Buenas noches. [Hasta mañana.]** *bwenas noches [asta mañana]*
Good-bye.	**Adiós.** *adeeyos*
Excuse me! (getting attention)	**¡Disculpe!** *deeskoolpeh*
Excuse me!/Sorry!	**¡Disculpe!/¡Perdón!** *deeskoolpeh/Perdon*
It was an accident.	**Fue un accidente.** *fweh oon akseedenteh*
Don't mention it.	**No fue nada. [No hay de qué.]** *no fweh nada [no eye deh keh]*
Never mind.	**No importa.** *no eemporta*

INTRODUCTIONS ➤ 118

Communication difficulties
Dificultades en la comunicación

Do you speak English?
¿Habla usted inglés?
abla oosteth eengles

Does anyone here
speak English?
¿Hay alguien aquí que hable inglés?
eye algeeyen akeeh keh ableh eengles

I don't speak (much) Spanish.
No hablo (mucho) español.
no ablo (moocho) español

Could you speak more slowly?
¿Podría hablar más despacio, por favor?
podreea ablar mas despaseeyo por fabor

Could you repeat that?
¿Podría repetírmelo, por favor?
podreea repeteermelo por fabor

Pardon?/What was that?
¿Perdón? *perdon*

Could you spell it?
¿Podría deletreármelo?
podreea deletrearmelo

Please write it down.
Escríbalo, por favor. *eskreebalo por fabor*

Can you translate this for me?
¿Puede traducirme esto, por favor?
pwedeh tradooseermeh esto por fabor

What does this/that mean?
**¿Qué significa esto/eso? [¿Qué quiere
decir esto/eso?]**
*keh seegneefeeka esto/eso [keh keeyereh
deseer esto/eso]*

Please point to the phrase
in the book.
Muéstreme la frase en el libro, por favor.
*mwestrameh la fraseh en el leebro
por fabor*

I understand.
Ya entiendo. *ya enteeyendo*

I don't understand.
No entiendo. *no enteeyendo*

Do you understand?
¿Entiende? [¿comprende?]
enteeyendeh [komprendeh]

– Eso cuesta ciento treinta y cinco pesos.
– No entiendo.
– Son ciento treinta y cinco pesos.
– Escríbamelo, por favor...
Ah. "P135" ... Aquí tiene.

11

Questions Preguntas

Questions can be formed in Spanish:

1. By a questioning intonation; often the personal pronoun is left out, both in affirmative sentences and in questions:

Hablo español.	I speak Spanish.
¿Habla español?	Do you speak Spanish?

2. By using a question word (▶12-18) + the inverted order:

¿Cuándo llega el tren?	When does the train arrive?

Where? ¿Dónde?

Where is it?	**¿Dónde está?** _dondeh esta_
Where are you going?	**¿Adónde va usted?** _adondeh ba oosteth_
to the meeting place	**al sitio de reunión** _al seeteeyo deh reooneeyon_
away from me	**lejos de mí** _lekhos deh mee_
downstairs	**abajo** _abakho_
from the U.S.	**de los Estados Unidos** _deh los estados ooneedos_
here (to here)	**aquí** _akee_
in the car	**en el carro** _en el karro_
in Mexico	**en México** _en mekheeko_
inside	**adentro** _adentro_
near the bank	**cerca del banco** _serka del banko_
opposite the market	**enfrente del mercado** _enfrenteh del merkado_
on the right/left	**a la derecha/a la izquierda** _a la derecha/a la eeskeeyerda_
outside the café	**fuera del café/de la cafetería** _fwera del kafeh/deh la kafetereeya_
there (to there)	**allá** _al-ya_
to the hotel	**al hotel** _al otel_
toward Bogota	**en dirección a Bogotá** _en deerekseeyon a Bogotah_
upstairs	**arriba** _arreeba_

When? ¿Cuándo?/ ¿A qué hora?

When does the museum open?	**¿A qué hora se abre el museo?** *a keh ora seh abreh el mooseo*
When does the train arrive?	**¿A qué hora llega el tren?** *a keh ora l-yega el tren*
10 minutes ago	**hace diez minutos** *aseh deeyes meenootos*
after lunch	**después de la comida [el almuerzo]** *despwes deh la komeeda [el almwerso]*
always	**siempre** *seeyempreh*
around midnight	**cerca [alrededor] de la medianoche** *serka [alrededor] deh la medeeyanocheh*
at 7 p.m.	**a las siete de la noche** *a las seeyeteh deh la nocheh*
on weekends	**los fines de semana** *los feenes deh semana*
before Friday	**antes del viernes** *antes del beeyernes*
by tomorrow	**para mañana** *para mañana*
early	**temprano** *temprano*
every week	**todas las semanas** *todas las semanas*
frequently	**frecuentemente** *frekwentementeh*
from 9 a.m. to 6 p.m.	**de nueve de la mañana a seis de la tarde** *deh nwebeh deh la mañana a seys deh la tardeh*
immediately	**inmediatamente** *eenmedeeyatamenteh*
in 20 minutes	**dentro de veinte minutos** *dentro deh beynteh meenootos*
never	**nunca** *noonka*
not yet	**todavía no** *todabeeya no*
now	**ahora** *aora*
often	**a menudo** *a menoodo*
on March 8	**el ocho de marzo** *el ocho deh marso*
on weekdays	**los días de la semana** *los deeyas deh la semana*
sometimes	**algunas veces** *algoonas beses*
soon	**pronto** *pronto*
then	**luego** *lwego*

13

What sort of?   ¿Qué clase de …?

I'd like something …	**Quisiera algo …**	_keeseeyera algo_
It's …	**Es …**	_es_
beautiful/ugly	**hermoso(-a)/feo(-a)**	_ermoso(-a)/feo(-a)_
better/worse	**mejor/peor**	_mekhor/peor_
big/small	**grande/pequeño(-a)**	_grandeh/pekeño(-a)_
cheap/expensive	**barato(-a)/caro(-a)**	_barato(-a)/karo(-a)_
clean/dirty	**limpio(-a)/sucio(-a)**	_leempeeyo(-a)/ sooseeyo(-a)_
dark/light	**oscuro(-a)/claro(-a)**	_oskooro(-a)/klaro(-a)_
delicious/revolting	**delicioso(-a)/asqueroso(-a)**	_deleeseeyoso(-a)/askeroso(-a)_
easy/difficult	**fácil/difícil**	_faseel/deefeeseel_
empty/full	**desocupado(-a)/lleno(-a)**	_desokoopado(-a)/l-yeno(-a)_
good/bad	**bueno(-a)/malo(-a)**	_bweno(-a)/malo(-a)_
heavy/light	**pesado(-a)/liviano(-a)**	_pesado(-a)/leebeeyano(-a)_
hot/warm/cold	**muy caliente/caliente/frío(-a)**	_mwee kaleeyenteh/kaleeyenteh/ freeyo(-a)_
modern/old-fashioned	**moderno(-a)/pasado(-a) de moda**	_moderno(-a)/pasado(-a) deh moda_
narrow/wide	**angosto(-a)/ancho(-a)**	_angosto(-a)/ancho(-a)_
old/new	**viejo(-a)/nuevo(-a)**	_beeyekho(-a)/nwebo(-a)_
open/shut	**abierto(-a)/cerrado(-a)**	_abeeyerto(-a)/serado(-a)_
pleasant, nice/unpleasant	**agradable/desagradable**	_agradableh/desagradableh_
quick/slow	**rápido(-a)/lento(-a)**	_rapeedo(-a)/lento(-a)_
quiet/noisy	**tranquilo(-a)/ruidoso(-a)**	_trankeelo(-a)/rooeedoso(-a)_
right/wrong	**correcto(-a)/incorrecto(-a)**	_korekto(-a)/eenkorekto(-a)_
tall/short	**alto(-a)/bajo(-a)**	_alto(-a)/bakho(-a)_
vacant/occupied	**disponible [libre]/ocupado(-a)**	_deesponeebleh [leebreh]/okoopado(-a)_

GRAMMAR

Nouns in Spanish are either masculine or feminine and the adjectival endings change accordingly. See page 169 for more explanation.

How much/Many?   ¿Cuánto(s)?

How much is that?	**¿Cuánto cuesta eso?/¿Cuánto es?** *kwanto kwesta eso/kwanto es*
How many are there?	**¿Cuántos hay?** *kwantos eye*
1/2/3	**uno/dos/tres** *oono/dos/tres*
4/5	**cuatro/cinco** *kwatro/seenko*
none	**ninguno(-a)** *neengoono(-a)*
about 100 pesos	**alrededor de cien pesos** *alrededor deh seeyen pesos*
a little	**un poquito** *oon pokeeto*
a lot of traffic	**mucho tráfico** *moocho trafeeko*
enough	**suficiente** *soofeeseeyenteh*
few/a few of them	**poco(-a)/unos(-as) pocos(-as)** *poko(-a)/oonos(-as) pokos(-as)*
more than that	**más** *mas*
less than that	**menos** *menos*
much more	**mucho más** *moocho mas*
nothing else	**nada más** *nada mas*
too much	**demasiado(-a)** *demaseeyado(-a)*

Why?   ¿Por qué?

Why is that?	**Y eso, ¿por qué?** *ee eso por keh*
Why not?	**¿Por qué no?** *por keh no*
because of the weather	**por el clima** *por el kleema*
because I'm in a hurry	**porque tengo prisa [estoy de prisa]** *porkeh tengo preesa [estoy deh preesa]*
I don't know why.	**Yo no sé por qué.** *yo no seh por keh*

NUMBERS ➤ 216

Who?/Which? ¿Quién?/¿Cuál?

Who's there?	**¿Quién es?** *keeyen es*
It's me!	**¡Soy yo!** *soy yo*
It's us!	**¡Somos nosotros!** *somos nosotros*
someone	**alguien** *algeeyen*
no one	**nadie** *nadeeyeh*
Which one do you want?	**¿Cuál desea usted?** [**¿Cuál quiere?**] *kwal deseya oosteth* [*kwal keeyereh*]
one like that	**uno(-a) como ese(-a)** *oono(-a) komo eseh(-a)*
that one/this one	**ése(-a)/éste(-a)** *ese(-a)/este(-a)*
not that one	**ése(-a) no** *ese(-a) no*
something	**algo** *algo*
nothing	**nada** *nada*
none	**ninguno(-a)** *neengoono(-a)*

Whose? ¿De quién es eso?

Whose is that?	**¿De quién es eso?** *Deh keeyen es eso*
It's ...	**Es ...** *es*
mine/ours	**mío/nuestro** *meeyo/nwestro*
yours (sing/fam/pl)	**suyo/tuyo/de ustedes** *sooyo/tooyo/deh oostedes*
his/hers/theirs	**de él/de ella/de ellos(-as)** *deh el/deh el-ya /deh el-yos(-as)*
It's ... turn.	**Es ... turno.** *es ... toorno*
my/our/your (sing)	**mi/nuestro/su** *mee/nwestro/soo*
his/her/your (pl)/their	**su** *soo*

GRAMMAR

Possessive pronouns	*singular*	*plural*
mine	**mío(-a)**	**míos(-as)**
yours (fam. sing.)	**tuyo(-a)**	**tuyos(-as)**
yours (polite form)	**suyo(-a)**	**suyos(-as)**
his/hers/its	**suyo(-a)**	**suyos(-as)**
ours	**nuestro(-a)**	**nuestros(-as)**
yours (fam. plur.)	**vuestro(-as)**	**vuestros(-as)**
theirs	**suyo(-a)**	**suyos(-as)**

How? ¿Cómo?

How would you like to pay?	**¿Cómo desea pagar?** *komo deseea pagar*
How are you getting here?	**¿En qué se viene?** *en keh seh beeyeneh*
by car	**en carro** *en karro*
by credit card	**con tarjeta de crédito** *kon tarkheta deh kretheeto*
by chance	**por casualidad** *por kasualeedath*
equally	**por partes iguales** *por partes eegwales*
extremely	**demasiado [extremadamente]** *demaseeyado [ekstremadamenteh]*
on foot	**a pie** *a peeyeh*
quickly	**rápidamente** *rapeedamenteh*
slowly	**lentamente** *lentamenteh*
too fast	**demasiado rápido(-a)** *demaseeyado rapeedo(-a)*
totally	**totalmente** *totalmenteh*
very	**muy** *mwee*
with a friend	**con un(a) amigo(-a)** *kon oon(a) ameego(-a)*
without a passport	**sin pasaporte** *seen pasaporteh*

Is it ...?/Are there ...? ¿Está ...?/¿Hay...?

Is it ...?	**¿Está ...?** *esta*
Is it free?	**¿Esto es gratis?** *esto es gratees*
It isn't ready.	**Esto no está listo.** *esto no esta leesto*
Is there ...?	**¿Hay ...?** *eye*
Are there ...?	**¿Hay ...?** *eye*
Are there any buses into town?	**¿Hay buses a la ciudad?** *eye booses a la seeoodath*
Here it is/they are.	**Aquí está/están.** *akee esta/estan*
There it is/they are.	**Allá está/están.** *al-ya esta/estan*

17

Can/May? Poder

Can I have …?	**¿Me puede traer …?** _meh pwedeh trayer_
Can we have …?	**¿Nos puede traer …?** _nos pwedeh trayer_
Can you tell me?	**¿Puede decirme?** _pwedeh deseermeh_
Can you help me?	**¿Puede ayudarme?** _pwedeh ayoodarmeh_
Can I help you?	**¿Puedo ayudarlo?** _pwedo ayoodarlo_
Can you direct me to …?	**¿Puede decirme cómo llegar a …?** _pwedeh deseermeh komo l-yegar a_

What do you want? ¿Qué desea usted?

I'd like …	**Quisiera …** _keeseeyera_
Could I have …?	**¿Podría traerme …?** _podreeya trayermeh_
We'd like …	**Queremos …** _keremos_
Give me …	**Tráigame …** _traeegameh_
I'm looking for …	**Estoy buscando …** _estoy booskando_
I need to …	**Necesito …** _neseseeto_
go …	**ir …** _eer_
find …	**encontrar …** _enkontrar_
see …	**ver …** _behr_
speak to …	**hablar con …** _ablar kon_

GRAMMAR

In Spanish, there are three forms for "you" (taking different verb forms):
tú (singular) and **vosotros** (plural) are used when talking to
relatives, close friends and children (and between young people);
usted (singular) and **ustedes** (plural) – often abbreviated to
Vd./**Vds**. – are used in all other cases. If in doubt; use **usted**/**ustedes**.

– Disculpe.
– ¿Sí?
– ¿Puedo?
– Sí, por supuesto.
– Gracias.
– De nada.

Other useful words
Otras palabras útiles

fortunately	**afortunadamente** *afortoonadamenteh*
hopefully	**¡ojalá!** *okhala*
of course	**por supuesto [claro que sí]** *por soopwesto [klaro keh see]*
perhaps/possibly	**tal vez/es posible** *tal bes/es poseebleh*
probably	**probablemente** *probablementeh*
unfortunately	**desafortunadamente** *desafortoonadamenteh*

Exclamations   Exclamaciones

At last!	**¡Por fin!** *por feen*
Carry on.	**Continúa. [Adelante.]** *konteenooa [athelanteh]*
Damn!	**¡Maldición! [¡Maldita sea!]** *maldeeseeyon [maldeeta seh-a]*
Good God!	**¡Santo Dios!** *santo deeyos*
I don't mind.	**Me da igual. [No hay cuidado.]** *meh da eegwal [no eye kweedado]*
No way!	**¡Ni hablar! [¡De ninguna manera!]** *nee ablar [deh neengoona manera]*
Really?	**¿De verdad? [¿De veras?]** *de berdath [deh beras]*
Rubbish.	**Mentiras. [Tonterías.]** *menteeras [tontereeas]*
That's enough.	**Es suficiente.** *es soofeeseeyenteh*
That's true.	**Es cierto.** *es seeyerto*
I can't believe it!	**¡No te creo! [¡No lo puedo creer!]** *no teh kreo [no lo pwedo kreyer]*
How are things?	**¿Qué tal?** *keh tal*
Fine, thank you.	**Bien, gracias.** *beeyen graseeyas*
great/brilliant	**excelente/de maravilla** *exelenteh/deh marabeel-ya*
fine/not bad/okay	**bien** *beeyen*
not good	**no muy bien** *no mwee beeyen*
terrible	**terrible** *terreebleh*

Early reservation and confirmation are essential in most major tourist centers, especially during high season or special events.

Most ports of entry and other larger towns have a tourist information office, which should be able to help if you're having difficulty finding a room.

Prices charged are generally per room; a single (**sencillo**) is therefore cheaper than a large family room with several beds. Rooms with air conditioning generally cost more, though a ceiling fan (**ventilador**) is often sufficient.

Hotel *otel*
Prices and facilities vary according to the six categories: **Gran Turismo**, five, four, three, two or one stars.

Motel *motel*
Local automobile associations (e.g. **AMA** in Mexico) have lists of recommended motels.

Apartamento amueblado/sin amueblar
apartamento amweblado/seen amweblar
Furnished/Unfurnished apartment (flat); consult a real estate agent.

Casa de huéspedes *kassa deh wespedes*
Guest house, usually for stays of several days or even months. The choice is between **pensión completa** (full board) or **media pensión** (bed and breakfast plus one other meal). Generally provides a friendly, relaxed atmosphere.

Hospedajes *ospedakhes*
A large family home that has an extra bedroom rented out; provides inexpensive accommodations, shared bathroom and local hospitality.

Pensión *penseeyon*
The equivalent of a boardinghouse, often offering **pensión completa** or **media pensión**. May have permanent lodgers.

Residencial *reseedenseeal*
Modest short-term budget accommodations. Facilities are usually shared with other guests.

Albergue juvenil *albergeh deh khoobeneel*
Youth hostels can generally be found in most major towns in Central and
    South America.

Reservations/Booking Reservaciones

In advance Por adelantado

Can you recommend a
hotel in …?

**¿Puede recomendarme un
hotel en …?** _pwedeh
rekomen<u>dar</u>meh oon o<u>tel</u> en

Is it near the center/
centre of town?

¿Está cerca del centro?
esta <u>ser</u>ka del <u>sen</u>tro

How much is it per night?

¿Cuál es el precio por noche?
kwal es el <u>pre</u>seeyo por <u>no</u>cheh

Is there anything cheaper?

¿Hay algo más barato?
eye <u>al</u>go mas ba<u>ra</u>to

Could you book me a
room there, please?

**¿Podría reservarme una habitación
en ese hotel, por favor?**
po<u>dree</u>a reser<u>bar</u>meh <u>oo</u>na abeetasee<u>yon</u>
en <u>e</u>seh o<u>tel</u> por fa<u>bor</u>

How do I get there?

¿Cómo se llega allá? <u>ko</u>mo seh <u>l-ye</u>ga al-ya

At the hotel En el hotel

Do you have any vacancies?

¿Tiene usted habitaciones disponibles?
tee<u>ye</u>neh oos<u>teth</u> abeetasee<u>yo</u>nes
dees<u>po</u>nee<u>bles</u>

I'm sorry, we're full.

Lo siento. Todo está ocupado [lleno].
lo see<u>yen</u>to <u>to</u>do esta okoo<u>pa</u>do [<u>l-ye</u>no]

Is there another hotel nearby?

¿Hay algún otro hotel por aquí?
eye al<u>goon</u> <u>o</u>tro o<u>tel</u> por a<u>kee</u>

I'd like a single/double room.

Quisiera una habitación sencilla/doble.
keesee<u>ye</u>ra <u>oo</u>na abeetasee<u>yon</u> sen<u>seel</u>-
yah/<u>do</u>bleh

I'd like a room with …

Quisiera una habitación con …
keesee<u>ye</u>ra <u>oo</u>na abeetasee<u>yon</u> kon

a double bed/twin beds

cama matrimonial [doble]/dos camas
<u>ka</u>ma matreemonee<u>al</u> [<u>do</u>bleh]/dos <u>ka</u>mas

a bath/shower

baño/ducha <u>ba</u>ño/<u>doo</u>cha

– ¿Tiene habitaciones [cuartos] disponibles?
Quisiera una habitación doble.
– Lo siento. Todo está ocupado [lleno].
– ¡Ah! ¿Hay algún otro hotel por aquí?
– Sí. El Hotel Plaza está por aquí.

Reception/Registration
Recepción/Registro

I have a reservation.	**Tengo una habitación reservada.** *tengo oona abeetaseeyon reserbada*
My name is …	**Me llamo…** *meh l-yamo*
We've reserved a double and a single room.	**Hemos reservado una habitación doble [cuarto doble] y una sencilla.** *emos reserbado oona abeetaseeyon dobleh [kwarto dobleh] ee oona senseel-ya*
I confirmed my reservation by mail.	**Confirmé mi reservación por escrito.** *konfeermeh mee reserbaseeyon por eskreeto*
Could we have adjoining rooms?	**¿Podríamos tener habitaciones contiguas [cuartos contiguos]?** *podreeamos tener abeetaseeyones konteegwas [kwartos konteegwos]*

Amenities and facilities Comodidades e instalaciones

Is there … in the room?	**¿Hay … en la habitación [el cuarto]?** *eye … en la abeetaseeyon [el kwarto]*
air conditioning	**aire acondicionado** *ayreh akondeeseeyonado*
TV/telephone	**televisión/teléfono** *telebeeseeyon/telefono*
Does the hotel have (a) …?	**¿El hotel tiene …?** *el otel teeyeneh*
satellite TV	**televisión satélite** *telebeeseeyon sateleeteh*
laundry service	**servicio de lavandería** *serbeeseeyo deh labandereea*
solarium	**solario** *solareeo*
swimming pool	**piscina** *peeseena*
Could you put … in the room?	**¿Podría poner … en la habitación [el cuarto]?** *podreea poner … en la abeetaseeyon [el kwarto]*
an extra bed	**una cama adicional** *oona kama adeeseeonal*
a crib/child's cot	**una cuna para bebé** *oona koona para bebeh*
Do you have facilities for children/the disabled?	**¿Hay servicios especiales para niños/personas incapacitadas?** *eye serbeeseeyos espeseeyales para neeños/personas eenkapaseetadas*

How long? ¿Cuánto tiempo?

We'll be staying …	**Pensamos quedarnos …** *pensamos kedarnos*
overnight only	**solamente esta noche** *solamenteh esta nocheh*
a few days	**unos pocos días** *oonos pokos deeas*
a week (at least)	**(por lo menos) una semana** *(por lo menos) oona semana*
I'd like to stay an extra night.	**Quisiera quedarme una noche más.** *keeseeyera kedarmeh oona nocheh mas*
What does this mean?	**¿Qué quiere decir esto?** *keh keeyereh deseer esto*

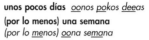

– Buenas tardes. Mi nombre es John Newton.
– Ah, buenas tardes, señor Newton.
– Quisiera quedarme dos noches.
– No hay problema. Firme aquí, por favor.

¿Su pasaporte, por favor?	May I see your passport, please?
Llene esta hoja de registro, por favor.	Please fill in this registration form.
¿Cuál es el número de placas de su carro?	What is your car's license plate/ registration number?

HABITACIÓN P…	room only … pesos
DESAYUNO INCLUIDO	breakfast included
SERVICIO DE RESTAURANTE	meals available
NOMBRE/APELLIDO	first-name/surname
DOMICILIO/CALLE/NÚMERO	home address/ street/number
NACIONALIDAD/PROFESIÓN	nationality/profession
FECHA/LUGAR DE NACIMIENTO	date/place of birth
PROCEDENCIA/DESTINO	coming from/going to
NÚMERO DE PASAPORTE	passport number
NÚMERO DE PLACAS	car license plate/ registration number
LUGAR/FECHA	place/date
FIRMA	signature

Price Precio

How much is it …?	**¿Cuánto cuesta …?** *kwanto kwesta*
per night/week	**la noche/la semana** *la noche/la semana*
for bed and breakfast	**la noche con desayuno incluido** *la noche kon desayoono eenklooeedo*
excluding meals	**la noche sin las comidas** *la noche seen las komeedas*
for full board (American Plan{A.P.})	**la pensión completa** *la penseeyon kompleta*
for half board (Modified American Plan {M.A.P.})	**la media pensión** *la medeea penseeyon*
Does the price include …?	**¿El precio incluye …?** *el preseeo eenklooyeh*
breakfast	**el desayuno** *el desayoono*
VAT	**el IVA** *el eeba*
Do I have to leave a deposit?	**¿Tengo que dejar un depósito?** *tengo keh dekhar oon deposeeto*
Is there a discount for children?	**¿Hay algún descuento especial para niños?** *eye algoon deskwento espeseeyal para neeños*

Decision Decisión

May I see the room?	**¿Puedo ver la habitación [el cuarto]?** *pwedo ber la abeetaseeyon [el kwarto]*
That's fine. I'll take it.	**Está bien. La tomo.** *esta beeyen. la tomo*
It's too …	**Es demasiado …** *es demaseeyado*
dark/small	**oscura/pequeña** *oskoora/pekeña*
noisy	**ruidosa** *rooeedosa*
Do you have anything …?	**¿Tiene algo …?** *teeyeneh algo*
bigger/cheaper	**más grande/más barato** *mas grandeh/mas barato*
quieter/warmer	**más tranquilo/más caliente** *mas trankeelo/mas kaleeyenteh*
No, I won't take it.	**No. No la tomo.** *no. no la tomo*

Problems Problemas

The … doesn't work.	**… no funciona.** *… no foonseeona*
air conditioning	**El aire acondicionado** *el ayreh akondeeseeonado*
fan	**El ventilador** *el benteelador*
heating	**La calefacción** *la kalefakseeyon*
light	**La luz** *la loos*
I can't turn the heat on/off.	**No puedo encender/apagar la calefacción.** *no pwedo ensender/apagar la kalefakseeyon*
There is no hot water/ toilet paper.	**No hay agua caliente/papel higiénico.** *no eye agwa kaleeyenteh/papel eekheeyeneeko*
The faucet/tap is dripping.	**El grifo [La llave] está goteando.** *el greefo [la l-yabeh] esta goteando*
The sink/toilet is blocked.	**El lavamanos/baño está tapado.** *el labamanos/baño esta tapado*
The window/door is jammed.	**La ventana/puerta está atascada.** *la bentana/pwerta esta ataskada.*
My room has not been made up.	**No han ordenado mi cuarto.** *no an ordenado mee kwarto*
The … is broken.	**… está roto(-a).** *… esta roto(-a)*
blind	**La persiana** *la perseeana*
lock	**La cerradura** *la seradoora*
There are insects in our room.	**Hay insectos en nuestra habitación.** *eye eensektos en nwestra abeetaseeyon*

Action ¡Hay que hacer algo!

Could you have that seen to?	**¿Podría hacer revisar eso también?** *podreea asehr rebeesar eso tambeeyen*
I'd like to move to another room.	**Quisiera trasladarme a otra habitación [otro cuarto].** *keeseeyera trasladarmeh a otra abeetaseeyon [otro kwarto]*
I'd like to speak to the manager.	**Quisiera hablar con el gerente [administrador] del hotel.** *keeseeyera ablar kon el kherenteh [admeeneestrador] del otel*

Requirements Exigencias generales

The 110-volt, 60-cycle AC is the norm throughout Mexico, Central America, Colombia, Venezuela. Further south, the 220-volt, 50-cycle operates in Peru, Bolivia (except La Paz), Paraguay, Uruguay, Chile and Argentina.

If you bring your own electrical appliances in Mexico, you may need to buy an adaptor to fit the various types of electrical sockets.

About the hotel Acerca del hotel

Where's the…?	**¿Dónde está …?** _dondeh esta_
bar	**el bar** _el bar_
bathroom	**el baño** _el baño_
parking lot / car park	**el estacionamiento [el parqueadero]** _el estaseeonameeyento [el parkeadero]_
dining room	**el comedor** _el komedor_
elevator / lift	**el ascensor** _el asensor_
shower	**la ducha** _la doocha_
swimming pool	**la piscina** _la peeseena_
tour operator's bulletin board	**la cartelera de anuncios del operador de viajes** _la kartelera deh anoonseeos del operador deh beeyakhes_
Where are the bathrooms/ toilets?	**¿Dónde están los baños?** _dondeh estan los baños_
What time is the front door locked?	**¿A qué hora se cierra con llave la puerta principal?** _a keh ora seh seeyera la pwerta preenseepal_
What time is breakfast served?	**¿A qué hora se sirve el desayuno?** _a keh ora seh seerbeh el desayoono_
Is there room service?	**¿Ofrecen ustedes servicio a la habitación?** _ofresen oostedes serbeesyo a la abeetaseeyon_

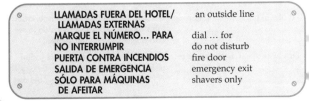

LLAMADAS FUERA DEL HOTEL/ LLAMADAS EXTERNAS	an outside line
MARQUE EL NÚMERO… PARA	dial … for
NO INTERRUMPIR	do not disturb
PUERTA CONTRA INCENDIOS	fire door
SALIDA DE EMERGENCIA	emergency exit
SÓLO PARA MÁQUINAS DE AFEITAR	shavers only

Personal needs Necesidades personales

The key to room ..., please.	**La llave de la habitación ..., por favor.** *la l-yabeh deh la abeetaseeyon ... por fabor.*
I've lost my key.	**Se me perdió mi llave.** *se meh perdeeyo mee l-yabeh*
I've locked myself out of my room.	**Me he quedado fuera de la habitación.** *meh eh kedado fwera deh la abeetaseeyon.*
Could you wake me at ...?	**¿Podría despertarme a las ...?** *podreea despertarmeh a las*
I'd like breakfast in my room.	**Quisiera tomar el desayuno en la habitación.** *keeseeyera tomar el desayoono en la abeetaseeyon*
Can I leave this in the safe?	**¿Puedo dejar esto en la caja de seguridad [caja fuerte]?** *pwedo dekhar esto en la kakha deh segooreedath [kakha fwerteh]*
Could I have my things from the safe?	**¿Podría entregarme las cosas que he dejado en la caja de seguridad?** *podreea entregarmeh las kosas keh eh dekhado en la kakha deh segooreedath*
Where is our tour representative?	**¿Dónde puedo encontrar a nuestro representante?** *dondeh pwedo enkontrar a nwestro representanteh*
maid	**un(-a) empleado(-a)** *oon(-a) empleado(-a)*
May I have a(n) (extra) ...?	**¿Me puede traer ... (adicional)?** *meh pwedeh trayer ... (adeeseeonal)*
bath towel	**una toalla** *oona toal-ya*
blanket	**una manta** *oona manta*
hangers	**una percha** *oona percha*
pillow	**una almohada** *oona almoada*
soap	**un jabón** *oon khabon*
Is there any mail for me?	**¿Hay alguna carta para mí?** *eye algoona karta para mee*
Are there any messages for me?	**¿Hay algún recado [alguna razón] para mí?** *eye algoon rekado [algoona rason] para mee*

BREAKFAST ➤ 43; CHANGING MONEY ➤ 138

Renting Alquilar

We've reserved an apartment/cottage in the name of …	**Hemos reservado un departamento [apartamento]/cabaña a nombre de …** *emos reserbado oon departamento [apartamento]/kabaña deh a nombre deh*
Where do we pick up the keys?	**¿Dónde reclamamos las llaves?** *dondeh reklamamos las l-yabes*
Which is the front door key?	**¿Cuál es la llave de la puerta principal?** *kwal es la l-yabeh deh la pwerta preenseepal*
Where is the…?	**¿Dónde está …?** *dondeh esta*
electricity meter	**el medidor [contador] eléctrico** *el medeedor [kontador] elektreeko*
fuse box	**la caja de fusibles** *la kakha deh fooseebles*
valve	**la llave de cierre** *la l-yabeh deh seeyereh*
water heater	**el calentador** *el kalentador*
Are there any spare …?	**¿Tiene … de repuesto?** *teeyeneh …de repwesto*
fuses	**algunos fusibles** *algoonos fooseebles*
gas bottles	**algunos cilindros de gas [bombona]** *algoonos seeleendros deh gas [bombona]*
sheets	**algunas sábanas** *algoonas sabanas*
Which day does the cleaner come?	**¿Qué día viene la aseadora?** *keh deeya beeyeneh la aseadora*
Where/When do I put out the trash/rubbish?	**¿Dónde/Cuándo se saca la basura?** *dondeh/kwando seh saka la basoora]*

Problems? ¿Hay problemas?

Where can I contact you?	**¿Dónde puedo localizarlo(-la)?** *dondeh pwedo lokaleesarlo(-la)*
How does the water heater/stove/work?	**¿Cómo funciona la estufa/el calentador?** *komo foonseeyona la estoofa/el kalentador*
The … is/are dirty.	**El/la … está sucio(-a).** *el/la … esta sooseeo(-a)*
We have accidentally broken/lost …	**Se nos rompió/perdió … por accidente.** *se nos rompeeo/perdeeo … por akseedenteh*
That was already damaged when we arrived.	**Eso no funcionaba cuando nosotros llegamos.** *eso no foonseeyonaba kwando nosotros l-yegamos*

HOUSEHOLD ARTICLES, CLEANING ITEMS ➤ 148

Useful terms Palabras útiles

boiler	**la caldera** *la kaldera*
crockery	**la loza [vajilla]** *la losa [bakheel-ya]*
cutlery	**los cubiertos** *los koobeeye tos*
freezer	**el congelador** *el konkhelador*
refrigerator	**la nevera** *la nebera*
frying pan	**la sartén** *la sarten*
kettle	**la tetera** *la tetera*
lamp	**la lámpara** *la lampara*
saucepan	**la cacerola** *la kaserola*
stove	**la estufa** *la estoofa*
toilet paper	**el papel higiénico** *el papel eekheeyeneeko*
washing machine	**la lavadora** *la labadora*

Rooms Las habitaciones

balcony	**el balcón** *el balkon*
bathroom	**el baño** *el baño*
bedroom	**la alcoba [el dormitorio]** *la alkoba [el dormeetoreeyo]*
dining room	**el comedor** *el komedor*
kitchen	**la cocina** *la koseena*
living room	**la sala** *la sala*
toilet	**el baño** *el baño*

Youth hostel Albergue juvenil

Do you have any places left for tonight?	**¿Tiene cupos disponibles para esta noche?** *teeyeneh koopos deesponeebles para esta nocheh*
Do you rent/hire out bedding?	**¿Alquila usted la ropa de cama?** *alkeela oosteth la ropa deh kama*
What time are the doors locked?	**¿A qué hora se cierra con llave la puerta?** *a keh ora seh seeyera kon l-yabeh la pwerta*
I have an International Student Card.	**Tengo credencial [tarjeta] internacional de estudiante.** *tengo kredenseeal [tarkheta] eenternaseeonal deh estoodeeanteh*

GENERAL REQUIREMENTS ➤ 26; CAMPING ➤ 30

Camping De campamento

In some parts of Latin America, camping isn't allowed without a permit. However, there are many authorized campsites with excellent facilities. In Argentina, most cities have sites where tents can be pitched. Camping and sleeping on the beach is allowed in Mexico, but isn't recommended, for safety reasons.

Booking Instalarse

Is there a camp site near here?	**¿Hay alguna zona de campamento por aquí?** eye algoona sona deh kampamento por akee
Do you have space for a tent/trailer/caravan?	**¿Tiene sitio para una tienda de campaña/casa móvil?** teeyeneh seeteeyo para oona teeyenda deh kampaña/kasa mobeel
What is the charge …?	**¿Cuál es el precio …?** kwal es el preseeo
per day/week	**por día/por semana** por deeya/por semana
for a tent/a car	**por tienda/por carro** por teeyenda/por karro
for a mobile home/camper	**por casa móvil** por kasa mobeel

Facilities Servicios

Are there cooking facilities on site?	**¿Se puede cocinar en la zona de campamento?** se pwedeh koseenar en la sona deh kampamento
Are there any electric outlets/power points?	**¿Hay alguna toma de corriente?** eye algoona toma deh koreeyenteh
Where is/are the …?	**¿Dónde está(n) …?** dondeh esta(n)
drinking water	**el agua potable** el agwa potableh
trash cans/garbage cans	**los botes de la basura [las canecas]** los botes deh la basoora [las kanekas]
laundry facilities	**el servicio de lavandería** el serbeeseeo deh labandereeya
showers	**las duchas** las doochas

AGUA POTABLE	drinking water
PROHIBIDO ACAMPAR	no camping
PROHIBIDO PRENDER FUEGO [HACER HOGUERAS] EN ESTE LUGAR	no fires/barbecues here

RESERVATIONS ➤ 21; LENGTH OF STAY ➤ 23

Complaints Quejas [Reclamos]

It's too sunny/shady/ crowded here.

Hace demasiado sol/ demasiada sombra/ Hay demasiada gente aquí.
aseh demaseeyado sol/demaseeyada sombra/eye demaseeyada khenteh akee

The ground's too hard/uneven.

El terreno está demasiado duro/ irregular. *el terreno esta demaseeyado dooro/eeregoolar*

Do you have a more level spot?

¿Hay algún sitio más plano? *eye algoon seeteeyo mas plano*

You can't camp here.

Usted no puede acampar aquí. *oosteth no pwedeh akampar akee*

Camping equipment Equipo de campamento

butane gas	**el gas butano** *el gas bootano*
campbed	**la cama plegable** *la kama plegableh*
charcoal	**el carbón vegetal** *el karbon bekhetal*
flashlight	**la antorcha** *la antorcha*
groundcloth/groundsheet	**la tela impermeable** *la tela impermeableh*
guy rope	**la cuerda** *la kwerda*
hammer	**el martillo** *el marteel-yo*
knapsack	**la mochila** *la mocheela*
mallet	**el mazo** *el maso*
matches	**los fósforos** *los fosforos*
(air) mattress	**el colchón (inflable)** *el kolchon (eenflableh)*
paraffin	**la parafina** *la parafeena*
primus stove	**la cocineta** *la koseeneta*
sleeping bag	**el saco de dormir [el sleeping]** *el sako de dormeer [el sleepeen]*
tent	**la tienda [la carpa]** *la teeyenda [la karpa]*
tent pegs	**las estacas de la tienda [la carpa]** *las estakas deh la teeyenda [la karpa]*
tent pole	**el poste de la tienda [la carpa]** *el posteh deh la teeyenda [karpa]*

Checking out
Pagar e irse del hotel

What time do we need to vacate the room?	**¿A qué hora debemos desocupar el cuarto?** *a keh ora debemos desokoopar el kwarto*
Could we leave our baggage/luggage here until … p.m.?	**¿Podemos dejar nuestro equipaje aquí hasta las … de la tarde?** *podemos dekhar nwestro ekeepakheh akee asta las … deh la tardeh*
I'm leaving now.	**Ya me voy.** *ya meh boy*
Could you order us a taxi, please?	**¿Podría pedirnos un taxi, por favor?** *podreea pedeernos oon taxi por fabor*
It's been a very enjoyable stay.	**Ha sido una estancia muy agradable.** *a seedo oona estanseea mwee agradableh*

Paying Pagar

May I have my bill, please?	**¿Me trae la cuenta, por favor?** *meh trayeh la kwenta por fabor*
I think there's a mistake in this bill.	**Creo que hay un error en esta cuenta.** *kreo keh eye oon error en esta kwenta*
I've made … telephone calls.	**Hice …llamadas.** *eeseh … l-yamadas.*
I've taken … from the minibar.	**Tomé … del mini-bar.** *tomeh … del mini-bar*
Can I have an itemized bill?	**¿Me puede dar una factura [un recibo detallado]?** *meh pwedeh dar oona faktoora [oon reseebo detal-yado]*
Could I have a receipt, please?	**¿Me podría dar un recibo, por favor?** *meh podreea dar oon reseebo por fabor*

Tipping: a service charge is generally included in hotel and restaurant bills. However, if the service has been particularly good, you may want to leave an extra tip.

Eating Out

Restaurants   Restaurantes

Cafetería *kafetereeya*
A small café serving both alcoholic and non-alcoholic drinks; varied menus. Sit at the counter or – for a little more money – choose a table. The **menú del día** (set menu) may be very good.

Cantina *kanteena*
Roughly equivalent to an English pub or an American tavern; standards vary; always a wide variety of appetizers on hand. A cantina is a great place for meeting friends and discussing the world. But one thing: cantinas are for men only.

Fonda *fonda*
Similar to an inn; food is plentiful and service usually good.

Fresquería *freskereeya*
Serves refreshments and drinks. It may also be called **refresquería**.

Hacienda *asseeyenda*
Some old **haciendas** (big ranches), dating back to colonial times in Mexico, have been transformed into first class, luxurious restaurants. You will find fountains, gardens, tropical flowers and exotic birds in what may be compared with a real museum of old furniture and paintings. Regional and international dishes are served; music is played by **mariachi** orchestras.

Hostería *ostereeya*
Restaurant, often specializing in regional dishes.

Lonchería *lonchereeya*
Bar where you get snacks and small meals.

Pastelería *pastele<u>ree</u>ya*

A cake shop, also called confitería. Some serve coffee, tea and non-alcoholic drinks.

Posada *po<u>ssa</u>da*

Similar to **fondas**, these inns specialize in local cuisine.

Restaurante *restor<u>an</u>teh*

Classified according to the standard of cuisine and service: **de lujo** (deluxe), **de primera**, **de segunda** and **de tercera** (first, second and third class).

Salón de té *sa<u>lon</u> deh teh*

Smart, expensive tea shop.

Snack-bar *"snack bar"*

The English word has been taken over to describe fast-food establishments.

Meal times Horas de comida

el desayuno *el dessa<u>yoo</u>no*

Breakfast: generally served from 8 to 10 a.m.. Traditionally a light meal, usually consisting of a selection of sweet breads with milky coffee (**café con leche**) or hot chocolate (**chocolate caliente**); hotels are now offering more filling fare for tourists, serving a buffet breakfast ➤ 43.

el almuerzo *el al<u>mwer</u>so*

Lunch is generally served between 1 and 4 p.m.. In Latin America people like to linger over a meal, so service may seem on the leisurely side. In a hurry, go for fast-food outlets, pizzerias or cafés ➤ 40.

la cena *la <u>se</u>na*

Dinner is usually served later than at home, starting around 8.00 p.m. and continuing until late. However, in tourist areas you can get a meal at most places just about any time of day.

Latin-American cuisine
Cocina latinoamericana

Latin-American cuisine in all its rich variety arose from a collision of two cooking worlds, that of the natives and the conquerors. Avocado, chocolate, peanuts, potatoes, tomatoes and turkeys are some of the culinary gifts that Latin America has presented to the world.

Sweet corn (**maíz**) and chilies form the basis of the cooking in all Latin-American countries. Here are some of the dishes using these two ingredients: **tacos** (Mexico), **tamales** (Colombia), **hallacas** (Venezuela).

Many delicious dishes are prepared with seafood; for example, **cazuela de mariscos**, **ceviche**, etc.

A table for …	**Una mesa para …**
	oona mesa para
1/2/3/4	**uno/dos/tres/cuatro**
	oono/dos/tres/kwatro
Thank you.	**Gracias.** *graseeas*
The bill, please.	**La cuenta, por favor.** *la kwenta por fabor*

Finding a place to eat
Buscar un sitio para comer

Can you recommend a good restaurant?	**¿Puede recomendarme un buen restaurante?** *pwedeh rekomendarmeh oon bwen restoranteh*
Is there … near here?	**¿Hay … cerca de aquí?** *eye … serka deh akee*
traditional local restaurant	**un restaurante típico de la región** *oon restoranteh teepeeko deh la rekheeyon*
Chinese restaurant	**un restaurante chino** *oon restoranteh cheeno*
fish restaurant	**un restaurante con especialidad en pescado** *oon restoranteh kon espeseeyaleedath en peskado*
a steak house	**un restaurante especializado en carnes** *oon restoranteh espeseeyaleesado en karnes*
inexpensive/vegetarian restaurant	**un restaurante barato/vegetariano** *oon restoranteh barato/begetareeyano*
Where can I find …?	**¿Dónde puedo encontrar …?** *dondeh pwedo enkontrar …*
a café	**un café [una cafetería]** *oon kafeh [oona kafetereeya]*
a café/restaurant with outdoor tables	**un café/un restaurante con mesas al aire libre** *oon kafeh/oon restoranteh kon mesas al ayreh leebreh*
a fast food restaurant	**un restaurante de comidas rápidas** *oon restoranteh deh komeedas rapeedas*
a pizzeria	**una pizzería** *oona peesereeya*
an ice-cream parlor/parlour	**una heladería** *oona eladereeya*

35

Reservations Reservar

I'd like to reserve a table for two.	**Quisiera reservar una mesa para dos.** *keeseeyera reser<u>bar</u> <u>oo</u>na <u>me</u>sa <u>pa</u>ra dos*
For this evening/ tomorrow at …	**Para esta noche/mañana a las …** *<u>pa</u>ra <u>es</u>ta <u>no</u>cheh/ma<u>ña</u>na a las …*
We'll come at 8:00.	**Llegaremos a las 8:00.** *l-yega<u>re</u>mos a las <u>o</u>cho*
A table for two, please.	**Una mesa para dos, por favor.** *<u>oo</u>na <u>me</u>sa <u>pa</u>ra dos por fa<u>bor</u>*
We have a reservation.	**Tenemos una reservación.** *te<u>ne</u>mos <u>oo</u>na reserbasee<u>yon</u>*

¿A nombre de quién, por favor?	What's the name, please?
Lo siento. Todo está reservado/no tenemos mesas disponibles/libres.	I'm sorry. We're very busy/full.
Tendremos una mesa disponible/ libre en … minutos.	We'll have a free table in … minutes.
Va(n) a tener que regresar en … minutos.	You'll have to come back in … minutes.

Where to sit Un lugar donde sentarse

Could we sit …?	**¿Podemos sentarnos …?** *po<u>de</u>mos sen<u>tar</u>nos*
over there	**allá** *al-<u>ya</u>*
outside	**afuera** *af<u>we</u>ra*
in a non-smoking area	**en la sección de no fumadores** *en la seksee<u>yon</u> deh no fooma<u>do</u>res*
by the window	**cerca de la ventana** *<u>ser</u>ka deh la ben<u>ta</u>na*
Smoking or non-smoking?	**¿Fumadores o no fumadores?** *fooma<u>do</u>res o no fooma<u>do</u>res*

– Quisiera reservar una mesa para esta noche.
– *¿Para cuántas personas?*
– Para cuatro.
– *¿Para qué hora?*
– Para las ocho.
– *¿A nombre de quién, por favor?*
– Macdonald.
– *Muy bien [Perfecto]. Los esperamos por la noche.*

Ordering Pedir

Waiter!/Waitress!	**¡Mesero!/¡Mesera!** _mesero/mesera_
May I see the wine list?	**¿Me trae la lista de vinos?** _meh traeh la leesta deh beenos_
Do you have a set menu?	**¿Tienen el menú del día?** _teeyenen el menoo del deeya_
Can you recommend some typical local dishes?	**¿Puede recomendarme algunos platos típicos de la región?** _pwedeh rekomendarmeh algoonos platos teepeekos deh la rekheeyon_
Could you tell me what ... is?	**¿Podría explicarme qué es ...?** _podreea espleekarmeh keh es_
What is in it?	**¿Qué ingredientes tiene?** _keh eengredeeyentes teeyeneh_
What kind of ... do you have?	**¿Qué clase de ... tiene?** _keh klaseh deh ... teeyeneh_
I'd like ...	**Quisiera ...** _keeseeyera_
a bottle/glass/carafe of ...	**una botella/un vaso/una jarra de ...** _oona botel-ya/oon baso/oona kharra deh_

¿Desean pedir?	Are you ready to order?
¿Qué desea(n) comer?	What would you like?
¿Desea(n) pedir las bebidas primero?	Would you like to order drinks first?
Le(s) recomiendo ...	I recommend ...
No tenemos ...	We haven't got ...
Eso demorará ... minutos	That will take ... minutes.
Buen provecho. Espero que disfruten la comida.	Enjoy your meal.

– _¿Desean pedir?_
– _¿Puede recomendarnos un plato típico de la región?_
– _Por supuesto. Les recomiendo el ceviche._
– _De acuerdo._
– _Muy bien. Y, ¿qué desean tomar?_
– _Una jarra de vino rojo, por favor._

DRINKS ➤ 49; MENU READER ➤ 52

Side dishes
Platos adicionales

Could I have … without …?	**¿Podría traerme … sin …?** _podreea trayermeh…seen …_
With a side order of …	**Con una porción adicional de …** _kon oona porseeyon adeeseeyonal deh_
Could I have salad instead of vegetables, please?	**¿Podría traerme ensalada en vez de verduras, por favor?** _podreea trayermeh ensalada en bes deh berdooras por fabor_
Does the meal come with vegetables/potatoes?	**¿La carne viene con verduras/papas?** _la karneh beeyeneh kon berdooras/papas_
Do you have any sauces?	**¿Tiene salsas?** _teeyeneh salsas_
Would you like … with that?	**¿Desea … también?** _deseea … tambeeyen_
vegetables/salad	**verduras/ensalada** _berdooras/ensalada_
potatoes/French fries	**papas/papas a la francesa** _papas/papas a la fransesa_
sauce	**salsa** _salsa_
ice	**hielo** _eeyelo_
May I have some …?	**¿Podría traerme un poco de …?** _podreea trayermeh oon poko deh_
bread	**pan** _pan_
butter	**mantequilla** _mantekeel-ya_
lemon	**limón** _leemon_
mustard	**mostaza** _mostasa_
pepper	**pimienta** _peemeeyenta_
salt	**sal** _sal_
seasoning	**aderezo** _adereso_
sugar	**azúcar** _asookar_
(artificial) sweetener	**endulzador** _endoolsador_
vinaigrette/French dressing	**salsa vinagreta** _salsa beenagreta_

MENU READER ➤ 52

General questions Preguntas generales

Could I have a(n) (clean) …, please?	**¿Podría traerme un(-a) … limpio(-a), por favor?** _podreea trayermeh oon(-a) … leempeeyo(-a) por fabor_
ashtray	**un cenicero** _oon seneesero_
cup/glass	**una taza/un vaso** _oona tasa/oon baso_
fork/knife	**un tenedor/cuchillo** _oon tenedor/koocheel-yo_
napkin/serviette	**una servilleta** _oona serbeel-yeta_
plate/spoon	**un plato/una cuchara** _oon plato/oona koochara_
I'd like some more …, please.	**Quisiera un poco más de …, por favor.** _keeseeyera oon poko mas deh… por fabor_
Nothing more, thanks.	**Nada más. Gracias.** _nada mas. graseeas_
Where are the bathrooms/toilets?	**¿Dónde están los baños?** _dondeh estan los baños_

Special requirements Exigencias especiales

I mustn't eat food containing …	**No puedo consumir alimentos que contengan …** _no pwedo konsoomeer aleementos keh kontengan_
salt/sugar	**sal/azúcar** _sal/asookar_
Do you have meals/drinks for diabetics?	**¿Tiene comidas/bebidas especiales para diabéticos?** _teeyeneh komeedas/bebeedas espeseeyales para deeabeteekos_
Do you have vegetarian meals?	**¿Tiene comida vegetariana?** _teeyeneh komeeda bekhetareeyana_

For the children Para los niños

Do you do children's portions?	**¿Tiene porciones especiales para niños?** _teeyeneh porseeyones espeseeyales para neeños_
Could we have a child's seat, please?	**¿Podría traernos un asiento para niños?** _podreea trayernos oon aseeyento para neeños_
Where can I feed/change the baby?	**¿Dónde puedo alimentar/cambiar al bebé?** _dondeh pwedo aleementar/kambeeyar al bebeh_

CHILDREN ➤ 113

Fast food/Café   Café [Cafetería]/ Restaurante de comidas rápidas

Something to drink   Algo para beber [tomar]

I'd like (a cup of) …	**Quisiera …** *keeseeyera*
coffee/tea	**un café/un té** *oon kafeh/oon teh*
black/with milk	**un café negro [tinto]/un café con leche** *oon kafeh negro [teento]/oon kafeh kon lecheh*
I'd like a … of red/white wine.	**Quisiera un(-a) … de vino tinto/blanco.** *keeseeyera oon(-a) … deh beeno teento/blanko.*
carafe/bottle/glass	**garafa/botella/vaso** *kharafa/botel-ya/baso*
Do you have … beer?	**¿Tiene … cerveza?** *teeyeneh … serbesa*
bottled/draft (draught)	**en botella/de barril** *en botel-ya/deh barreel*

And to eat …   Y para comer …

A piece of …, please.	**Un pedazo de…, por favor.** *oon pedaso deh… por fabor*
I'd like two of those.	**Quiero dos de ésos, por favor.** *keeyero dos deh esos por fabor*
burger/French fries	**una hamburguesa/unas papas a la francesa** *oona amboorgesa/oonas papas a la fransesa*
sandwich/cake	**un sandwich/un pastel** *oon sandweech/oon pastel*
an ice cream	**un helado de …** *oon elado deh …*
vanilla	**vainilla** *bayneel-ya*
chocolate	**chocolate** *chokolateh*
strawberry	**fresa** *fresa*
A … portion, please.	**Una porción …, por favor.** *oona porseeyon … por fabor*
small	**pequeña** *pekeña*
medium/regular	**mediana** *medeeyana*
large	**grande** *grandeh*
It's to take out.	**Es para llevar.** *es para l-yebar*
That's all, thanks.	**Eso es todo, gracias.** *eso es todo, graseeyas*

OTHER DRINKS ➤ 49-51

> – ¿Qué desean?
> – Dos cafés, por favor.
> – ¿Café negro [tinto] o café con leche?
> – Café con leche, por favor.
> – ¿Y para comer?
> – Eso es todo, gracias.

Complaints Quejas [reclamos]

I have no knife/fork/spoon.	**No tengo cuchillo/tenedor/cuchara.** _no tengo koocheel-yo/tenedor/koochara_
There must be some mistake.	**Debe haber una equivocación [un error].** _debeh aber oona ekeebokaseeyon [oon error]_
That's not what I ordered.	**Esto no es lo que yo pedí.** _esto no es lo keh yo pedee_
I asked for …	**Yo pedí …** _yo pedee_
I can't eat this.	**Yo no puedo comer esto.** _yo no pwedo komer esto._
The meat is …	**La carne está …** _la karne esta_
overdone	**demasiado asada** _demaseeyado asada_
underdone	**poco hecha [cruda]** _poko echa [krooda]_
too tough	**demasiado dura** _demaseeyado doora_
This is too …	**Esto está demasiado …** _esto esta demaseeyado_
bitter/sour	**amargo/ácido** _amargo/aseedo_
The food is cold.	**La comida está fría.** _la komeeda esta freea_
This isn't fresh.	**Esto no está fresco.** _esto no esta fresko_
How much longer will our food be?	**¿Cuánto tiempo más va a tardar nuestra comida?** _kwanto teeyempo mas ba a tardar nwestra komeeda_
We can't wait any longer. We're leaving.	**No podemos esperar más. Nos vamos.** _no podemos esperar mas. nos bamos_
This isn't clean.	**Esto no está limpio.** _esto no esta leempeeo_
I'd like to speak to the head waiter/manager.	**Quisiera hablar con el gerente [el administrador].** _keeseeyera ablar kon el kherenteh [el admeeneestrador]_

Paying Pagar

In Mexico, most bills have 10% **IVA (Impuesto de Valor Aña-dido)** added.

I'd like to pay.
¿Me trae la cuenta, por favor?
meh traeh la kwenta por fabor

We'd like to pay separately.
Queremos pagar por separado.
keremos pagar por separado

It's all together, please.
Todo junto, por favor.
todo khoonto por fabor

I think there's a mistake in this bill.
Creo que hay un error en esta cuenta.
kreo keh kye oon error en esta kwenta

What is this amount for?
¿A qué corresponde esta cantidad?
a keh korrespondeh esta kanteedath

I didn't have that. I had …
Yo no comí eso. Yo comí …
yo no komee eso. yo komee

Is service included?
¿Está incluido el servicio?
esta eenklooeedo el serbeeseeo

Can I pay with this credit card?
¿Puedo pagar con esta tarjeta de crédito?
pwedo pagar kon esta tarkheta deh kredeeto

I've forgotten my wallet.
He olvidado mi billetera.
eh olbeedado mee beel-yetera

I haven't got enough money.
No tengo suficiente dinero.
no tengo soofeeseeyenteh deenero.

Could I have a VAT receipt, please?
¿Me podría dar el recibo del IVA, por favor?
me podreea dar el reseebo del eeba por fabor

That was a very good meal.
La comida estuvo deliciosa.
la komeeda estoobo deleeseeyosa

– ¡Mesero(-a)! ¿Me trae la cuenta, por favor?
– Con mucho gusto [por supuesto]. Aquí tiene.
– ¿Está incluido el servicio?
– Sí, señor(a).
– ¿Puedo pagar con esta tarjeta de crédito?
– Por supuesto…
– ¿Muchas gracias. La comida estuvo deliciosa.

Course by course Platos

Breakfast Desayuno

I'll have …	**Tomaré …** _tomareh_
bread	**pan** _pan_
butter	**mantequilla** _mantekeel-ya_
eggs	**huevos** _webos_
fried eggs	**huevos fritos** _webos freetos_
scrambled eggs	**huevos revueltos** _webos rebweltos_
grapefruit juice	**jugo de toronja** _khoogo deh toronkha_
orange juice	**jugo de naranja** _khoogo deh narankha_
jam	**mermelada** _mermelada_
honey	**miel** _meeyel_
marmalade	**mermelada de naranja** _mermelada deh narankha_
milk	**leche** _lecheh_
rolls	**bollitos** _bol-yeetos_
toast	**pan tostado** _pan tostado_

Appetizers/Starters Entradas [Entremeses]

When in Mexico, try some special appetizers. Ask for **antojitos mexicanos**. A few examples:

guacamole _gwakamoleh_
Mashed avocado, lime juice and chilies with **totopos** (small fried pieces of tortilla).

quesadilla _kesadeel-ya_
Tortilla filled with cheese or any other filling you want; it can be fried and it is often served with chili sauce, cream and cheese.

tostadas _tostadas_
Fried tortilla with different fillings on top (a **tortilla** is a dry cornmeal pancake).

tacos _takos_
Tacos are as popular in Mexico as hot dogs in the United States. They are made from tortillas stuffed with all kinds of meat, vegetables or cheese fillings. They can be fried (**tacos dorados**) in hot oil and spiced with chili-pepper sauce, guacamole, cream, cheese and lettuce. Tacos can be had in any kind of restaurant.

Soups and stews Sopas y guisados

cazuela de mariscos	a flavorful seafood stew (Argentina)
chipi-chipi	clam soup (Venezuela)
chupe de mariscos	a superb shellfish dish (Chile, Peru)
crema de lima	lima bean soup
menudo	tripe in chili-pepper sauce (Mexico)
pozole	pork and ground-corn soup (Mexico)
sopa de ajo	soup with fried bread, paprika, garlic
sopa de arroz	rice soup
sopa de cebolla	onion soup
sopa de espárragos	asparagus soup
sopa de fideos [sopa de pasta]	vermicelli soup
sopa de frijoles	bean soup
sopa de mariscos	seafood soup
sopa de papas	potato, onion, parsley and sherry soup
sopa de pescado	fish soup
sopa de tortuga	turtle soup
sopa de verduras	green vegetable soup

cazuela de ave _kaswela deh abeh_
a rich chicken soup with green vegetables cooked in stock (Chile)

chupe de camarones _choopeh deh kamarones_
a soup made of potatoes, milk, prawns, hot chilies, peppers and eggs (Peru)

cocido [sancocho] _koseedo [sankocho]_
a stew made with chunks of beef, chicken or fish and local vegetables or roots (Peru)

Fish and seafood Pescado y mariscos

In coastal areas, try the wide variety of fresh fish and seafood.

atún	atoon	tuna
bacalao	bakalao	cod
besugo	besoogo	(sea) bream
bonito	boneeto	striped tuna
boquerones	bokerones	herring (whitebait)
caballa	kabal-ya	mackerel
calamares	kalamares	squid
camarones grandes	kamarones grandes	prawns
gambas	gambas	shrimps
huachinango	wacheenango	red snapper
langosta	langosta	lobster
lenguado	lengwado	sole
merluza	merloosa	hake
mero	mero	bass
mújol	mookhol	mullet
pez espada	pes espada	swordfish
pulpo	poolpo	octopus
rape	rapeh	monkfish
rodaballo	rodabal-yo	turbot
salmón (ahumado)	salmon (ahoomado)	(smoked) salmon
salmonetes	salmonetes	red mullet
trucha	troocha	trout

cazuela de mariscos *kaswela deh mareeskos*
all kinds of fish in a bechamel sauce

ceviche *sebeecheh*
raw fish, marinated in lemon juice and served with onions and hot peppers

ceviche de langostinos *sebeecheh deh langosteenos*
a ceviche (all kinds of shellfish) with crayfish as main ingredient

ceviche mixto *sebeecheh meeksto*
a ceviche with a mixture of shrimp, fish and shellfish

pescado a la veracruzana *peskado a la berakroosana*
red snapper with tomatoes and pimientos

viudo de pescado *beeoodo deh peskado*
fish stew, traditionally cooked in holes dug in the ground and covered
with hot stones (Colombia)

Meat Carne

Many Latin-American countries are beef and pork producers.
Lamb is common in mountainous countries and chicken is
universal. Apart from the standard dishes, there are many
regional specialties.

I'd like some …	**Quisiera …** _keeseeyera_
bacon	**panceta [tocino]** _panseta [toseeno]_
beef	**carne de res [carne vacuna]** _karneh deh res [karneh bakoona]_
chicken	**pollo** _pol-yo_
duck	**pato** _pato_
goose	**ganso** _ganso_
ham	**jamón** _khamon_
lamb	**cordero** _kordero_
liver	**hígado** _eegado_
mutton	**carnero** _karnero_
pork	**chancho [cerdo, puerco]** _chancho [serdo, pwerko]_
sausages	**salchichas** _salcheechas_
steak	**filete, lomo** _feeleteh, lomo_
turkey	**pavo** _pabo_
veal	**ternera** _ternera_

Meat cuts Clases de carne

chuleta	_chooleta_	chop
costilla	_kosteel-ya_	cutlet/scallop
carne molida	_karneh moleeda_	chopped/minced meat
biftec	_beeftek_	steak
filete	_feeleteh_	fillet steak
pierna	_peeyerna_	leg
riñones	_reeñones_	kidneys

Meat dishes Platos de carne

anticucho _anteekoocho_ squares of beef heart on skewers, broiled over
charcoal and served with hot sauce (Peru)

pollo en mole _pol-yo en moleh_ chicken in a sauce made of chilies, oil,
sugar, sesame seeds, peanuts, cocoa, cinnamon and other spices, served
with small pieces of bread (Mexico)

Vegetables/Fruit Verduras/Fruta

ajo	_akho_	garlic
alcachofas	_alkachofas_	artichokes
berenjena	_berenkhena_	eggplant
calabaza	_kalabasa_	squash
cebollas	_sebol-yas_	onions
col	_kol_	cabbage
champiñones	_champeeñones_	mushrooms
chícharos	_cheecharos_	peas
ejotes	_ekhotes_	green (French) beans
elote	_eloteh_	corn
flores de calabaza	_flores deh kalabasa_	zucchini/courgette flowers
frijoles	_freekholes_	beans
garbanzos	_garbansos_	chickpeas
lechuga	_lechooga_	lettuce
pepino	_pepeeno_	cucumber
rábanos	_rabanos_	radishes
repollo	_repol-yo_	cabbage
zanahorias	_sanahoreeyas_	carrots
zapallitos	_sapal-yeetos_	zucchini/courgette
zapallo	_sapal-yo_	pumpkin
cerezas	_seresas_	cherries
duraznos	_doorasnos_	peaches
fresas	_fresas_	strawberries
granadas	_granadas_	pomegranates
higos	_eegos_	figs
manzanas	_mansanas_	apples
naranjas	_narankhas_	oranges
piña	_peeña_	pineapple
plátanos	_platanos_	bananas

chile _cheeleh_
Chili peppers or hot peppers – call them what you like. They come in
many varieties; the most popular are: **poblano chipotle, jalapeño, largo,
piquín**; but you'll also see **habanero, serrano, pimento**
papas [patatas] _papas [patatas]_
Potatoes; may be ~ **fritas** (fries), ~ **hervidas** (boiled), **puré de** ~ (mashed);
and sweet potatoes such as: **batatas, camotes, yame** and **yuca**

Cheese Queso

Popular Mexican cheeses

asadero	a soft, creamy cheese
queso añejo	hand-pressed and salted. The flavor is sharp, the texture close-grained and hard with a few small holes; made from ewe's milk
queso de bola	a soft cheese made in the form of a ball
queso de Chihuahua	a popular soft cheese named after the province from which it originates
queso de Oaxaca	very popular in the south of Mexico, especially used to make **quesadillas**
queso enchilado	same as **queso añejo** but a little sharper in taste; the exterior is colored with red chili peppers
queso fresco	fresh white cheese; made and sold the same day

Dessert Postre

alborotos	*alborotos*	sweet made of roasted corn
ante	*anteh*	pastry with coconut and almonds
bizcocho	*beeskocho*	sponge cake
buñuelos	*booñwelos*	fritters
cocada	*kokada*	sweet made of coconut
espumilla	*espoomeel-ya*	a sort of meringue
flan	*flan*	caramel custard
galletas	*gal-yetas*	cookies/biscuits
pastel	*pastel*	layer cake
ponqué [queque]	*ponkeh [kekeh]*	pound cake

capirotada *kapeerotada*
Bread pudding with cheese, apples, banana and peanuts (Mexico).

helado *elado*
Ice cream; popular flavors include ~ **de chocolate**, ~ **de fresa** (strawberry), and ~ **de vainilla**.

frutas tropicales *frootas tropeekales*
Tropical fruits. Among the many exotic and wonderful types you may encounter, are **anona** (custard-tasting fruit), **carambola** (star fruit), **chirimoya** (custard apple), **fruta de pan** (bread fruit), **guayaba** (guava), **mamey** (sweet fruit), **maracuyá** (passion fruit) and **tamarindo** (sour fruit).

Drinks Bebidas

Wine Vino

You'll find imported European wines all over Latin America, but try the local ones as well, particularly in Chile, Argentina and Mexico. Latin America produces almost one tenth of the world's wines.

As a general rule, white wine goes better with fish and light meats, while red wine accompanies dark meats such as beef or lamb. If you need help in choosing a wine, don't hesitate to ask the waiter.

South American and Mexican wines

Argentina The fourth largest wine producer in the world. Best wines called **vinos finos**. Major wine areas are **La Rioja, Mendoza, Rio Negro, Salta** and **San Juan**. The most common grape varieties are **Malbec** (red) and **Criollas** (white). Proprietary names include **Etchart, Orfila, Suter** and **Santa Ana**.

Chile The leading quality wine-producer in South America. Produces excellent red wines, esp. **Merlot** and **Cabernet Sauvignon**; and white: **Chardonnay, Sauvignon Blanc** and **Riesling**. The best wines are from **Aconcagua, Maule, Maipo** and **Rapel regions**. The geographic diversity of the country allows a wide variety of wines.

Mexico The most popular wines are red: **Cepa Urbiñon, Calafía** and **Chatillon**. For a sparkling wine, try **Chambrule**. The best wines are from the **North Baja California** and **Querétaro** regions, such as **Pedro Domecq**.

Reading the label

seco _seko_	dry	**espumoso** _espoomoso_	sparkling
fuerte _fwerteh_	full-bodied	**dulce** _doolseh_	sweet
ligero _leekhero_	light	**muy seco** _mwee seko_	very dry
tinto _teento_	red	**blanco** _blanko_	white
rosado _rosado_	rosé		

Beer Cerveza

Beer is an excellent accompaniment for a spicy, hot dish; and local beers can be excellent. Popular brands to look for include **Escudo** (Chile), **Cuzqueña** (Peru), **Polar** (Venezuela), **Imperial** (C. Rica). In Mexico, look for **Bohemia**, **Dos Equis**, **Pacífico**, **Sol**, **Superior** and **Tecate** (served with lime and salt), **Negra Modelo** and **Tres Equis** (both dark beers).

Do you have … beer?   **¿Tienen cerveza …?** *teeyenen serbesa*

light/dark/chilled   **rubia/negra/fría** *roobeea/negra/freea*

Other alcoholic drinks Otras bebidas alcohólicas

Local drinks may provide you with a new experience. They are usually made from tropical fruit. Here are a few national specialties:

tequila *tekeela*

The most famous Mexican spirit, distilled from the maguey (**agave**) cactus and reminiscent of gin: ask your waiter how to drink it Mexican style (with lime and salt on the side). The best is **añejo** or **reposado** (aged). Tequila is the main constituent of margarita cocktails.

mescal [mexcal] *meskal*

A less refined version of tequila; the bottle contains a worm (**gusano**) to prove its authenticity.

pulque *poolkeh*

Thick, milky beer also made from maguey cactus; the unfermented version is called **aguamiel**.

Mexico	**chicha**, a strong drink made from fermented sweetened corn and various kinds of fruit
	tepache, a drink made from pulque, pineapple, and cloves
Argentina	**caña** (cane alcohol), also popular elsewhere in South America; **ginebra bols** are popular local spirits
Chile, Peru, Bolivia	**pisco**, a local brandy, served with lemon juice, bitters or syrup
Colombia	**aguardiente**, a fiery spirit
	pisco sour, with ginger ale (**chilcano**), or with vermouth (**capitán**)
Puerto Rico	**ron** is the word for rum here and Puero Ricans are justly proud of the wide variety available
	ron caldas, a rum comparable to the Jamaican type
	ron medellín, a lighter rum
Venezuela	**ponche de crema**, an eggnog punch, spiced with liqueur; **ron** comes in various varieties

Here's a list of standard drinks you'll find in most bars and hotels. Note that Mexican brandy is well worth trying. It's the most popular spirit of that country.

aperitif	**un aperitivo** *oon apereeteebo*
brandy	**un coñac** *oon koñak*
gin	**una ginebra [un gin]** *oona kheenebra [oon "gin"]*
gin and tonic	**una tónica con ginebra** *oona toneeka kon kheenebra*
liqueur	**un licor** *oon leekor*
port	**un oporto** *oon oporto*
rum	**un ron** *oon ron*
sherry	**un jerez** *oon kheres*
vermouth	**un vermut** *oon bermoot*
vodka	**un vodka** *oon bodka*
whisky	**un whisky** *oon weesky*
a glass	**un vaso [una copa]** *oon baso [oona kopa]*
a bottle	**una botella** *oona botel-ya*
ice cubes	**cubos de hielo** *koobos deh yelo*
straight/neat	**solo** *solo*
on the rocks/with water	**con hielo/con agua** *kon yelo/kon agwa*

Non-alcoholic drinks   Bebidas sin alcohol

I'd like a(n) …	**Quisiera un(-a) …** *keeseeyera oon(-a)*
(hot) chocolate	**chocolate (caliente)** *chokolateh (kaleeyenteh)*
lemonade/cola	**limonada/coca** *leemonada/koka*
milk shake	**batido de leche** *bateedo deh lecheh*
mineral water	**agua mineral** *agwa meeneral*
carbonated/non-carbonated	**con gas/sin gas** *kon gas/seen gas*
tonic water	**agua tónica [quina]** *agwa toneeka [keena]*

atole *atoleh* Drink made from the same paste as tortillas and flavored with walnuts and coconuts.

café *kafeh* Coffee types ~ **chico** (thick, dark in small cup); ~ **con crema** (with cream); ~ **con leche** (with milk); ~ **cortado** (light); ~ **descafeinado** (decaffeinated);~ **de olla** (with cane sugar, cinnamon and cloves); ~ **exprés [expreso]** (espresso); ~ **solo [negro]** (black); or ~ **tinto** (small, black cup).

Menu Reader

This Menu Reader is an alphabetical glossary of terms that you may find in a menu. Certain traditional dishes are cross-referenced to the relevant page in the *Course by course* section, where they are described in more detail. Items that are particularly associated with a region or country are indicated: e.g. *Arg.* – Argentina, *Carib.* – Caribbean, *Col.* – Colombia, *Mex.* – Mexico.

How is it cooked?

baked	al horno	al *orno*
fried	frito(-a)	*freeto*
boiled	cocido(-a)	*koseedo*
grilled	a la parrilla	a la pa*reel*-ya
roasted	asado(-a)	a*sado*(-a)
poached	hervido(-a)/ escalfado(-a)	er*beedo*(-a)/eskal*fado*(-a)
marinated	en escabeche	en eska*becheh*
sautéed	salteado(-a) [saltado(-a)]	salte*ado*(-a)[sal*tado*(-a)]
smoked	ahumado(-a)	aoo*mado*(-a)
spicy	condimentado(-a)	kondeemen*tado*(-a)
steamed	al vapor	al *bapor*
braised	a la brasa	a la *brasa*
stewed	guisado(-a) [estofado(-a)]	gee*sado*(-a)[esto*fado*]
stuffed	relleno(-a)	rel-*yeno*(-a)
creamed	en crema	en *krema*
diced	cortado(-a) en cubos	kor*tado*(-a) en *koobos*
oven-browned	tostado(-a) al horno	tos*tado*(-a) al *orno*
breaded	empanado(-a) [apanado(-a)]	empa*nado*(-a)[apa*nado*(-a)]
deep-fried	frito(-a)	*freeto*(-a)
very rare	muy crudo(-a)	mwe *kroodo*(-a)
rare/underdone	crudo(-a) [poco hecho (-a)]	*kroodo*(-a)[poko *echo*(-a)]
medium	medio hecho(-a) [a medio cocinar]	*medeeo echo*(-a)[a *medeeo koseenar*]
well done	bien hecha [bien cocinada]	*beeyen echa* [*beeyen koseenada*]

A

a elegir of your choice

a la brasa braised

a la parrilla grilled (broiled)

a medio cocinar medium

aceite oil

aceitunas olives

acelgas en crema Swiss chard sautéed with onion, carrot and potato *(Arg.)*

achicoria endive

adobo sauce made from two types of chili peppers *(chile ancho* and *chile pasilla)*, vegetable oil, sesame seeds, peanuts, sugar, salt and spices

adobado(-a) marinated

agua (caliente) (hot) water

agua de jamaica unfermented drink from a red flower

agua de panela hot sugar water

agua mineral mineral water

agua quina tonic water

agua tónica tonic water

aguacate avocado

aguardiente anise flavored spirit

ahumado(-a) smoked

ají red pepper

ají picante hot pepper

ajiaco a pimiento-based sauce; chicken and potato soup *(Col.)*

ajiaco criollo creole stew of ribs, steak, corn, sweet potatoes and cassava *(Carib.)*

ajo garlic

al carbón barbecued

al horno baked, roast

al mojo de ajo fried in butter and garlic

al vapor steamed

alambre kebab

albahaca basil

albóndiga meatball

alborotos candy made of roasted corn

alcachofas artichokes

alcaparras capers

aliado ham and cheese

almejas clams

almendras almonds

almuerzo lunch

ananá[s] pineapple

anchoas anchovies

anguila (ahumada) (smoked) eel

anís aniseed

anona tropical fruit tasting like custard

ante pastry with coconut and almonds

anticucho squares of beef heart on skewers, broiled over charcoal and served with hot sauce *(Peru)*

antojitos snacks, starters *(Mex.)*

apanado(-a) breaded

aperitivo aperitif

api sweet corn, lemon and cinnamon drink

apio celery

aporreado de tasajo salt-dried beef stew

arenque herring

arenques ahumados smoked herrings

arepa grilled corn dough stuffed with meat, seafood or cheese *(Ven., Col.)*

aromática herb tea *(Col.)*

arreglados meat sandwiches

arroz rice

arroz a la milanesa risotto *(Carib.)*

arroz con leche rice pudding

arvejas peas

asadero a soft, creamy cheese

asado(-a) grilled, roasted

atole hot drink made from the same paste as *tortillas* and flavored with walnuts, coconuts, etc.

atún tuna

avellanas hazelnuts

aves poultry

azafrán saffron

azúcar sugar

B **bacalaíto** small cod fritter

bacalao cod

barbacoa barbequed meat

batatas sweet potatoes

batido watered fruit juice

bebidas drinks

bebidas sin alcohol non-alcoholic drinks

berenjena eggplant/aubergine

besugo (sea) bream

betabel sugar beet

bien coci[na]do(-a) well done

bien hecho(-a) well done

bife beef steak

bife a caballo "horseback beef"; a steak topped by two fried eggs *(Arg.)*

bife de costilla T-bone steak

birria goat or mutton stew

bistec steak

bizcocho sponge cake

blanco white (wine)

blando soft (egg)

bocaditos small sandwiches with various fillings *(Carib.)*

boliche stuffed pot roast *(Carib.)*

bollitos bread rolls

boniato sweet potato

boniatos asados caramelized potatoes

bonito striped tuna

boquerones herring/whitebait

botella bottle

budín pudding

buñuelos doughnut fritters with sugar, anise and cinnamon

burrito filled wheat flour *tortilla (Mex.)*

C **caballa** mackerel

cabeza head

cabra goat

cabrito kid

cacahuetes peanuts

cachapa large corn pancake

café coffee; **~ americano** black; **~ chico** small strong, thick coffee *(Arg.)*; **~ con leche** with milk; **~ de olla** coffee with cane sugar, cinnamon and cloves; **~ marrón** milky coffee

cajeta milk, sugar and vanilla dessert

calabacita zucchini/courgette

calabaza squash, pumpkin

calamares squid

caldo verde kale soup *(Mex.)*

camarones shrimps; **~ al ajillo** garlic shrimp; **~ grandes** prawns

camotes sweet potatoes

caña cane alcohol

canela cinnamon

cangrejo crab

capirotada bread pudding with banana, apple, peanuts and cheese *(Mex.)*

capón capon

caracoles snails

carambola starfruit

caramelos candy, sweets

carbonada criolla beef slices sautéed with zucchini/courgette, sweet potatoes, peaches and sweet corn *(Arg.)*

carne meat

carne a la tampiqueña steak strips with *guacamole, tacos* and fried beans *(Mex.)*

carne claveteada pot-roast studded with almonds and bacon

carne con papas fragrant beef stew *(Carib.)*

carne de cangrejo crabmeat

carne de chancho pork

carne de res beef

carne molida minced meat

carne vacuna beef

carnero mutton

carnes frías cold cuts of meat

carnitas spicy pork

carta menu

castañas chestnuts

caza game

cazuela de ave a rich chicken soup with green vegetables cooked in stock *(Chile)*

cazuela de mariscos a flavorful seafood stew *(Arg.)*

cazuela de pescado all kinds of fish in a very spicy sauce

cebollas onions; ~ **encurtidos** pickled onion rings *(Mex.)*

cebolletas chives

centolla king crab

cerdo pork

cereales cereal

cerezas cherries

cerveza beer

ceviche raw fish, marinated in lemon juice and served with onions and hot peppers

ceviche de corvina marinated sea bass with yams or potatoes *(Peru)*

ceviche de langostinos shellfish *ceviche* with crayfish as main ingredient

ceviche mixto *ceviche* with a mixture of shrimp, fish and shellfish

chabacanos apricots

chacarero beef steak with vegetables

champiñones mushrooms

chancho pork

chayote avocado-like vegetable

chícharos peas

chicharrones pork rinds

chicha a strong drink made from fermented sweet corn, rice and various kinds of fruit

chicharrón fried salt pork

chilaquiles tortillas filled with beef, spices and egg

chile chili peppers, hot peppers or pimientos. Common varieties: *poblano chipotle, jalapeño, largo, piquín,* also *habanero, pimento, serrano.*

chile con carne stew of kidney beans and minced beef, well spiced with chili peppers

chiles en nogada stuffed green peppers, walnut sauce and sour cream with red pomegranate *(Mex.)*

chimichurri marinade

chipi-chipi a soup made with tiny clams *(Ven.)*

chirimoya custard apple

chirivías parsnips

chivito steak, bacon, cheese, lettuce and tomato sandwich *(Urug.)*

choclo corn

chocolate (caliente) (hot) chocolate

cholgas mussels

chopp draft beer or lager

chorizo a highly spiced type of smoked pork sausage

chuleta chop

chupe de camarones soup made of potatoes, milk, shrimp, hot chilies, peppers and eggs *(Peru)*

chupe de congrio conger eel stew *(Chile)*

chupe de marisco delicious shellfish dish *(Chile, Peru)*

churrasco steak

churros doughnuts

cilantro coriander

ciruelas plums

ciruelas secas prunes

clavos cloves

clericó white wine and fruit juice

cocada coconut cookie

cochinillo suckling pig; **~ pibil** slowly baked in a banana-leaf wrapping *(Mex.)*

cocido a stew made with chunks of beef, chicken or fish and local vegetables or roots *(Peru)*

cocido(-a) boiled, braised

coco coconut

coctel appetizer in sauce

codorniz quail

col cabbage; **~ morada** red cabbage

coles de Bruselas brussels sprouts

coliflor cauliflower

comino cumin

completo hot dog with all the extras

con agua with water

con crema with cream

con gas carbonated

con hielo on the rocks

con leche with milk

con limón with lemon

coñac brandy

condimentado(-a) spicy

condimentos spices

conejo rabbit

copa glass

cordero lamb

cortado small coffee light

cortado(-a) en cubos diced

corvina sea bass

costilla cutlet

crema de lima lima bean soup

crepa thin pancake

criadillas sweetbreads

croquetas croquettes; **~ de jamón** ham croquettes *(Carib.)*

crudo(-a) rare/underdone; raw

cubos de hielo ice cubes

culantro coriander

curuba tropical fruit

D

damascos apricots
dátiles dates
descafeinado decaffeinated
desayuno breakfast
dulce sweet
dulce de camote puréed yam with nuts and dried fruit *(Mex.)*
durazno peach
duro hard boiled (egg)

E

ejotes green (French) beans
elote corn on the cob *(Mex.)*
empanada turnover with egg, minced beef, ham, chicken, cheese, vegetables and other fillings; can be *al horno* (baked) or *frita* (fried); may be highly spiced
empanado(-a) breaded
en barbacoa barbecued, Mexican style
en crema creamed
en escabeche marinated
en salsa in casserole
en su jugo pot roasted
enchilada *tortilla* with filling and sauce, a type of *taco (Mex.)*; ~ **de pollo** with a chicken filling in a red or green chili-pepper or *mole* sauce; served with cheese; ~ **suiza** with sour cream
eneldo dill
enfrijolada *tortilla* with cheese, onion and bean sauce
ensalada salad; ~ **de aguacate** avocado; ~ **de camarones** shrimp; ~ **de fruta** fruit; ~ **de lechuga** green; ~ **de patatas [papas]** potato;

~ **de pepino** cucumber; ~ **de tomate [jitomate]** tomato
entomatada *tortilla* with cheese, onion and tomato sauce
entradas appetizers, starters
entremeses appetizers, starters
escabeche pickled or marinated dish
escalfado(-a) poached
escarola endive/chicory
espárragos asparagus
especialidades de la casa house specialties
especialidades locales local specialties
especias spices
espinacas spinach; ~ **con anchoas** sautéed with anchovies
espumilla sort of meringue
espumoso sparkling
estofado(-a) stewed
estragón tarragon
exprés/expreso espresso
exprimido(-a) fresh (fruit juice)

F

fainá baked chickpea dough
faisán pheasant
fiambres cold meat
filete fillet steak
flan caramel custard; ~ **casero** homemade
flor de calabaza zucchini/courgette flowers
foie-gras pâté
frambuesas raspberries
fresas strawberries
frijoles beans; ~ **negros** black beans

fritas French fries, chips; small fried hamburgers *(Carib.)*
frito(-a) fried
frituras fritters; **~ de carita** black-eyed pea fritters *(Carib.)*
fruta de pan bread fruit
frutas fruit; **~ tropicales** tropical fruit
fría cold
fuerte full-bodied
fugazza pizza with sweet onions *(Arg.)*

G
galletas cookies, biscuits
galletas saladas crackers
gallo pinto "painted rooster"; rice with red and white beans *(C. Rica)*
gambas shrimps
ganso goose
garbanzos chickpeas
gaseosas sodas, carbonated drinks
gazpacho chilled vegetable and chili soup
gelatina gelatine
ginebra [un gin] gin
granadas pomegranates
granadilla passion fruit
guacamole mashed avocado with lime juice, chilies and *totopos* (small fried pieces of *tortilla*)
guanábana soursop
guaro spirit *(C. Rica)*
guayaba guava (fruit)
guayabada guava paste
guisado(-a) stewed
guisado stew
guisantes peas

guiso de maíz rich corn stew
guiso de puerco pork stewed in onions, chilies, cloves, cinnamon, pepper, cumin, garlic and vinegar *(Mex.)*

H
hallaca chopped meat with vegetables in corn pancake wrapped in banana leaves *(Ven.)*
helada ice cream tart
helado ice cream
helado(-a) iced
hervidas boiled, steamed (potatoes)
hervido(-a) poached
hígado liver; **~ de pollo** chicken liver
higos figs
hoja de laurel bay leaf
hongos mushrooms
horchata cooling, unfermented drink made from almonds, cinnamon and rice
hormiga culona large fried ants *(Col.)*
huachinango red snapper *(Mex.)*
huauzontles vegetable coated and served with a cheese filling *(Mex.)*
huevos eggs; **~ con jamón** with ham and eggs; **~ con tocino** with bacon and eggs; **~ fritos** fried: **~ mexicanos** scrambled with tomatoes, chilies, garlic and onions *(Mex.)*; **~ rancheros** fried with hot chili sauce; **~ revueltos** scrambled
humita corn *tamale*
húngaro spicy sausage

J

jaiba crab
jamón ham; ~ ahumado smoked; ~ cocido boiled
jarra carafe
jerez sherry
jitomates tomatoes *(Mex.)*
jugo de fruta fruit juice
jugoso(-a) rare

L

lamprea eel
langosta lobster
langostino crayfish
leche milk
lechecillas sweetbreads
lechón suckling pig
lechón asado roast suckling pig
lechuga lettuce
legumbres vegetables
lengua tongue
lenguado sole
lentejas lentils
licor liqueur
licuado milky fruit drink
liebre hare
ligero light
lima lime
limón lemon
limonada lemonade
locos abalone
locro corn (maize) stew
lomito filet mignon
lomo steak
lomo a lo pobre beef with eggs and French fries/chips *(Chile)*
lomo de cerdo pork fillet
lomo saltado chopped steak, potatoes, tomatoes with rice
lulo tropical fruit

M

maíz sweet corn
macarrones macaroons
mamey sweet tropical fruit
mamoncillo tropical fruit
mamones chinos type of lychee
mandarina tangerine
mango mango
maníes peanuts
mantequilla butter
manzana apple
maracuyá passion fruit
marañón tropical fruit with cashew nut seed
mariquitas chips; ~ de plátanos plantain chips *(Carib.)*
mariscos seafood
masita pastries
masitas de puerco fritas fried pork chunks
matambre flank steak; ~ relleno stuffed, eaten cold or baked *(Arg.)*
mate herb tea; ~ de coca coca leaf tea
mazamorra corn mush
media botella half bottle
medialuna croissant
medio hecho(-a) medium
medio litro half a liter
mejillones mussels
melón melon
menta mint
menú del día set menu
menudencias chicken livers
menudo tripe, usually in chili-pepper sauce *(Mex.)*
merengada milk shake
merengue meringue
meriendas snacks
merluza hake

mermelada jam; **~ de naranja** marmalade

mero grouper

mescal/mezcal similar to *tequila*

miel honey

milanés chocolate fingers

milanesa breaded steak

mojarra sea bream

mojo criollo strong garlic sauce *(Carib.)*

mole a composition of chili peppers, oil, sugar, sesame seeds, peanuts, salt, cinnamon, cocoa and spices, with small pieces of toasted bread; **~ poblano** *mole* sauce with chili peppers *(Mex.)*

mondongo seasoned tripe *(Carib.)*

mora blackberry

morcilla blood sausage

mostaza mustard

mosto sugar-cane juice

mote con huesillo peach juice with barley kernels *(Chile)*

muchacho roast beef in sauce *(Ven.)*

mújol mullet

muslo de pollo chicken leg

muy crudo(-a) very rare

muy seco(-a) very dry

N **ñame** tropical yam

naranja orange

naranjilla bitter type of orange

natilla sour cream

negro(-a) black (coffee); dark (beer)

nieve flavored ice

níspero tropical fruit, medlar

nopales cactus, prickly pears

ñoquis gnocchi

nueces walnuts

nuez moscada nutmeg

O **olímpico** club sandwich

olla de carne meat stew

omelet omelette; **~ de cebolla** onion; **~ de hongos** mushroom; **~ de jamón** ham; **~ de queso** cheese

oporto port

orégano oregano

ostiones oysters

ostras oysters

P **pabellón** beef, beans, rice and plantain *(Ven.)*

paila marina fish chowder *(Chile)*

paleta popsicle/ice lolly

paleta de cordero breast of lamb

palitos de queso cheese sticks/straws

palmito palm heart

palta a la jardinera stuffed avocado with vegetables

pan bread; **~ tostado** toast

pan dulce sweet rolls; **~ chileno** frosted egg-bread *(Chile)*

panceta bacon

pancho hot dog

panecillos rolls

panqué pound cake

papas potatoes; **~ fritas/a la francesa** French fries (chips); **~ rellenas** mashed potato balls stuffed with meat hash *(Carib.)*

pargo relleno stuffed red snapper

parrillada mixed grill with everything from a steak to sausages grilled over charcoal *(Arg.)*

parrillada Machu Picchu beefsteak garnished with avocado, pineapple and papayas *(Peru)*

pasas raisins

pastas cookies, biscuits; noodles, pasta; pastries

pastel cake; **~ de moca** coffee cake; **~ de queso** cheese cake

pastel de carne meat pie

pastel de choclo corn/maize casserole with beef, chicken and vegetables

pastel de mapueyes yam pie *(Carib.)*

pastelería pastries

pasteles pastries

pastelitos cookies/biscuits; small puff pastries

patacones plantain chips

patas de cerdo pig's feet/trotters

patatas potatoes

pato duck

pavo turkey

pay fruit pie

pechuga de pollo chicken breast

pepinillos pickles/gherkins

pepino cucumber

pera pear

perca perch

perdiz partridge

perejil parsley

perico small milk coffee *(Col.)*

pescadilla whiting

pescado fish

pescado a la veracruzana red snapper with tomatoes and pimientos

pez espada swordfish

picadillo beef hash *(Carib.)*

pichón pigeon

pierna de cordero leg of lamb

pierna de puerco asada roast leg of pork creole *(Carib.)*

pimienta pepper

pimientos hot peppers

pimientos morrones sweet peppers

piña pineapple

pinolillo corn and milk drink

pipián pumpkin seeds, chili peppers, oil, sesame seeds, peanuts, salt, garlic, onions, coriander and caraway seeds, with small pieces of toasted bread

pisco brandy served with lemon juice, bitters or syrup *(Chile, Peru, Bol.)*

pitahayas tropical fruit

plátano plantains (type of banana); **~ fritos** pan-fried; **~ a la tentación** baked sweet

poco hecho(-a) rare (underdone)

pollo chicken; **~ a la brasa/al carbón/ al espiedo/rostizado/asado** roast chicken

pollo en adobo chicken in a red-pepper sauce *(Mex.)*

pollo en mole chicken in a *mole* sauce, made of chilies, oil, sugar, sesame seeds, peanuts, salt, cinnamon, cocoa and spices, with small pieces of toasted bread. *(Mex.)*

pomelo grapefruit

ponche fruit juice and rum punch (esp. for Christmas)

ponche de crema eggnog punch, spiced with liqueur *(Ven.)*

porotos beans
postre dessert
postre vigilante cheese and preserved fruit
pozole pork and ground-corn soup *(Mex.)*
puchero casserole of beef, sausage, bacon, chicken, peppers, tomatoes, sweet potatoes *(Arg.)*
pudín de bacalao cod casserole
puerco pork; ~ **en naranja** pork loin with mustard and orange sauce *(Mex.)*
puerros leeks
pulpo octopus
pulque fermented juice of the agave *(Mex.)*
pupusa pancake with cheese or bacon
puré de papa mashed potatoes

Q **quesadilla** *tortilla* filled with cheese or any other filling you want; it can be fried and it is often served with chili sauce, cream and cheese
queque (seco) pound cake
queso cheese
queso añejo hand-pressed and salted cheese; the flavor is sharp, the texture close-grained and hard with a few small holes; made from ewe's milk *(Mex.)*
queso de bola soft cheese made in the form of a ball *(Mex.)*
queso de Chihuahua popular soft cheese named after the province from which it originates *(Mex.)*

queso de Oaxaca cheese very popular in the south of Mexico, especially used to make *quesadillas* *(Mex.)*
queso enchilado same as *queso añejo* but a little sharper in taste; the exterior is colored with red chili peppers *(Mex.)*
queso fresco fresh white cheese; made and sold the same day *(Mex.)*
quinada tonic water

R **rábanos** radishes
rabo de buey oxtail
rabo encendido oxtail soup
rape monkfish
recomendamos … we recommend …
refrescos cold drinks, esp. made with fruit, ice and milk or water
relleno(-a) stuffed
remolacha beet
repollo cabbage
riñones kidneys
róbalo sea bass
rodaballo turbot
romero rosemary
ron rum; ~ **caldas** Jamaican-like rum *(Col.)*; ~ **medellín** light rum *(Col.)*
ropa vieja steak hash in tomato sauce
rosado rosé
rosquilla doughnut
rubia light (beer)
ruibarbo rhubarb

S **saice** spicy meat stew *(Bol.)*

sajta chicken in hot pepper sauce

sal salt

salchichas sausages

salmón (ahumado) (smoked) salmon

salmonetes red mullet

salsas sauces

salteado(-a), saltado(-a) sautéed

salteña meat and vegetable pasty

salvia sage

sancocho stew made with chunks of beef, chicken or fish and local vegetables or roots *(Ven.)*

sandía watermelon

sardinas sardines

seco dry

silpancho beef schnitzel

sin gas still, non-carbonated

sincronizada fried tortilla with ham and cheese filling

singani grape spirit *(Bol.)*

sofrito onion, tomato, garlic, herb and spice sauté *(Carib.)*

solo black (coffee); straight (neat)

solomillo pork fillet

sopa soup

sopa a la criolla spicy noodle soup with beef, egg and vegetables *(Peru)*

sopa azteca dried tortillas with cheese and chilli

sopa de ajo soup with fried bread, paprika and garlic

sopa de arroz rice soup

sopa de cebolla onion soup

sopa de elote corn soup *(Mex.)*

sopa de espárragos asparagus soup

sopa de fideos vermicelli soup

sopa de frijoles bean soup

sopa de mariscos seafood soup

sopa de papas potato, onion, parsley and sherry soup

sopa de pasta vermicelli soup

sopa de pescado fish soup

sopa de plátanos criolla creole plantain soup *(Carib.)*

sopa de tortuga turtle soup

sopa de verduras green vegetable soup

submarino milky chocolate drink

suplemento sobre ... ... extra

surubí type of freshwater fish *(Bol.)*

T

tableta de chocolate chocolate bar

taco *tortilla* with all kinds of meat, chicken or cheese filling

tamal asado corn flour cake

tamales chopped pork with vegetables and rice in a corn meal dough, wrapped in banana leaves or corn husks and steamed

tamarindo sour tropical fruit; unfermented drink from it

tarta tart; **~ de almendras** almond tart; **~ de manzana** apple tart

tartaletas small tarts

tasajo salt-dried beef; **~ a la cubana** stir-fried

té tea; **~ con leche** with milk; **~ de manzanilla** camomile

tenedor libre all you can eat

tepache a drink made of *pulque*, pineapple, and cloves *(Mex.)*

tequila alcoholic drink reminiscent of gin, distilled from agave

término medio medium

ternera veal

tiburón shark

tinto small black coffee *(Col.)*; red (wine)

tocino bacon

tomate tomato; green tomato *(Mex.)*

tónica con ginebra gin and tonic

toronja grapefruit

torrejas French toast

torta cake; white bread sandwich

torta de almidón grilled pancake *(Par.)*

torta del cielo almond sponge cake *(Mex.)*

tortilla corn meal pancake; ~ al ron rum; ~ de cebolla onion; ~ de hongos mushroom; ~ de jamón ham; ~ de papas potato; ~ de plátanos maduros plantain *(Carib.)*; ~ de queso cheese

tortilla de huevo omelette

tostada fried *tortilla* with sausage, beans or avocado

tostado cheese and ham toasted sandwich

tostado(-a) al horno oven-browned

tostones crispy fried plantains *(Carib.)*

tres leches cake soaked in syrup and milk

tripas tripe

trucha trout

tucumana meat and vegetable pastry

tumbo type of tropical fruit

tuna prickly pear

U **uvas** grapes

V **vaca** beef; ~ frita stir-fried *(Carib.)*

vainilla vanilla

vaso glass

venado venison

verduras vegetables

vermut vermouth

vinagre vinegar

vino wine

viudo de pescado fish stew, traditionally cooked in holes dug in the ground and covered with hot stones *(Col.)*

WXYZ **whisky con soda** whisky and soda

yame yam (sweet potato)

yogur yogurt

yuca cassava (a type of potato)

zanahorias carrots

zapallito zucchini/courgette

zapallo pumpkin

zapote tropical fruit

zarzuela de mariscos spicy shellfish stew *(Carib.)*

zuppa inglesa egg custard and lady fingers (sponge fingers)

Travel

Because of the often difficult terrain encountered in South America, rail services are generally less developed than bus and air services. However, Mexico, Argentina and Chile do have extensive rail networks.
Air travel is often the best option (and quickest, by far) for covering the vast distances involved. Alternatively, long-distance buses are comfortable and economical.
Don't be confused in Mexico when talking with the natives, who call their capital **México** or **el DF** (**Distrito Federal**), while their nation is generally referred to as **la República**.

ESSENTIAL

1/2/3 for ...	**Un/Dos/Tres para ...** *oon/dos/tres para*
To ..., please.	**A ..., por favor.** *a por fabor*
one-way/single	**de ida** *deh eeda*
round-trip/return	**de ida y vuelta** *deh eeda ee bwelta*
How much?	**¿Cuánto?** *kwanto*

Safety Seguridad

It is wise to take precautions against crime, particularly in major cities: don't wear expensive jewelry when traveling on public transport; do not take unofficial taxis on your own, especially at night; avoid carrying large amounts of money; and don't walk alone along empty streets.

EMERGENCY, POLICE ➤ 152

Arrival Llegada

To enter Mexico, travelers from most Western countries (excluding South Africa) require only a valid visa and a tourist card (**FMT** or **folleto de migración turística**, available from consulates, airports and border crossings). U.S. and Canadian citizens only require proof of citizenship.

For Argentina, most foreigners require only a passport, though Australians and New Zealanders need a visa.

West European and U.S. citizens need tourist cards; all other foreigners need visas for Uruguay.

Customs clearance systems vary. Some airports have adopted an honor system: follow the green arrow if you have nothing to declare, the red arrow for items to declare. Elsewhere, including Mexico, travelers are required to press a button: a green light means pass through, a red light means the baggage must be checked.

Passport control Control de pasaportes

We have a joint passport.	**Tenemos pasaporte conjunto.** *tenemos pasaporteh konkhoonto*
The children are on this passport.	**Los niños están en este pasaporte.** *los neeños estan en esteh pasaporteh*
I'm here on vacation/ holiday/business.	**Vengo de vacaciones/en viaje de negocios.** *bengo deh bakaseeyones/en beeyakheh deh negoseeos*
I'm just passing through.	**Estoy de paso.** *estoy deh paso*
I'm going to …	**Voy hacia …** *boy aseea*
I'm …	**Vengo …** *bengo*
on my own	**solo(-a)** *solo(-a)*
with my family	**con mi familia** *kon mee fameeleeya*
with a group	**con un grupo** *kon oon groopo*

FAMILY ➤ 120

Customs Aduana

I have only the
normal allowances.

**No tengo nada que
declarar.** *no tengo nada
keh deklarar*

It's a gift.

Es un regalo. *es oon regalo*

It's for my personal use.

Es de uso personal.
es deh ooso personal

I would like to declare …

Quisiera declarar … *keeseeyera deklarar*

¿Tiene algo que declarar?	Do you have anything to declare?
Tiene que pagar impuesto por esto.	You must pay duty on this.
¿Dónde compró usted esto?	Where did you buy this?
Abra esta bolsa, por favor.	Please open this bag.
¿Tiene más equipaje?	Do you have any more luggage?

I don't understand.

No entiendo. *no enteeyendo*

Does anyone here
speak English?

¿Hay alguien aquí que hable inglés?
eye algeeyen akee keh ableh eengles

CONTROL DE PASAPORTES	passport control
CRUCE DE FRONTERA	border crossing
ADUANA	customs
NADA QUE DECLARAR	nothing to declare
ARTÍCULOS PARA DECLARAR	goods to declare
ARTÍCULOS LIBRES DE IMPUESTOS	duty-free goods

Duty-free shopping Tiendas libres de impuestos

What currency is this in?

¿En qué moneda hay que pagar?
en keh moneda eye keh pagar

Can I pay in …

¿Puedo pagar en …
pwedo pagar en

dollars

dólares *dolares*

Mexican pesos

pesos mexicanos
pesos mekheekanos

pounds

libras esterlinas *leebras esterleenas*

Plane Avión

Tickets and reservations Boletos y reservaciones

The main hubs for international flights into Mexico are from Miami, Houston, Dallas and Los Angeles.

There are more than 50 airports in Mexico with regular internal passenger flights. Popular flights within Mexico are cheap; *Mexicana*, *Aeroméxico* and *Inter* offer multi-flight airpasses, ony available outside Mexico. Air passes can greatly reduce the cost of air travel within South America, though check their conditions and restrictions first. Some national airlines (e.g. *Aerolíneas Argentinas*, *AeroPerú*, *LanChile* and *Líneas Aéreas Paraguayas*) offer multi-country air passes.

When is the flight ... to ...?	**¿A qué hora sale el vuelo ... a ...?** *a keh ora saleh el bwelo a*
first/next/last	**primero/próximo/último** *preemero/prokseemo/oolteemo*
I'd like 2 ... tickets to ...	**Quiero dos boletos [tiquetes] ... para ...** *keeyero dos boletos [teeketes]...para*
one-way/single	**de ida** *deh eeda*
return/round-trip	**de ida y vuelta** *deh eeda ee bwelta*
first class	**primera clase** *preemera klaseh*
business class	**clase ejecutiva** *klaseh ekhekooteeba*
economy class	**clase económica [clase de turista]** *klaseh ekonomeeka [klaseh deh tooreesta]*
How much is a flight to ...?	**¿Cuánto cuesta el pasaje a ...?** *kwanto kwesta el pasakheh a*
I'd like to ... my reservation for flight number ...	**Quisiera ... mi reservación para el vuelo número ...** *keeseeyera ... mee reserbaseeyon para el bwelo noomero*
cancel/change/confirm	**cancelar/cambiar/confirmar** *kanselar/kambeeyar/konfeermar*
Are there any supplements/ reductions?	**¿Hay algún sobrecargo [recargo]/ descuento?** *eye algoon sobrekargo [rekargo]/deskwento*
What time does the plane leave?	**¿A qué hora sale el avión?** *a keh ora saleh el abeeyon*
What time will we arrive?	**¿A qué hora llegamos?** *a keh ora l-yegamos*
What time do I have to check in?	**¿A qué hora tengo que presentarme?** *a keh ora tengo keh presentarmeh*

TIME ➤ 220; DAYS OF THE WEEK ➤ 218

Checking in Registrarse

Where is the check-in
desk for flight …?

**¿Dónde queda la ventanilla
para el vuelo número …?**
*dondeh keda la bentaneel-ya
para el bwelo noomero*

I have …

Tengo … *tengo*

3 cases to check in

tres maletas para registrar
tres maletas para rekheestrar

2 pieces of hand luggage

dos maletas de mano
dos maletas deh mano

Me permite su boleto [tiquete]/ pasaporte, por favor.	Your ticket/passport please.
¿Desea un asiento cerca de la ventanilla o del pasillo?	Would you like a window or an aisle seat?
¿Fumadores o no fumadores?	Smoking or non-smoking?
Diríjase/pase, por favor a la sala de embarque	Please go through to the departure lounge.
¿Cuántas maletas tiene?	How many pieces of luggage do you have?
Tiene exceso de equipaje.	You have excess luggage.
Tiene que pagar un sobrecargo [sobrecupo] de … pesos mexicanos	You'll have to pay a supplement of … Mexican pesos
Esto está demasiado pesado/ grande para llevar en la mano.	That's too heavy/ large for hand luggage.
¿Empacó usted mismo su equipaje?	Did you pack these bags yourself?
¿Contienen artículos cortantes o aparatos eléctricos?	Do they contain any sharp or electrical items?

LLEGADAS	arrivals
NO DESCUIDE SU EQUIPAJE	do not leave bags unattended
SALIDAS	departures
SEGURIDAD	security check

LUGGAGE/BAGGAGE➤ 71

Information Información

Is there any delay on flight …?	¿Está retrasado el vuelo …?
	esta retrasado el bwelo
How late will it be?	¿Cuánto se demora en llegar?
	kwanto seh demora en l-yegar
Has the flight from … landed?	¿Ha llegado ya el vuelo de …?
	a l-yegado ya el bwelo deh
Which gate does flight … leave from?	¿De qué puerta sale el vuelo …?
	de keh pwerta sale el bwelo …

Boarding/In-flight Embarque/A bordo

Your boarding card, please.	Me permite su tarjeta de embarque, por favor. *meh permeeteh soo tarkheta deh embarkeh por fabor*
Could I have something to drink/eat, please?	¿Podría traerme algo para tomar/comer, por favor? *podreea trayermeh algo para tomar/komer por fabor*
Please wake me for the meal.	Despiérteme a la hora de la comida, por favor. *despeeyertemeh a la ora deh la komeeda por fabor*
What time will we arrive?	¿A qué hora llegamos? *a keh ora l-yegamos*
A vomit/sick bag, please.	Una bolsa para el mareo, por favor. *oona bolsa para el mareo por fabor*

Arrival Llegada

Where is/are …?	¿Dónde puedo encontrar …?
	dondeh pwedo enkontrar
currency exchange	una oficina de cambio [una casa de cambio] *oona ofeeseena deh kambeeo [oona kasa deh kambeeo]*
buses	las paradas de autobuses *las paradas deh aootobooses*
rental/car hire agency	un local de alquiler de carros *oon lokal deh alkeeler deh karros*
exit	la salida *la saleeda*
taxis	un taxi *oon taksi*
Is there a bus into town?	¿Hay algún bus que entre a la ciudad? *eye algoon boos keh entreh a la seeoodath*

Luggage Equipaje

Porter! Excuse me!	**¡Disculpe, señor!**
	deeskoolpeh señor
Could you take my luggage to …?	**¿Podría llevar mi equipaje hasta …?** *podreea l-yebar mee ekeepakheh asta*
a taxi/bus	**un taxi/bus** *oon taksi/boos*
Where is/are …?	**¿Dónde está(n) …?** *dondeh esta(n)*
luggage carts/trolleys	**los carritos de equipaje** *los karreetos deh ekeepakheh*
luggage lockers	**los casilleros [los lóckers]** *los kaseel-yeros [los lokers]*
luggage check/ left-luggage office	**el depósito de equipaje** *el deposeeto deh ekeepakheh*
Where is the luggage from flight …?	**¿Dónde está el equipaje del vuelo …?** *dondeh esta el ekeepakheh del bwelo*

Loss, damage and theft Pérdidas, daños y robos

I've lost my luggage.	**Mi equipaje se me perdió.** *mee ekeepakheh seh meh perdeeo*
My luggage has been stolen.	**Me han robado mi equipaje.** *meh an robado mee ekeepakheh*
My suitcase was damaged.	**Mi maleta se dañó.** *mee maleta seh daño*
Our luggage has not arrived.	**Nuestro equipaje no ha llegado.** *nwestro ekeepakheh no a l-yegado*

¿Cómo es su equipaje?	What does your luggage look like?
¿Tiene la etiqueta de reclamo?	Do you have the claim check/ reclaim tag?
Su equipaje …	Your luggage …
pudo haberse llevado a …	may have been sent to …
puede llegar más tarde	may arrive later today
Vuelva mañana, por favor.	Please come back tomorrow.
Llame a este número para averiguar si su equipaje ya llegó.	Call this number to check if your luggage has arrived.

POLICE ➤ 152; DIRECTIONS ➤ 94

Train Tren

Autovía *aootoveeya*
Fast intercity trains. In Mexico, they resemble track-bound buses rather than trains, and space is limited (3 cars).

Tren de lujo *tren deh lookho*
Long-distance expresses; can also be called **tren de larga distancia**. The trains are generally very comfortable and well equipped, with bars, sleeping cars and lounges. Compartments, with reclining seats, are air conditioned.

Tren directo *tren deerekto*
Fast train stopping at main stations.

Ómnibus *omneeboos*
Train stopping at all stations; also called **tren local**. Not very comfortable; all second-class.

Coche cama *kocheh kama*
Sleeping car with individual compartments (single or double) and washing facilities.

Coche comedor *kocheh komedor*
Dining car. Not all trains have a dining car, even night trains. However, if not, trolley service is common, and there may be a small bar.

Mexico, Argentina and Chile have extensive railway networks. If you have time to travel around, the train can be a convenient means of transport and it certainly gives you a better feel for the country and the people.

Children aged 5-12 travel half-fare, those under 5 travel free.

In Mexico, there are special overnight trains such as **El Tapatio** (Mexico City to Guadalajara) with waitress service.

For a spectacular train journey, take the Lima to Huancayo train on the highest normal gauge railway in the world. However, most of the rail service in Peru can often be unreliable.

Reservations are essential during vacation times.

To the station Hacia la estación

How do I get to the (main) rail station?	¿Cómo se llega a la estación (principal) de tren? *komo seh l-yega a la estaseeyon (preenseepal) deh tren*
Do trains to … leave from … station?	¿Los trenes para … salen de la estación de …? *los trenes para … salen deh la estaseeyon deh …*
How far is it?	¿A qué distancia está? *a keh deestantheeya esta*
Can I leave my car there?	¿Puedo dejar mi carro allí? *pwedo dekhar mee karro al-yee*

At the station En la estación

Where is/are …?	¿Dónde está(n) …? *dondeh esta(n)*
currency-exchange office	la oficina [casa] de cambio *la ofeeseena [kasa] deh kambeeo*
information desk	la oficina [ventanilla] de información *la ofeeseena [betaneel-ya] deh eenformaseeyon*
luggage check/ left-luggage office	el depósito de equipaje *el deposeeto deh ekeepakhe*
lost-and-found/ lost property office	la oficina de objetos perdidos *la ofeeseena deh obkhetos perdeedos*
luggage lockers	los casilleros [los lóckers] *los kaseel-yeros [los lokers]*
platforms	los andenes *los andenes*
snack bar	la cafetería *la kafetereeya*
ticket office	la venta de boletos [tiquetes] *la benta deh boletos [teeketes]*
waiting room	la sala de espera *la sala deh espera*

A LOS ANDENES	to the platforms
ENTRADA	entrance
INFORMACIÓN	information
RESERVACIONES	reservations
LLEGADAS	arrivals
SALIDA	exit
SALIDAS	departures

DIRECTIONS ➤ 94

Tickets Boletos

Where can I buy a ticket?	**¿Dónde puedo comprar un boleto [tiquete]?** *dondeh pwedo komprar oon boleto [teeketeh]*
I'd like a … ticket to...	**Quisiera un boleto [tiquete] … para ...** *keeseeyera oon boleto [teekete] … para ...*
one-way/single	**de ida** *de eeda*
round-trip/return	**de ida y vuelta** *de eeda ee bwelta*
first/second class	**de primera/segunda clase** *de preemera/segoonda klaseh*
concessionary	**concesionario** *konseseeyonareeo*
I'd like to reserve a seat.	**Quisiera reservar un asiento.** *keeseeyera reserbar oon aseeyento*
aisle seat	**un asiento cerca del pasillo** *oon aseeyento serka del pasil-yo*
window seat	**un asiento cerca de la ventanilla** *oon aseeyento serka deh la bentaneel-ya*
Is there a sleeping car/sleeper?	**¿Hay algún coche cama en el tren?** *eye algoon kocheh kama en el tren*
I'd like a … berth.	**Quisiera una litera …** *keeseeyera oona leetera*
upper/lower	**superior/inferior** *soopereeyor/eenfereeyor*

Price Tarifas

How much is that?	**¿Cuánto es?** *kwanto es*
Is there a discount for …?	**¿Hay descuentos para …?** *eye deskwentos para*
children/families	**niños/familias** *neeños/fameeleeas*
senior citizens	**ancianos** *anseeyanos*
students	**estudiantes** *estoodeeyantes*
Do you offer a cheap same-day round-trip/return?	**¿Hay una tarifa especial para viajes de ida y vuelta en el mismo día?** *eye oona tareefa espeseeyal para beeyakhes deh eeda ee bwelta en el meesmo deeya*
Is it cheaper to travel after a certain time?	**¿Sale más barato viajar después de determinada hora?** *saleh mas barato beeakhar despwes deh determeenada ora*

Queries Dudas relacionadas

Do I have to change trains?	**¿Tengo que cambiar de tren?** _tengo keh kambeeyar deh tren_
It's a direct train.	**Es un tren directo.** _es oon tren deerekto_
You have to change at …	**Tiene que cambiar en …** _teeyeneh keh kambeeyar en_
Can I return on the same ticket?	**¿Puedo regresar con el mismo boleto [tiquete]?** _pwedo regresar kon el meesmo boleto [teeketeh]_
How long is this ticket valid for?	**¿Por cuánto tiempo es válido este boleto [tiquete]?** _por kwanto teeyempo es baleedo esteh boleto [teeketeh]_
Can I take my bicycle on to the train?	**¿Puedo subir mi bicicleta al tren?** _pwedo soobeer mee beeseekleta al tren_
Which car/coach is my seat in?	**¿En qué coche [vagón] está mi asiento?** _en keh kocheh esta mee eseeyento_
Is there a dining car on the train?	**¿Hay un coche comedor en el tren?** _eye oon kocheh komedor en el tren_

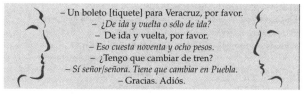

– Un boleto [tiquete] para Veracruz, por favor.
– ¿De ida y vuelta o sólo de ida?
– De ida y vuelta, por favor.
– Eso cuesta noventa y ocho pesos.
– ¿Tengo que cambiar de tren?
– Sí señor/señora. Tiene que cambiar en Puebla.
– Gracias. Adiós.

Train times Horario de trenes

Could I have a timetable?	**¿Podría darme un horario de trenes?** _podreeya darmeh oon orareeo deh trenes_
When is the … train to …?	**¿A qué hora sale el … tren para …?** _a keh ora saleh el … tren para_
first/next/last	**primer/próximo/último** _preemer/prokseemo/oolteemo_

How frequent are the trains to …?	**¿Con qué frecuencia salen los trenes con destino a …?** kon keh frekwenseea salen los trenes kon desteeno a
once/twice a day	**una vez/dos veces al día** oona bes/dos beses al deeya
5 times a day	**cinco veces al día** seenko beses al deeya
every hour	**cada hora** kada ora
What time do they leave?	**¿A qué hora salen?** a keh ora salen
on the hour	**a la hora en punto** a la ora en poonto
20 minutes past the hour	**a la hora y veinte [a las y veinte]** a la ora ee beynteh [a las ee beynteh]
What time does the train stop at …?	**¿A qué hora para el tren en …?** a keh ora para el tren en
What time does the train arrive in …?	**¿A qué hora llega el tren a …?** a keh ora l-yega el tren a
How long is the trip/journey?	**¿Cuánto dura el viaje?** Kwanto doora el beeyakheh
Is the train on time?	**¿Viene a tiempo el tren ?** beeyeneh a teeyempo el tren

Departures Salidas

Which platform does the train to … leave from?	**¿De qué andén sale el tren para …?** de keh anden sale el tren para
Where is platform 4?	**¿Dónde está el andén 4?** dondeh esta el anden kwatro
over there	**por allá** por al-ya
on the right/left	**a la derecha/izquierda** a la derecha/eeskeeyerda
Where do I change for …?	**¿Dónde puedo cambiar de tren para ir a …?** dondeh pwedo kambeeyar deh tren para eer a
How long will I have to wait for a connection?	**¿Cuánto tiempo tengo que esperar para hacer el trasbordo?** kwanto teeyempo tengo keh esperar para aser el trasbordo

Boarding Subir al tren

Is this the right platform for the train to …?
¿Es éste el andén para el tren a …? *es esteh el andén para el tren a*

Is this the train to …?
¿Es éste el tren a …? *es esteh el tren a*

Is this seat taken?
¿Está ocupado este asiento? *esta okoopado esteh aseeyento*

I think that's my seat.
Creo que ése es mi asiento. *kreyo keh eseh es mee aseeyento*

Here's my reservation.
Aquí está mi reservación. *akee esta mee reserbaseeyon*

Are there any seats/berths available?
¿Queda algún asiento/alguna litera disponible? *keda algoon aseeyento/ algoona leetera deesponeebleh*

Do you mind if …?
¿Le molesta si…? *le molesta see*

I sit here
me siento aquí *me seeyento akee*

I open the window
abro la ventana *abro la bentana*

On the journey Durante el viaje

How long are we stopping here for?
¿Cuánto tiempo vamos a parar aquí? *kwanto teeyempo bamos a parar akee*

When do we get to …?
¿A qué hora llegamos a …? *a keh ora l-yegamos a*

Have we passed …?
¿Hemos pasado …? *emos pasado*

Where is the dining/ sleeping car?
¿Dónde está el coche comedor/el coche cama? *dondeh esta el kocheh komedor/ el kocheh kama*

Where is my berth?
¿Dónde está mi litera? *dondeh esta mee leetera*

I've lost my ticket.
Se me perdió mi boleto [tiquete]. *seh meh perdeeyo mee boleto [teeketeh]*

⊙ **FRENO DE EMERGENCIA**	emergency brake
ALARMA	alarm
⊙ **PUERTAS AUTOMÁTICAS**	automatic doors

Long-distance bus/Coach Autocar

Mexico, Chile and Argentina provide good regional coach (bus) services. Most cities have a **terminal de autobuses**. Service is categorized as first, second and third class; and **sin escalas** (nonstop), **directo** (few stops), and **ordinario** (stops on demand).

Where is the bus station?	**¿Dónde queda la estación de autobuses?** *dondeh keda la estaseeyon deh aootobooses*
When's the next bus to …?	**¿A qué hora sale el próximo autobús para …?** *a keh ora saleh el prokseemo aootoboos para*
Which terminal does it leave from?	**¿De qué parada [paradero] sale el bus?** *deh keh parada [paradero] saleh el aootoboos*
Does the bus stop at …?	**¿Se detiene el autobús en …?** *seh deteeyeneh el aootoboos en*
How long does the trip/ journey take?	**¿Cuánto dura el viaje?** *kwanto doora el beeyakheh*

Bus/Tram Bus/Tranvía

Most towns have a bus station (**Central de Autobuses** or **Central Camionera**), but city buses vary in name: **el bus/autobús** (the general term), **el camión** (Mexico), **el ómnibus** (Peru), **el micro** (Chile) and **la guagua** (Carribean).

Where can I get a bus/ tram to …?	**¿Dónde puedo tomar un autobús/tranvía para…?** *dondeh pwedo tomar oon aootoboos/tranbeeya para*
What time is the … bus to …?	**¿A qué hora sale el … autobús para …?** *a keh ora sale el …aootoboos para*

Tiene que esperar el autobús en el paradero que está allá/bajando la calle.	You need that stop over there/down the road.
Tiene que tomar el autobús número …	You need bus number …
Tiene que cambiar de autobús en …	You must change buses at …

PARADA DE AUTOBUSES	bus stop
PROHIBIDO FUMAR	no smoking
SALIDA (DE EMERGENCIA)	(emergency) exit
SOLICITE LA PARADA	request stop

Buying tickets
Comprar boletos [tiquetes]

Where can I buy tickets? **¿Dónde se compran los boletos [tiquetes]?** *dondeh seh kompran los boletos [teeketes]*

A … ticket to …, please. **Un boleto [tiquete] … para …, por favor.** *oon boleto [teeketeh] … para … por fabor*

one-way/single **de ida** *deh eeda*

round-trip/return **de ida y vuelta** *deh eeda ee bwelta*

day/weekly/monthly **para el día/la semana/el mes** *para el deeya/la semana/el mes*

How much is the fare to …? **¿Cuál es la tarifa para …?** *kwal es la tareefa para*

Traveling De viaje

Is this the right bus/tram to …? **¿Es éste el autobús/tranvía para …?** *es este el aootoboos/tranbeeya para*

Could you tell me when to get off? **¿Podría avisarme cuándo tengo que bajarme?** *podreeya abeesarmeh kwando tengo keh bakharmeh*

Do I have to change buses? **¿Tengo que cambiar de autobús?** *tengo keh kambeeyar deh aootoboos*

How many stops are there to …? **¿Cuántas paradas [paraderos] hay hasta …?** *kwantas paradas [paraderos] eye asta*

Next stop, please! **¡La próxima parada, por favor!** *la prokseema parada por fabor*

○ **CONVALIDE SU TIQUETE**   validate your ticket ○

– ¿Disculpe, es éste el bus que va hasta la catedral?
– Sí, el número 8. Allá viene, por allá...
– Un boleto a la catedral, por favor.
– Son 20 pesos.
– ¿Podría avisarme cuándo bajarme?
– Son cuatro paraderos más.

NUMBERS ➤ 216; *DIRECTIONS* ➤ 94

Subway/Metro Metro

There are metro systems in Mexico City, Buenos Aires, Santiago and Caracas. Buy a single flat-rate ticket or a book of tickets (**un abono**) at ticket offices or automatic machines, found in every station.

The Mexico City metro runs from 5 a.m. till midnight (7 a.m. on Sundays); but try to avoid it during rush hour; passengers are allowed to carry only one package (no bigger than a briefcase) each.

General Inquiries Información general

Where's the nearest subway/metro station?	**¿Dónde queda la estación de metro más cercana?** _dondeh <u>ke</u>da la estasee<u>yon</u> deh <u>metro mas ser<u>ka</u>na_
Where do I buy a ticket?	**¿Dónde se compran los boletos [tiquetes]?** _dondeh seh <u>kom</u>pran los bo<u>le</u>tos [tee<u>ke</u>tes]_
Could I have a subway/metro map?	**¿Me podría dar un mapa del metro, por favor?** _meh po<u>dree</u>ya dar oon <u>ma</u>pa del metro por fa<u>bor</u>_

Traveling De viaje

Which line should I take for …?	**¿Qué línea debo tomar para ir a…?** _keh <u>lee</u>nea <u>de</u>bo to<u>mar</u> para eer a_
Is this the right train for …?	**¿Es éste el metro para …?** _es <u>es</u>teh el <u>me</u>tro para_
Which stop is it for …?	**¿Qué parada [paradero] es ésta?** _keh pa<u>ra</u>da [para<u>de</u>ro] es <u>es</u>ta [<u>es</u>teh]_
How many stops is it to …?	**¿Cuántos paraderos faltan para llegar a …?** _<u>kwan</u>tos para<u>de</u>ros <u>fal</u>tan para l-ye<u>gar</u> a_
Is the next stop …?	**¿Es … la próxima parada?** _es…la <u>prok</u>seema pa<u>ra</u>da_
Where are we?	**¿Dónde estamos?** _dondeh es<u>ta</u>mos_
Where do I change for …?	**¿Dónde debo cambiar para …?** _dondeh <u>de</u>bo kambee<u>yar</u> para_
What time is the last train to …?	**¿A qué hora sale el último metro para …?** _a keh <u>o</u>ra <u>sa</u>leh el <u>ool</u>teemo metro para_

CONEXIÓN CON OTRAS LÍNEAS	to other lines

NUMBERS ➤ 216; BUYING TICKETS ➤ 74, 79

Ferry Transbordador [Ferry]

Cruises sail between Los Angeles and Acapulco, and Miami and the Caribbean coast. Ferries run between mainland Mexico and Baja California, and Cozumel and Isla Mujeres and the Yucatán peninsula.

When is the … car ferry to …?	**¿A qué hora sale el … transbordador de carros para …?** *a keh ora saleh el … transbordador deh karros para*
first/next/last	**primero/próximo/último** *preemero/prokseemo/oolteemo*
hovercraft/ship	**el hidrodeslizador/el barco** *el eedrodesleesador/el barko*
A round-trip/return ticket for …	**Un boleto [tiquete] de ida y vuelta para …** *oon boleto [teeketeh] deh eeda ee bwelta para*
1 car and 1 trailer/camper	**un carro y una casa móvil** *oon karro ee oona kasa mobeel*
2 adults and 3 children	**dos adultos y tres niños** *dos adooltos ee tres neeños*
I want to reserve a … cabin.	**Quiero reservar una cabina …** *keeyero reserbar oona kabeena*
single/double	**sencilla/doble** *senseel-ya/dobleh*

BOTE SALVAVIDAS	life boat
CINTURÓN SALVAVIDAS	life preserver/belt
SITIO DE CONCENTRACIÓN DE PASAJEROS	muster station
PROHIBIDO EL ACCESO A LOS ESTACIONAMIENTOS	no access to car decks

Boat trips Viajes en barco

Is there a …?	**¿Hay …?** *eye*
boat trip/river cruise	**un viaje en barco/un crucero por el río** *oon beeyakheh en barko/oon kroosero por el reeyo*
What time does it leave/return?	**¿A qué hora se sale/se regresa?** *a keh ora seh saleh/seh regresa*
Where can we buy tickets?	**¿Dónde se pueden comprar los boletos [tiquetes]?** *dondeh seh pweden komssprar los boletos [teeketes]*

TIME ➤ 220; BUYING TICKETS ➤ 74, 79

1 brake pad **la pastilla de frenos**
2 bicycle bag **la mochila**
3 saddle **el asiento**
4 pump **la bomba**
5 water bottle **la cantimplora**
6 frame **el cuadro [la armadura]**
7 handlebars **los manubrios**
8 bell **la campana**
9 brake cable **el cable de los frenos**
10 gear shift/lever **la barra de cambios**
11 gear/control cable
    el cable de los cambios
12 inner tube **cámara de aire/llanta**
13 front/back wheel
    la rueda delantera/trasera
14 axle **el eje**
15 tire/tyre **la llanta**
16 wheel **la rueda**
17 spoke **el radio/rayo**
18 bulb **la bombilla/el foco**
19 headlamp **faro**

20 pedal **el pedal**
21 lock **la cerradura contra robos**
22 generator/dynamo **el dínamo**
23 chain **la cadena**
24 rear light **el faro trasero/luz**
25 rim **la llanta**
26 reflectors **los reflectores**
27 fender/mudguard **el guardafango**
28 helmet **el casco**
29 visor **la visera**
30 fuel tank **el tanque de la gasolina**
31 clutch lever **el pedal de embrague**
32 mirror **el espejo**
33 ignition switch **la llave de encendido**
34 turn signal/switch **la direccional**
35 horn **la bocina [el pito]**
36 engine **el motor**
37 gear shift/stick **la barra de cambios**
38 main stand **la varilla de la bicicleta**
39 exhaust pipe **el tubo de escape**
40 chain guard **la barra**

CAR REPAIRS ➤ 89

Bicycle/Motorbike
Bicicletas/motocicletas

I'd like to rent/hire a …	**Quisiera alquilar …** *keeseeyera alkeelar*
3-/10-gear bicycle	**una bicicleta de cambio 3-/10** *oona beeseekleta deh kambeeo tres/deeyes*
moped	**un velomotor** *oon belomotor*
motorbike	**una motocicleta** *oona motoseekleta*
How much does it cost per day/week?	**¿Cuál es el precio por día/semana?** *kwal es el preseeyo por deeya/semana*
Do you require a deposit?	**¿Hay que pagar un depósito?** *eye keh pagar oon deposeeto*
The brakes don't work.	**Los frenos no funcionan.** *los frenos no foonseeyonan*
There are no lights.	**No tiene luces.** *no teeyene looses*
The front/rear tire/tyre has a flat/puncture.	**La llanta delantera/trasera está pinchada.** *la l-yanta trasera/delantera esta peenchada*

Hitchhiking Autostop

Hitchhiking is not very safe in Mexico; you are advised not to hitch alone.

Where are you heading?	**¿Adónde va usted?** *adondeh ba oosteth*
I'm heading for …	**Voy hacia …** *boy aseeya*
Is that on the way to …?	**¿Está eso en la vía a …?** *esta eso en la beeya a*
Could you drop me off …?	**¿Podría dejarme …?** *podreeya dekharmeh*
here/at …	**aquí/en …** *akee/en*
at the … exit	**en la salida …** *en la saleeda*
in the center/centre	**en el centro** *en el sentro*
Thanks for the lift.	**Gracias por el aventón [el viaje].** *graseeyas por el abenton [el beeyakheh]*

DIRECTIONS ➤ 94; NUMBERS ➤ 216

Taxi/Cab Taxi

Most taxis have meters, but it is generally wise to ask the fare beforehand. Extra charges are added for night trips and often for baggage. In most major cities there are official taxis (at airports, bus stations, etc.) which should be used for your security. Tipping suggestions: No tip is generally required for taxi drivers in most Central and South American countries; it is considered optional in Argentina.

Where can I get a taxi?	**¿Dónde puedo tomar un taxi?** _dondeh pwedo tomar oon taksi_
Do you have the number for a taxi?	**¿Tiene el número de alguna empresa de taxis?** _teeyeneh el noomero deh algoona empresa deh taksis_
I'd like a taxi ...	**Quisiera un taxi ...** _keeseeyera oon taksi_
now	**para ahora mismo** _para aora meesmo_
in an hour	**para dentro de una hora** _para dentro deh oona ora_
for tomorrow at 9:00	**para mañana a las nueve** _para mañana a las nwebeh_
The address is ... We're going to ...	**La dirección es ... Nos dirigimos a ...** _la deerekseeyon es ... nos deereekheemos a_

> ◎ **SE ALQUILA**   for hire ◎

Please take me to the ...	**Por favor, lléveme a ...** _por fabor l-yebemeh a_
airport	**el aeropuerto** _el aeropwerto_
rail station	**la estación de tren** _la estaseeyon deh tren_
this address	**esta dirección** _esta deerekseeyon_
How much will it cost?	**¿Cuánto va a costar el viaje [la carrera]?** _kwanto ba a kostar el beeyakheh [la karrera]_
How much is that?	**¿Cuánto es?** _kwanto es_
On the meter it's ...	**Según el taxímetro son ...** _segoon el takseemetro son_
Keep the change.	**Guarde el cambio.** _gwardeh el kambeeo_

> – ¿Me podría llevar a la estación, por favor?
> – Con mucho gusto.
> – ¿Cuánto va a costar el viaje?
> – Catorce pesos. ... Aquí estamos.
> – Gracias. Guarde el cambio.

NUMBERS ➤ 216; TIME ➤ 220

Car/Automobile Automóvil

Most foreign driver's licenses/licences are valid in Mexico.

If driving into Mexico, take out insurance on your own car, available from agencies at the border.

You are not allowed to sell your car in Mexico; you will be required to fill out a vehicle import form at the border.

Carry a spare tire, a jack and water for your radiator; and spare parts, if possible.

Speed limits kmph (mph)	Built-up area	Outside built-up area	Highway
Mexico	25 (40)	43 (70)	68 (110)

Don't drive at night in Mexico, to avoid any dangers of banditry or road hazards.

Watch out for speed bumps (**topes**) on entering most towns in Mexico; they should generally be approached at walking pace.

Check that gas/petrol pumps are set at zero before pumping. Have enough cash for your fuel: credit cards are not accepted at filling stations.

Gas/Petrol (Octane)	Leaded	<u>Unleaded</u>	Diesel (gas-oil)
Mexico (Pemex)	Nova (80)	Magna Sin (87)	Gas-oil
	Blue pump	Green pump	Red/Purple pump

Conversion Chart

km	1	10	20	30	40	50	60	70	80	90	100	110	120	130
miles	0.62	6	12	19	25	31	37	44	50	56	62	68	74	81

Parking (➤ 87 for phrases)

In Mexico, illegal parking may result in your license plate being removed. Pay an on-the-spot fine to the nearby policeman to retrieve it.

In Mexico City, vehicles are banned from driving one day per week, which is set according to the final digit of their license plate.

Car rental Alquiler de carros

Car rental firms will require to see a valid driver's license/licence and identification. The minimum age varies between countries.

Local firms tend to be cheaper than major chains, but check the cost of insurance, tax and mileage when comparing prices.

Where can I rent/hire a car?	**¿Dónde puedo alquilar un carro?** _dondeh pwedo alkeelar oon karro_
I'd like to rent/hire a(n) ...	**Quisiera alquilar ...** _keeseeyera alkeelar_
2-/4-door car	**un carro de dos/cuatro puertas.** _oon karro deh dos/kwatro pwertas_
an automatic	**un carro automático** _oon karro aootomateeko_
with air conditioning	**con aire acondicionado** _kon ayreh akondeeseeonado_
I'd like it for a day/a week.	**Lo quiero para un día/una semana.** _lo keeyero para oon deeya/oona semana_
How much does it cost per day/week?	**¿Cuál es el precio por día/ semana?** _kwal es el preseeo por deeya/semana_
Is mileage/insurance included?	**¿Está incluido el kilometraje/el seguro?** _esta eenklooeedo el kilometrakheh/ el segooro_
Are there special weekend rates?	**¿Hay precios especiales para los fines de semana?** _eye preseeos espeseeyales para los feenes deh semana_
Can I leave the car at your office in ...?	**¿Puedo dejar el carro en la sucursal de ...?** _pwedo dekhar el karro en la sookoorsal deh_
What sort of fuel does it take?	**¿Qué clase de gasolina consume?** _keh klaseh deh gasoleena konsoomeh_
Where's the high/full low/dipped beam?	**¿Dónde están las luces altas/las luces bajas?** _dondeh estan las looses altas/ las looses bakhas_
Could I have full insurance, please?	**Quiero seguro completo, por favor.** _keeyero segooro kompleto por fabor_

PAYING ➤ 89; DAYS OF THE WEEK ➤ 218

Gas Gasolinera [Estación de gasolina]

Where's the next filling station, please?	**¿Dónde está la próxima gasolinera [estación de gasolina], por favor?** _dondeh esta la prokseema gasoleenera [estaseeyon deh gasoleena] por fabor_
Is it self-service?	**¿Es autoservicio?** _es aootoserbeeseeo_
Fill it up, please.	**Llene el tanque, por favor.** _l-yeneh el tankeh por fabor_
… liters/litres of gasoline, please.	**… litros de gasolina, por favor.** _leetros deh gasoleena por fabor_
What grade of gas would you like?	**¿Qué clase de gasolina desea?** _keh klaseh deh gasoleena deseea_
premium (super)/regular	**súper/normal** _sooper/normal_
lead-free/diesel	**sin plomo/diesel** _seen plomo/deesel_
I'm pump number …	**Bomba número …** _bomba noomero_
Where is the air pump/water?	**¿Dónde está la bomba de aire/agua?** _dondeh esta la bomba deh ayreh/agwa_

> ◎ **PRECIO POR LITRO**   price per liter/litre   ◎

Parking Estacionamiento [parqueo]

Is there a parking lot nearby?	**¿Hay un estacionamiento [parqueadero] de carros por aquí?** _eye oon estaseeonameeyento [parkeadero] deh karros por akee_
What's the charge per hour/per day?	**¿Cuál es la tarifa por hora/día?** _kwal es la tareefa por ora/deeya_
Do you have some change for the parking meter?	**¿Tiene cambio para el parquímetro/contador de estacionamiento?** _teeyeneh kambeeo para el parkeemetro/kontador deh estaseeonameeyento_
My car has been booted/clamped. Who do I call?	**Han inmobilizado [bloqueado] mi carro. ¿Con quién tengo que hablar?** _an eenmobeeleesado [blokeado] mee karro. kon keeyen tengo keh ablar_

DIRECTIONS ➤ 94; _NUMBERS_ ➤ 216;   **87**

Breakdown Averías

For help in the event of a breakdown: refer to your breakdown assistance documents; or contact the national automobile association.

In the event of a breakdown in Mexico, contact the Green Angels (**Ángeles Verdes**), a free mechanic service. Within Mexico City, contact the Mexican Automobile Association (**AAM**).

Where is the nearest garage?	**¿Dónde está el taller de mecánica más cercano?** _dondeh esta el tal-yer deh mekaneeka mas serkano_
I've had a breakdown.	**Mi carro se ha descompuesto. [Estoy varado(-a).]** _mee karro seh a deskompwesto [estoy barado(-a)]_
Can you send a mechanic/ tow/breakdown truck?	**¿Puede enviar un mecánico/una grúa?** _pwedeh enbeear oon mekaneeko/oona grooa_
I belong to … recovery service.	**Estoy afiliado al servicio de rescate …** _estoy afeeleeyado al serbeeseeo deh reskate_
My registration number is …	**Mi número de matrícula es …** _mee noomero deh matreekoola es_
The car is …	**El carro está…** _el karro esta_
on the highway/motorway	**en la autopista** _en la aootopeesta_
2 km from …	**a dos kilómetros de…** _a dos kilometros de_
How long will you be?	**¿Cuánto se demorará?** _kwanto seh demorara_

What is wrong? ¿Qué anda mal?

My car won't start.	**Mi carro no quiere arrancar.** _mee karro no keeyere arrankar_
The battery is dead.	**La batería está descargada.** _la batereeya esta deskargada_
I've run out of gas/petrol.	**Se me acabó la gasolina.** _seh meh akabo la gasoleena_
I have a flat/puncture.	**Tengo una llanta pinchada.** _tengo oona l-yanta peenchada_
There is something wrong with …	**Algo anda mal con …** _algo anda mal kon_
I've locked the keys in the car.	**Dejé las llaves dentro del carro.** _dekheh las l-yabes dentro del karro_

Repairs Reparaciones

Do you do repairs?	**¿Hace usted reparaciones?** *aseh oostteth reparaseeyones*
Can you repair it?	**¿Podría repararlo?** *podreeya repararlo*
Please make only essential repairs.	**Por favor haga sólo las reparaciones indispensables.** *por fabor aga solo las reparaseeyones eendeespensables*
Can I wait for it?	**¿Puedo esperar a que lo repare?** *pwedo esperar a keh lo repareh*
Can you repair it today?	**¿Puede repararlo hoy mismo?** *pwedeh repararlo oy meesmo*
When will it be ready?	**¿Cuándo estará listo?** *kwando estara leesto*
Come back next Tuesday.	**Regrese el próximo martes.** *regreseh el prokseemo martes*
How much will it cost?	**¿Cuánto me va a costar la reparación?** *kwanto meh ba a kostar la reparaseeyon*
That's outrageous!	**¡Es un precio escandaloso!** *es oon preseeyo eskandaloso*
Can I have a receipt for the insurance?	**¿Podría darme un recibo para el trámite de seguro?** *podreeya darmeh oon reseebo para el trameeteh deh segooro*

... no está funcionando.	The ... isn't working.
No tengo los repuestos necesarios.	I don't have the necessary parts.
Tendría que encargar los repuestos.	I will have to order the parts.
Sólo puedo repararlo temporalmente.	I can only repair it temporarily.
Su carro no sirve para nada.	Your car is a write-off.
No se puede reparar.	It can't be repaired.
Estará listo ...	It will be ready ...
dentro de un rato/más tarde	later today
mañana	tomorrow
dentro de ... días	in ... days

DAYS OF THE WEEK ➤ 218; NUMBERS ➤ 216

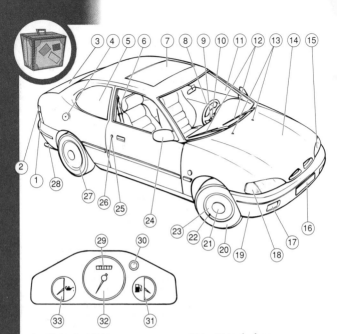

1 tail lights/back lights
   las luces traseras
2 brakelights **las luces de los frenos**
3 trunk/boot
   la cajuela [el maletero/el baúl]
4 gas tank door
   la tapa del depósito de gasolina
5 window **la ventana**
6 seat belt **el cinturón de seguridad**
7 sunroof **el techo solar**
8 steering wheel **el volante**
9 starter/ignition **el encendido**
10 ignition key **la llave (de encendido)**
11 windscreen **el parabrisas**
12 windshield/windscreen wipers
   las escobillas
13 windshield/windscreen washer
   el limpiaparabrisas
14 hood/bonnet **el capó**

15 headlights **los faros**
16 registration plate **las placas**
17 fog lamp **el faro antiniebla**
18 turn signals/indicators
   las direccionales
19 bumper **el parachoques**
20 tires/tyres **las llantas**
21 hubcap/wheel cover **el tapacubos**
22 valve **la válvula**
23 wheels **las ruedas**
24 outside/wing mirror
   el espejo retrovisor
25 central locking **el cierre centralizado**
26 lock **el seguro [la cerradura]**
27 wheel rim **el rin de la rueda**
28 exhaust pipe **el tubo de escape**
29 odometer/milometer
   el medidor de kilometraje

90

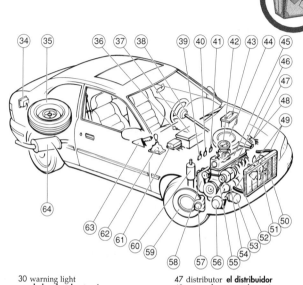

30 warning light
   la luz de advertencia
31 fuel gauge/pump **el indicador/**
   la bomba de la gasolina
32 speedometer **el velocímetro**
33 oil gauge
   el indicador del nivel de aceite
34 backup lights **las luces de reversa**
35 spare wheel **la llanta de repuesto**
36 choke **el estárter [ahogador]**
37 heater **la calefacción**
38 steering column
   la columna de dirección
39 accelerator **el acelerador**
40 pedal **el pedal**
41 clutch **el embrague [el cloche]**
42 carburetor **el carburador**
43 battery **la batería**
44 alternator **el alternador**
45 camshaft **el árbol de levas**
46 air filter **el filtro de aire**

47 distributor **el distribuidor**
48 points **las tomas de corriente**
49 radiator hose (top/bottom)
   la manguera del radiador
   (arriba/abajo)
50 radiator **el radiador**
51 fan **el ventilador**
52 engine **el motor**
53 oil filter **el filtro de aceite**
54 starter motor **el motor de arranque**
55 fan belt **la correa del ventilador**
56 horn **la bocina [el pito]**
57 brake pads **las pastillas de los frenos**
58 transmission/gear box
   la caja de cambio
59 brakes **los frenos**
60 shock absorbers **los amortiguadores**
61 fuses **los fusibles**
62 gear shift/lever **la barra de cambios**
63 handbrake **el freno de mano**
64 muffler **el silenciador**

Accidents Accidentes

In the event of a minor accident in Mexico, you may find it simpler to sort things out with the other driver without involving the police. For a serious incident, contact your consulate and Mexican Insurance Company.

There has been an accident.	**Ha habido un accidente.**
	a a_beedo oon aks_eedenteh
It's …	**Ocurrió…** *okoor_eeyo*
on the highway/motorway	**en la autopista**
	en la aootopeesta
near …	**cerca de …** *serka deh*
Where's the nearest telephone?	**¿Dónde está el teléfono más cercano?**
	dondeh esta el telefono mas serkano
Call …	**Llame a …** *l-yameh a*
an ambulance	**una ambulancia**
	oona amboolanseea
a doctor	**un doctor** *oon doktor*
the fire station/brigade	**los bomberos** *los bomberos*
the police	**la policía** *la poleeseeya*
Can you help me please?	**¿Puede ayudarme, por favor?**
	pwedeh ayoodarmeh por fabor

Injuries Heridas

There are people injured.	**Hay personas heridas.**
	eye personas ereedas
No one is hurt.	**Nadie resultó herido.**
	nadeeyeh resoolto ereedo
He is seriously injured.	**Él está gravemente herido.**
	el esta grabementeh ereedo
She's unconscious.	**Ella está inconsciente.**
	el-ya esta eenkonseeyenteh
He can't breathe/move.	**Él no puede respirar/moverse.**
	el no pwedeh respeerar/moberseh
Don't move him.	**No lo mueva.**
	no lo mweba

Legal matters Asuntos legales

What's your insurance company? **¿Cuál es su compañía de seguros?** *kwal es soo kompañeeya deh segooros*

What's your name and address? **¿Cuál es su nombre y dirección?** *kwal es soo nombreh ee deerekseeyon*

He ran into me. **Él me chocó.** *el meh choko*

She was driving too fast/too close. **Ella estaba conduciendo [manejando] demasiado rápido/demasiado cerca.** *el-ya estaba kondooseeyendo [manekhando] demaseeyado rapeedo/demaseeyado serka*

I had the right of way. **Yo tenía el derecho a la vía.** *yo teneeya el derecho a la beeya*

I was (only) driving at … km/h. **Yo sólo estaba conduciendo [manejando] a … kilómetros por hora.** *yo solo estaba kondooseeyendo [manekhando] a … kilometros por ora*

I'd like an interpreter. **Quisiera un intérprete.** *keeseeyera oon eenterpreteh*

I didn't see the sign. **Yo no vi la señal.** *yo no bee la señal*

He/She saw it happen. **Él/ella vio lo que sucedió.** *el/el-ya beeo lo keh soosedeeyo*

¿Me permite su …?	Can I see your …?
licencia de conducir	driver's license/licence
certificado del seguro	insurance certificate
número de matrícula	license plate number
¿A qué hora sucedió?	What time did it happen?
¿Dónde sucedió?	Where did it happen?
¿Hubo alguien más involucrado en el accidente?	Was anyone else involved?
¿Hay testigos?	Are there any witnesses?
Usted estaba conduciendo [manejando] a gran velocidad.	You were speeding.
Sus luces no están funcionando.	Your lights aren't working.
Usted tendrá que pagar una multa ahora mismo.	You'll have to pay a fine (on the spot).
Necesitamos que haga una declaración en la estación.	We need you to make a statement at the station.

TIME ➤ 220

Asking directions
Pedir direcciones

Excuse me, please.	**Disculpe, por favor.** *deeskoolpeh por fabor*
How do I get to …?	**¿Cómo se llega a …?** *komo se l-yega a*
Where is …?	**¿Dónde queda …?** *dondeh keda*
Can you show me on the map where I am?	**¿Puede mostrarme en el mapa dónde estoy ahora?** *pwedeh mostrarmeh en el mapa dondeh estoy aora*
I've lost my way.	**Estoy perdido(-a).** *estoy perdeedo(-a)*
Can you repeat that please?	**¿Puede repetirmelo, por favor?** *pwedeh repeteermelo por fabor*
More slowly, please.	**Más despacio, por favor.** *mas despaseeo por fabor*
Thanks for your help.	**Gracias por su ayuda.** *graseeas por soo ayooda*

Traveling by car Viajar en carro

Is this the right road for …?	**¿Es ésta la carretera que va a…?** *es esta la karretera keh ba a*
How far is it to … from here?	**¿A qué distancia queda … de aquí?** *a keh distancia keda deh akee*
Where does this road lead?	**¿Adónde va esta carretera?** *adondeh ba esta karretera*
How do I get onto the freeway/motorway?	**¿Cómo puedo llegar a la autopista?** *komo pwedo l-yegar a la aootopeesta*
What's the next town called?	**¿Cómo se llama el próximo pueblo?** *komo seh l-yama el prokseemo pweblo*
How long does it take by car?	**¿Cuánto dura el viaje en carro?** *kwanto doora el beeyakheh en karro*

- Disculpe, por favor.
¿Cómo se llega a la estación de tren?
- Tome el tercer giro a la izquierda y siga derecho.
- Tercer giro a la izquierda. ¿Queda muy lejos?
- Son cinco minutos a pie.
- Gracias por su ayuda.
- De nada.

Location Ubicación

Está...	It's ...
derecho	straight ahead
a la izquierda	on the left
a la derecha	on the right
al otro lado de la calle	on the other side of the street
en la esquina	on the corner
a la vuelta de la esquina	round the corner
en dirección a...	in the direction of ...
enfrente de.../detrás de...	opposite .../behind ...
al lado de.../después de...	next to .../after ...
Baje ...	Go down ...
la calle lateral/la calle principal	side street/main street
Cruce ...	Cross the ...
la plaza/el puente	square/bridge
Tome el tercer giro a la derecha	Take the third turning on the right
gire a la izquierda...	Turn left ...
después del primer semáforo	after the first traffic lights
en el segundo cruce de carreteras	at the second crossroad (intersection)

By car En carro

Está al ... de aquí.	It's ... of here.
norte/sur	north/south
oriente/occidente	east/west
Tome la carretera hacia ...	Take the road for ...
Usted está en la carretera equivocada.	You're on the wrong road.
Tiene que regresar a...	You'll have to go back to ...
Siga las señales para ...	Follow the signs for ...

How far? ¿A qué distancia ...?

Está ...	It's ...
cerca/muy lejos	close/a long way
a cinco minutos a pie/en carro	5 minutes on foot/by car
a diez kilómetros de aquí	about 10 km away
bajando alrededor de 100 metros	about 100m down the road

TIME ➤ 220; NUMBERS ➤ 216

Road signs Señales de carretera

CAMINO CERRADO	road closed
DE [CEDA] LA VÍA	yield (give way)
DESVÍO	detour (diversion)
ESCUELA/COLEGIO	school
MÉTASE AL CARRIL	stay in lane (get in lane)
PUENTE BAJO	low bridge
RUTA ALTERNATIVA	alternative route
UNA SOLA VÍA	one-way street
ENCIENDA LOS FAROS	use headlights
VÍA DE ACCESO SOLAMENTE	access only

Town plans Mapa de la ciudad/del pueblo

aeropuerto (m)	airport
calle (f) principal	main/high street
campos (mpl) deportivos	playing field/sports ground
cine (m)	movie theater/cinema
ciudad (f) vieja	old town
cruce (m) peatonal	pedestrian crossing
edificio (m) público	public building
estación (f)	station
estación (f) del metro	subway/metro station
estación (f) de policía	police station
estacionamiento [parqueadero] (m)	parking lot
estadio (m)	stadium
iglesia (f)	church
oficina (f) de correo	post office
oficina (f) de información	information office
parada (f) de autobús	bus stop
parque (m)	park
parada (f) de taxi	taxi rank
pasadizo (m) subterráneo	underpass/subway
ruta (f) de buses	bus route
teatro (m)	theater
usted está aquí	you are here
zona (f) peatonal	pedestrian zone/precinct

Sightseeing

Tourist information office Oficina de turismo

Tourist offices (**turismos**) are very helpful with plenty of free leaflets about services and attractions.

Where's the tourist office?	**¿Dónde queda la oficina de turismo?** _dondeh keda la ofeeseena deh tooreesmo_
What are the main points of interest?	**¿Cuáles son los principales sitios de interés?** _kwales son los preenseepales seeteeos deh eenteres_
We're here for …	**Vamos a estar aquí …** _bamos a estar akee_
only a few hours	**sólo un par de horas** _solo oon par deh oras_
a day	**un día** _oon deeya_
a week	**una semana** _oona semana_
Can you recommend …?	**¿Puede recomendarme … por favor?** _pwedeh rekomendarmeh … por fabor_
a sightseeing tour	**un recorrido por los lugares turísticos** _oon rekorreedo por los loogares tooreesteekos_
an excursion	**una excursión** _oona eskoorseeyon_
a boat trip	**un viaje en barco** _oon beeyakheh en barko_
Do you have any information on …?	**¿Tiene alguna información sobre …?** _teeyeneh algoona eenformaseeyon sobreh_
Are there any trips to …?	**Hay algún viaje a …?** _eye algoon beeyakheh a_

Excursions Excursiones

How much does the tour cost?	**¿Cuánto cuesta el tour?** _kwanto kwesta el toor_
Is lunch included?	**¿Está incluida la comida [el almuerzo]?** _esta eenklooeeda la komeeda [el almwerso]_
Where do we leave from?	**¿De dónde salimos?** _deh dondeh saleemos_
What time does the tour start?	**¿A qué hora empieza el recorrido?** _a keh ora empeeyesa el rekoreedo_
What time do we get back?	**¿A qué hora regresamos?** _a keh ora regresamos_
Do we have free time in …?	**¿Tenemos tiempo libre en …?** _tenemos teeyempo leebreh en_
Is there an English-speaking guide?	**¿Hay algún guía que hable inglés?** _eye algoon geeya keh able eengles_

On tour Durante la visita

Are we going to see …?	**¿Vamos a ver …?** _bamos a ber_
We'd like to have a look at …	**Quisiéramos echar un ojo [vistazo] al/a la …** _keeseeyeramos echar oon okho [beestaso] al/a la_
Can we stop here …?	**¿Podemos parar aquí?** _podemos parar akee_
to take photographs	**para tomar fotografías** _para tomar fotografeeyas_
to buy souvenirs	**para comprar recuerdos** _para komprar rekwerdos_
for the bathrooms/toilets	**para ir al baño** _para eer al baño_
Would you take a photo of us, please?	**¿Podría tomarnos una fotografía, por favor?** _podreeya tomarnos oona fotografeeya por fabor_
How long do we have here/in …?	**¿Cuánto tiempo vamos a estar aquí?** _kwanto teeyempo bamos a estar akee_
Wait! … isn't back yet.	**¡Un momento! …no ha regresado …** _oon momento… no a regresado_

98

Sights Lugares de interés

Where is the ...?	¿Dónde está ... _dondeh esta_
abbey	la abadía *la aba<u>dee</u>ya*
art gallery	la galería de arte *la gale<u>ree</u>ya deh <u>ar</u>teh*
battle site	el campo de batalla *el <u>kam</u>po deh ba<u>tal</u>-ya*
botanical garden	el jardín botánico *el khar<u>deen</u> bo<u>ta</u>neeko*
castle	el castillo *el kas<u>teel</u>-yo*
cathedral	la catedral *la kate<u>dral</u>*
cemetery	el cementerio *el semen<u>tereeo</u>*
church	la iglesia *la ee<u>glee</u>seea*
downtown area	el centro (de la ciudad) *el <u>sen</u>tro (deh la seeoo<u>dath</u>)*
fountain	la fuente *la <u>fwen</u>te*
market	el mercado *el mer<u>ka</u>do*
(war) memorial	el monumento conmemorativo *el mono<u>o</u>mento konmemora<u>tee</u>bo*
monastery	el monasterio *el mona<u>stereeo</u>*
museum	el museo *el moo<u>se</u>yo*
old town	la ciudad vieja *la seeoo<u>dath</u> bee<u>ye</u>kha*
opera house	el teatro de la ópera *el te<u>a</u>tro deh la <u>o</u>pera*
palace	el palacio *el pa<u>la</u>seeo*
park	el parque *el <u>par</u>keh*
parliament building	la Cámara de Senadores [la Cámara de Representantes/Asamblea Nacional] *la <u>ka</u>mara deh sena<u>do</u>res [la <u>ka</u>mara deh represen<u>tan</u>tes/asam<u>ble</u>a naseeo<u>nal</u>]*
ruins	las ruinas *las roo<u>ee</u>nas*
shopping area	la zona comercial *la <u>so</u>na komer<u>see</u>yal*
statue	la estatua *la esta<u>too</u>a*
theater/theatre	el teatro *el te<u>a</u>tro*
tower	la torre *la <u>to</u>rreh*
town hall	la casa del ayuntamiento [el consejo municipal] *la <u>ka</u>sa del ayoontamee<u>yen</u>to [el kon<u>se</u>kho mooneesee<u>pal</u>]*
vantage point	el mirador *el meera<u>dor</u>*

DIRECTIONS ➤ 94

Admission Admisiones

Museums in Mexico are generally closed on Monday; some shut on Sunday afternoon. General opening hours are 9 a.m. to 1 p.m. to 3 p.m. to 6 p.m..

Is the ... open to the public?	¿Está ... abierto(-a) al público? esta ... abeeyerto(-a) al poobleeko
Can we look around?	¿Podemos dar una vuelta? podemos dar oona bwelta
What are the opening hours?	¿Cuáles son los horarios? kwales son los orareeos
When does it close?	¿A qué hora cierran? a keh ora seeyeran
Is ... open on Sundays?	¿Está abierto(-a) ... los domingos? esta abeeyerto(-a) ... los domeengos
When's the next guided tour?	¿Cuándo es el próximo tour con guía? kwando es el prokseemo toor kon geeya
Have you a guide book (in English)?	¿Tiene usted una guía turística en inglés? teeyeneh oosteth oona geeya tooreesteeka en eengles
Can I take photos?	¿Puedo tomar fotografías? pwedo tomar fotografeeyas
Is there access for the disabled?	¿Hay una entrada especial para personas incapacitadas? eye oona entrada espeseeyal para personas eenkapaseetadas
Is there an audio-guide in English?	¿Hay alguna guía grabada en inglés? eye algoona geeya grabada en eengles

Paying/Tickets Comprar/Boletos [tiquetes]

How much is the entrance fee?	¿Cuánto cuesta la entrada? kwanto kwesta la entrada
Are there any discounts for ...?	¿Hay descuentos/concesiones para ...? eye deskwentos/konseseeyones para
children/students	niños/estudiantes neeños/estoodeeyantes
disabled	personas incapacitadas personas eenkapaseetadas
groups/pensioners	grupos/pensionados groopos/penseeyonados
1 adult and 2 children, please.	un boleto [tiquete] para adulto y dos para niño, por favor. oon boleto [teekete] para adoolto ee dos para neeño por fabor

ABIERTO	open
CERRADO	closed
ENTRADA LIBRE [GRATUITA]	admission free
HORAS DE VISITA	visiting hours
PROHIBIDA LA ENTRADA	no entry
PROHIBIDO TOMAR FOTOGRAFÍAS CON FLASH	no flash photography
PRÓXIMO TOUR A LAS …	next tour at …
TIENDA DE REGALOS	gift shop
ÚLTIMA ENTRADA A LAS 5 P.M.	latest entry at 5 p.m.

Impressions Impresiones

It's …	**Es …** *es*
amazing	**asombroso(-a)** *asom<u>bro</u>so(-a)*
beautiful/ugly	**hermoso(-a)/feo(-a)** *er<u>mo</u>so(-a)/<u>feo</u>(-a)*
bizarre	**extraño(-a)** *es<u>tra</u>ño(-a)*
boring	**aburrido(-a)** *aboor<u>ree</u>do(-a)*
brilliant	**brillante** *breel-<u>yan</u>teh*
great fun	**divertido(-a)** *deeber<u>tee</u>do(-a)*
interesting	**interesante** *intere<u>san</u>teh*
magnificent	**suntuoso(-a) [majestuoso(-a)]** *soontoo<u>o</u>so(-a) [makhestoo<u>o</u>so(-a)]*
romantic	**romántico(-a)** *ro<u>man</u>teeko(-a)*
strange	**raro(-a)** *<u>ra</u>ro(-a)*
stunning	**sensacional** *sensaseeo<u>nal</u>*
superb	**magnífico(-a)** *mag<u>nee</u>feeko(-a)*
terrible	**terrible** *ter<u>ree</u>bleh*
It's good value.	**Es dinero bien gastado.** *es dee<u>ne</u>ro bee<u>yen</u> gas<u>ta</u>do*
It's a rip-off.	**Es una estafa.** *es <u>oo</u>na es<u>ta</u>fa*
I like it.	**Me gusta.** *meh <u>goo</u>sta*
I don't like it.	**No me gusta** *no meh <u>goo</u>sta*

AC BC
acuarela watercolor
alfiz frame around arch
al estilo de in the style of
ala wing (of building)
alfarería pottery
almenas battlements
antigüedades antiquities
aposentos reales
 apartments (royal)
arco arch
arma weapon
arquitecto architect
arsenal armory/armoury
arte moderno modern art
artesanías crafts
artista artist
atlas sculpted figure support
auditorio auditorium
azulejo glazed tile
balcón balcony
baluarte defensive wall
baño baths
biblioteca library
boleadoras bolas, weighted thongs
bosquejo sketch
bóveda vault
cacique Indian chief
camarín side chapel
camarote stateroom
capilla abierta open-air chapel
casona large colonial mansion
cementerio churchyard
cenotafio cenotaph
cerámica ceramic, pottery
Chac Mayan rain god
chac-mool recumbent stone
 sculpture
chapitel spire

chinampas Aztec floating gardens
colección collection
completado(-a) en completed in
conferencia lecture
construido-(a) en built in
contrafuerte buttress
corona crown
cripta crypt
cuadro picture
cúpula dome
DC A.D.
de oro gold(en)
decoración decoration
decorado(-a) por decorated by
demostración demonstration
descubierto(-a) en discovered in
destruido(-a) por destroyed by
detalle detail
dibujo drawing
diseñado(-a) por designed by
diseño design
disfraz costume
documento document
donado(-a) por donated by
dorado(-a) gilded
edificio building
emperador emperor
emperatriz empress
empezó en started in
encargado(-a) por commissioned by
escala de 1 a 100 scale 1:100
escalera staircase
escenario stage
escuela de school of
escultor sculptor
escultura sculpture, carving
estela standing stone monument
estípite pedestal
exhibición display

exponer exhibit
exposición exhibition
exposición temporal
 temporary exhibit
fachada facade
figura de cera waxwork
fósil fossil
foso moat
fotografía photograph
friso frieze
fundado(-a) en founded in
gárgola gargoyle
grabado engraving, etching
guaca burial ground, tomb
joyas jewelry
juego de pelota ball court
laberinto formal garden
lápida headstone
lienzo canvas
manuscrito manuscript
mármol marble
miniatura miniature
modelo model
moneda coin
muebles furniture
muerto(-a) en died in
mural mural
muro wall
na Mayan hut
nacido(-a) en born in
obra maestra masterpiece
óleos oils
órgano organ
pabellón pavilion
paisaje landscape (painting)
palacio palace
parroquia parish church
pastel pastel
patio courtyard
piedra stone
piedra preciosa gemstone
pila bautismal font

pilar pillar
pintado(-a) por
 painted by
pintor(-a) painter
pintura painting
pirámide pyramid
placa plaque
plata silver
por by (person)
porcelana porcelain
portal doorway
presidio fort, garrison
prestado(-a) a on loan to
primer nivel level 1
puerta gate
púlpito pulpit
quero Maya vase
quipu Inca knotted cord
reconstruido(-a) en rebuilt in
reina queen
reinado reign
reloj clock
representa represents
restaurado(-a) en restored in
retablo altar (piece)
retrato portrait
rey king
sacbe Maya sacred causeway
siglo century
silla de coro choir (stall)
tapiz tapestry
telamon sculpted figure support
templo church, temple
toqui Indian chieftain
torre tower
tumba grave, tomb
vajilla de plata silverware
vestíbulo foyer
vitral stained-glass window
vivió lived
yácata ceremonial structure

Who/What/When?
¿Quién?/¿Qué?/¿Cuándo?

What's that building?
¿Qué es ese edificio?
keh es eseh edeefeesyo

Who was the ...?
architect/artist
¿Quién fue ...? *keeyen fweh*
el/la arquitecto/el/la artista
el/la arkeetekto/el/la arteesta

When was it built?
¿En qué época fue construido(-a)?
en keh epoka fweh konstrooeedo(-a)

What style is that?
¿Qué estilo es ése? *keh esteelo es eseh*

la cultura maya 2000 b.c.–1500 a.d.
The great Mayan culture flowered in the Classic period (250-900 a.d.). Excavated ruins reveal grand monuments, pyramids, ceremonial buildings, stone causeways, stelae and altars. Surviving artifacts include stone carvings and mosaics, multicolored pottery and murals.

la cultura azteca 1400s–1520s
The Aztecs, or Mexica, centered their empire on the vast, regulated ancient city of Tenochtitlan (in the Mexico City valley). Among the few remains of their culture are mural and frescoes, huge pyramids adorned with stylized carved heads of the god Quetzalcoatl (plumed serpent), and records of extensive human sacrifice.

la civilización inca 1430–1530s
The Incas extended their Andean empire from Ecuador to Chile. Major sites at Machu Picchu and Cuzco feature temples, courtyards, trapezoidal stonework, terraces and zigzag walls. Surviving cultural artifacts include ceramics, textiles and vases.

gótico-renacimiento ca.16–17
Very elaborate Gothic and Renaissance styles (esp. Plateresque intricate lacelike carving) predominated in the colonial cities of Mexico and South America, particularly in the religious architecture.

barroco ca.17–18
An exuberant architectural style, evident in the great cathedrals of Mexico City and Puebla, and also in Zacatecas. This developed in Latin America into a more extravagant Churriqueresque style.

neoclásico ca.19
The influence of neoclassical art can be seen in the grandiose public buildings in Mexico City: e.g. **Palacio de Bellas Artes** and the Post Office.

modernismo late ca.19–20
The originality of modern architecture in Mexico is seen in the buildings of the National Archeology Museum and University City in Mexico City.

Rulers Gobernantes

What period is that?

¿Qué periodo es ése?
keh pereeyodo es eseh

prehispánico 2000 b.c.–1519 a.d.
Settlements by ancient Mexican cultures in the preclassic period
(2000 b.c.–300 a.d.): Olmecs (at San Lorenzo, La Venta, Tres Zapotes;
Monte Alban); the Mayans (across southern Mexico and Guatemala) and
the Zapotecs. The classic period (300–900) saw the flowering of Mayan cul-
ture in the Yucatan. The postclassic (900–1500) period: Toltecs (in Tula),
Mixtecs (Monte Alban, Mitla), and the Aztecs (at Tenochtitlan). The Incas
built up the most extensive empire, ruling about 12 million people from
Ecuador to Chile; the Picunche and Mapuche Indians predominated in
Argentina and Chile.

colonial ca.15–18
Cristóbal Colón (Christopher Columbus) "discovered" the Americas in
1492. The Treaty of Tordesillas (1494) split the continent into Spanish and
Portuguese influence. Prominent among the Conquistadors was Cortés,
who captured and destroyed the vast city of Teonochtitlan in central
Mexico (1519–21). Meanwhile, Pizarro plundered the Inca Empire.
Conquest was followed by centuries of economic exploitation of land and
native Indian labor. Cruelty and European diseases led to a catastrophic
collapse in the native Indian population.

independencia ca.19
Independence from Spanish control was prompted by Napoleon's military
occupation of Spain. Mexico fought a 10-year war for independence
(1810–21), while in South America the heroic campaigns of Simón Bolívar
brought independence to Colombia, Venezuela, Eduador, Peru and Bolivia
(1817–24). Other years of statehood: Paraguay (1811), Argentina (1816);
Chile (1818), Uruguay (1828).

dictadura ca.19–20
The history of Latin America since independence has rarely been peaceful.
Mexico suffered huge loss of territory to the U.S., French invasions (1838,
1863–66) and the Mexican Revolution (1910–21), when almost 2 million
died in civil war. Elsewhere, miliary coups and dicatorship, guerrilla war-
fare and economic crises have been the norm. Only recently has democ-
racy taken root in many countries.

Churches Iglesias

Central and South America are predominantly Roman Catholic.

Catholic/Protestant church	**la iglesia católica/protestante** *la eegleseea katoleeka/protestanteh*
mosque/synagogue	**la mezquita/la sinagoga** *la meskeeta/* *la seenagoga*
mass/the service	**la misa/el oficio** *la meesa/el ofeeseeyo*

In the countryside En el campo

I'd like a map of this region.	**Quisiera un mapa de esta región.**
	keeseeyera oon mapa deh esta rekheeyon
walking routes	**las rutas peatonales**
	las rootas peatonales
bicycle routes	**las rutas para tránsito de bicicletas**
	las rootas para transeeto deh beeseekletas
How far is it to …?	**¿A qué distancia está …?**
	a keh distancia esta
Is there a right of way?	**¿Está permitido el paso a particulares?**
	esta permeeteedo el paso a parteekoolares
Is there a trail/ scenic route to …?	**¿Hay alguna ruta pintoresca hacia …?**
	eye algoona roota peentoreska aseea
Can you show me on the map?	**¿Puede mostrarme en el mapa?**
	pwedeh mostrarmeh en el mapa
I'm lost.	**Estoy perdido(-a).**
	estoy perdeedo(-a)

Organized walks Caminatas

When does the guided walk/hike start?	**¿A qué hora empieza la caminata?**
	a keh ora empeeyesa la kameenata
When will we return?	**¿A qué hora regresamos?**
	a keh ora regresamos
What is the walk/hike like?	**¿Cómo es la caminata?**
	komo es la kameenata
gentle/medium/tough	**suave/media/dura**
	swabeh/medeea/doora
I'm exhausted.	**Estoy muy cansado(-a).**
	estoy mwee kansado(-a)
What kind of … is that?	**¿Qué clase de … es ese(-a)?**
	keh klase deh … es ese(-a)
animal/bird	**animal/pájaro**
	aneemal/pakharo
flower/tree	**flor/árbol** *flor/arbol*

HIKING GEAR ➤ 145

Geographic features
Características geográficas

bridge	**el puente** *el pwente*
cave	**la cueva** *la kweba*
cliff	**el acantilado [el precipicio]** *el akanteelado [el preseepeeseeo]*
farm	**la finca** *la feenka*
field	**el campo** *el kampo*
footpath	**el sendero** *el sendero*
forest	**la selva** *la selba*
hill	**la colina** *la koleena*
lake	**el lago** *el lago*
mountain	**la montaña** *la montaña*
mountain pass	**el cruce de montaña** *el kroose deh montaña*
mountain range	**la cordillera** *la kordeel-yera*
nature reserve	**la reserva natural** *la reserba natooral*
panorama	**el panorama** *el panorama*
park	**el parque** *el parkeh*
peak	**el pico** *el peeko*
picnic area	**la zona de picnic** *la sona deh peekneek*
pond	**la laguna** *la lagoona*
rapids	**los rápidos** *los rapeedos*
river	**el río** *el reeo*
sea	**el mar** *el mar*
stream	**el arroyo** *el arroyo*
tropical rain-forest	**la selva** *la selba*
valley	**el valle** *el bal-yeh*
vantage point	**el mirador** *el meerador*
village	**la aldea** *la aldeya*
vineyard/winery	**la viña** *la beeña*
waterfall	**la cascada [la catarata]** *la kaskada [la katarata]*
wood	**el bosque** *el boskeh*

Leisure

What's on? ¿Qué presentan?

Local papers and weekly entertainment guides will tell you what's on.

Do you have a program/ programme of events?	**¿Tiene usted el programa de eventos?** *teeyeneh oosteth el programa deh ebentos*
Can you recommend a good …?	**¿Puede recomendarme un buen …?** *pwedeh rekomendarmeh oon bwen*
Is there a … on somewhere?	**¿Presentan un(a)/algún(a) … en alguna parte?** *presentan oon(a)/algoon(a) … en algoona parteh*
ballet/concert	**algún ballet/algún concierto** *algoon baleh/algoon konseeyerto*
film/movie	**alguna película** *algoona peleekoola*
opera	**alguna ópera** *algoona opera*

Availability Disponibilidad

Are there any seats for tonight?	**¿Hay entradas para esta noche?** *eye entradas para esta nocheh*
Where can I get tickets?	**¿Dónde puedo conseguir boletos [tiquetes]?** *dondeh pwedo konsegeer boletos [teeketes]*
There are … of us.	**Somos …** *somos*
When does it start?	**¿A qué hora empieza?** *a keh ora empeeyesa*
When does it end?	**¿A qué hora termina?** *a keh ora termeena*

Tickets Boletos [tiquetes]

How much are the seats?
¿Cuánto cuestan las entradas?
kwanto kwestan las entradas

Do you have anything cheaper?
¿Hay entradas más baratas?
eye entradas mas baratas

I'd like to reserve …
Quisiera reservar … _keeseeyera reserbar_

3 for Sunday evening
tres entradas para la función del domingo por la noche. _tres entradas para la foonseeyon del domeengo por la nocheh_

1 for Friday matinée
una entrada para la función de matiné del viernes. _oona entrada para la foonseeyon deh mateeneh del beeyernes_

¿Cuál es su … de tarjeta de crédito?	What's your credit card …?
número	number
tipo	type
fecha de vencimiento	expiration/expiry date
Por favor, reclame sus boletos [tiquetes] …	Please pick up the tickets …
a la(s) … de la tarde	by … p.m.
en la taquilla/ventanilla	at the reservations desk

May I have a program/ programme, please?
¿Podría darme un programa, por favor?
podreeya darmeh oon programa por fabor

Where's the coat room/ cloakroom?
¿Dónde queda el guardarropa?
dondeh keda el gwardarropa

– Buenos días, Teatro Nacional a la orden [para servirle].
– Hola. Quisiera dos boletos [tiquetes] para la función de "Don Quijote" de esta noche.
– ¿Cuál es su número de tarjeta de crédito, por favor?
– 050365 7854.
– ¿Y cuál es la fecha de vencimiento?
– El séptimo mes del noventa y ocho.
– Gracias. Reclame su boleto [tiquete] en la oficina de reservaciones.

AGOTADOS(-AS) /VENDIDOS(-AS)	sold out
BOLETOS [TIQUETES] PARA LA FUNCIÓN DE HOY	tickets for today
RESERVACIONES POR ADELANTADO	advance bookings/ reservations

NUMBERS ➤ 216

109

Movies/Cinema Cine/Películas

Is there a multiplex cinema near here?
¿Hay un cine múltiple cerca de aquí?
eye oon seeneh moolteepleh serka deh akee

What's on at the cinema (What's playing at the movies) tonight?
¿Qué presentan en el cine hoy?
keh presentan en el seeneh oy

Is the film dubbed/subtitled?
¿Tiene subtítulos la película?
teeyeneh soobteetoolos la peleekoola

Is the film in the original English?
¿Presentan el original en inglés?
presentan el oreekheenal en eengles

A ..., please.
Un(a) ..., por favor
oon(a)... por fabor

box (carton) of popcorn
unas palomitas de maíz [maíz pira]
oonas palomeetas deh maees [maees peera]

chocolate ice cream
un helado de chocolate
oon elado deh chokolateh

hot dog
un hot dog [un perro caliente]
oon hot dog [oon perro kaleeyenteh]

soft drink/soda
un refresco [una gaseosa]
oon refresko [oona gaseyosa]

small
pequeño(-a) *pekeño(-a)*

regular
mediano(-a) *medeeyano(-a)*

large
grande *grandeh*

Theater Teatro

What's playing at the ... Theater?
¿Qué presentan en el teatro ...?
keh presentan en el teatro

Who's the playwright?
¿Quién es el autor?
keeyen es el aootor

Do you think I'd enjoy it?
¿Crees que la/lo voy a disfrutar?
kreyes keh la/lo boy a deesfrootar

I don't know much Spanish.
No sé mucho español.
no se moocho español

Opera/Ballet/Dance
Opera/Ballet/Danza [Baile]

Where's the opera house?	¿Dónde queda el teatro de la ópera? _dondeh keda el teatro deh la opera_
Who's the soloist/composer?	¿Quién es el/la solista/el compositor? _keeyen es el/la soleesta/el komposeetor_
Is formal dress expected?	¿Se exige traje de etiqueta? _seh ekseekheh trakheh deh eteeketa_
Who's dancing?	¿Quién baila? _keeyen baeela_
I'm interested in contemporary dance.	Me interesa la danza contemporánea _meh eenteresa la dansa kontemporanea_

Music/Concerts Música/Conciertos

Popular music styles include **mariachi** (brass, violin and guitar ensemble), **marimba** (played on xylophone), **música ranchera** (country music), **música tropical** (rhythmic dance music), and Andean pan-pipe music, played at Latin American folk evenings (**peñas**).

Where's the concert hall?	¿Dónde queda la sala de conciertos? _dondeh keda la sala deh konseeyertos_
Which orchestra/band is playing?	¿Qué orquesta/banda toca esta noche? _keh orkesta/banda toka esta nocheh_
What are they playing?	¿Qué presentan? _keh presentan_
Who is the conductor/soloist?	¿Quién es el director/el (la) solista? _keeyen es el deerektor/el (la) soleesta_
I really like …	Soy aficionado(-a) a … _soy afeeseeyonado(-a) a_
country music	la música country _la mooseeka kontree_
folk music/jazz	la música folklórica/el jazz _la mooseeka folkloreeka/el yas_
music of the 60s	la música de los años sesenta _la mooseeka deh los años sesenta_
pop/rock/soul music	la música pop/rock/soul _la mooseeka pop/rok/soool_
Have you ever heard of her/him?	¿Lo/La has oído nombrar/mencionar? _lo/la as oeedo nombrar/menseeonar_
Are they popular?	¿Son muy famosos? _son mwee famosos_

Nightlife Vida nocturna

What is there to do in the evenings?	**¿Qué se puede hacer por las noches?** *keh seh pwedeh aser por las noches*
Can you recommend a ...?	**¿Puede usted recomendarme un(a) ...** *pwedeh oosteth rekomendarme oon(a)*
Is there a ... in town?	**¿Hay ... en el pueblo?** *eye ... en el pweblo*
bar	**un bar** *oon bar*
casino	**un casino** *oon kaseeno*
discotheque	**una discoteca** *oona diskoteka*
gay club	**un club de gays** *oon kloo deh geys*
nightclub	**un club nocturno** *oon kloo noktoorno*
restaurant	**un restaurante** *oon restoranteh*
What type of music do they play?	**¿Qué clase de música tocan?** *keh klaseh deh mooseeka tokan*
How do I get there?	**¿Cómo se llega allí?** *komo seh l-yega al-yee*

Admission Admisiones

What time does the show start?	**¿A qué hora empieza la función?** *a keh ora empeeyesa la foonseeyon*
Is evening dress required?	**¿Se exige traje formal?** *seh ekseekheh trakheh formal*
Is there a cover charge?	**¿Hay consumo minimo [cover]?** *eye konsoomo meeneemo [kober]*
Is a reservation necessary?	**¿Hay que reservar?** *eye keh reserbar*
Do we need to be members?	**¿Hay que ser miembros?** *eye keh ser meeyembros*
How long will we have to stand in line/queue?	**¿Por cuánto tiempo tendremos que hacer cola [fila]?** *por kwanto teeyempo tendremos keh aser kola [feela]*
I'd like a good table.	**Quisiera una buena mesa.** *keeseeyera oona bwena mesa*

INCLUYE UNA BEBIDA DE CORTESÍA	includes one complimentary drink

Children Niños

Can you recommend something for the children?	**¿Me puede recomendar algo para los niños?** *meh pwedeh rekomendar algo para los neeños*
Are there changing facilities here for babies?	**¿Hay algún lugar especial para cambiar a los bebés?** *eye algoon loogar espeseeyal para kambeeyar a los bebes*
Where are the bathrooms/toilets?	**¿Dónde quedan los baños?** *dondeh kedan los baños*
amusement arcade	**el local de maquinitas [de juegos electrónicos]** *el lokal deh makeeneetas [deh khwegos elektroneekos]*
fairground	**el parque de atracciones** *el parkeh deh atrakseeyones*
kiddie/paddling pool	**la piscina para niños** *la peeseena para neeños*
playground	**el patio de recreo [el patio de juego]** *el pateeo deh rekreo [el pateeo deh khwego]*
play-group	**la guardería** *la gwardereeya*
zoo	**el zoológico** *el soo-olokheeko*

Baby-sitting Cuidado de niños

Can you recommend a reliable baby-sitter?	**¿Me puede recomendar una niñera confiable?** *meh pwedeh rekomendar oona neeñera konfeeyableh*
Is there full time supervision?	**¿Hay vigilancia continua?** *eye beekheelanseea konteenooa*
Are the helpers properly trained?	**¿Hay personal debidamente cualificado?** *eye personal debeedamenteh kaleefeekado*
When can I drop them off?	**¿A qué hora puedo dejar a los niños?** *a keh ora pwedo dekhar a los neeños*
I'll pick them up at …	**Paso a recogerlos a las …** *paso a rekokherlos a las*
We'll be back by …	**Regresamos a las …** *regresamos a las*
She's 3 and he's 18 months.	**Ella tiene tres años y él tiene dieciocho meses.** *el-ya teeyeneh tres años y el teeyeneh deeyes-ee-ocho meses*

113

Sports Deportes

The Central and South Americans are avid soccer fans. Successful club teams include Boca Juniors (Buenos Aires) and River Plate in Argentina; matches between América (Mexico City) and Guadalajara (nicknamed Las Chivas) raise tremendous passions. There are some huge stadiums, particularly Estadio Azteca in Mexico City.

Other spectator sports include baseball (**el béisbol**) in Central America; boxing (**el boxeo**) and show-biz wrestling (**lucha libre**) are also enjoyed in Mexico. In Argentina, popular participation sports (introduced by European immigrants) include polo, rugby and field hockey. For the adventurous, there is trekking in the Andes foothills, as well as hang-gliding and white-water rafting.

Spectating Ver deportes

Is there a soccer (football) game/match this Saturday?	**¿Hay algún partido de fútbol este sábado?** *eye algoon parteedo deh footbol esteh sabado*
Which teams are playing?	**¿Qué equipos juegan?** *keh ekeepos khwegan*
Can you get me a ticket?	**¿Puede conseguirme un tiquete?** *pwedeh konsegeermeh oon teeketeh*
What's the admission charge?	**¿Cuánto cuesta la entrada?** *kwanto kwesta la entrada*
Where's the racetrack/racecourse?	**¿Dónde queda la pista de carreras?** *dondeh keda la peesta deh karreras*
Where can I place a bet?	**¿Dónde puedo hacer una apuesta?** *dondeh pwedo aser oona apwesta*
What are the odds on …?	**¿Cuáles son las probabilidades para …?** *kwales son las probabeeleedades para*
athletics	**el atletismo** *el atleteesmo*
basketball	**el baloncesto** *el balonsesto*
cycling	**el ciclismo** *el seekleesmo*
soccer/football	**el fútbol** *el footbol*
golf	**el golf** *el golf*
horse race	**las carreras de caballos** *las karreras deh kabal-yos*
swimming	**la natación** *la nataseeyon*
tennis	**el tenis** *el tenees*
volleyball	**el voleibol** *el boleybol*

114

Playing Practicar deportes

Where's the nearest …?	**¿Dónde queda … más cercano(-a)?** _dondeh keda … mas serkano(-a)_
golf course	**el campo de golf** _el kampo deh golf_
sports club	**el club deportivo** _el kloo deporteebo_
Where are the tennis courts?	**¿Dónde quedan las canchas de tenis?** _dondeh kedan las kanchas deh tenees_
What's the charge per …?	**¿Cuál es el precio [la tarifa] de …?** _kwal es el preseeo [la tareefa] deh_
day/round/hour	**día/ronda/hora** _deeya/ronda/ora_
Do I need to be a member?	**¿Hay que ser miembro?** _eye keh ser meeyembro_
Where can I rent/hire …?	**¿Dónde puedo alquilar …?** _dondeh pwedo alkeelar_
boots	**unas botas** _oonas botas_
clubs	**unos palos de golf** _oonos palos deh golf_
equipment	**el equipo** _el ekeepo_
racket	**una raqueta** _oona raketa_
Can I get lessons?	**¿Puedo tener un entrenador?** _pwedo tener oon entrenador_
Do you have a fitness room?	**¿Tienen gimnasio?** _teeyenen kheemnaseeo_
Can I join in? (the game)	**¿Puedo jugar con ustedes?** _pwedo khoogar kon oostedes_

Lo siento, todo está reservado / no tenemos nada libre.	I'm sorry, we're booked up.
Hay que pagar un depósito de…	There is a deposit of …
¿Qué talla es usted?	What size are you?
Usted necesita una fotografía tamaño pasaporte	You need a passport size photo.

PERMISO CON LICENCIA	permit holders only
PROHIBIDA LA PESCA	no fishing
VESTIDORES	locker/changing rooms

At the beach En la playa

The Mexican resorts of Acapulco on the Pacific coast and Cancun and Cozumel in the Caribbean are famed for their beaches.

Is the beach …?	**¿La playa es …?** *la playa es*
pebbly/sandy	**de graba/de arena** *deh graba/deh arena*
Is there a … here?	**¿Hay … por aquí?** *eye … por akee*
children's pool	**un chapoteadero [una piscina para niños]** *oon chapoteadero [oona peeseena para neeños]*
swimming pool	**una piscina …** *oona peeseena*
indoor/open-air	**cubierta/al aire libre** *koobeeyerta/al ayreh leebreh*
Is it safe to swim/dive here?	**¿Se puede nadar/bucear aquí sin peligro?** *seh pwedeh nadar/boosear akee seen peleegro*
Is it safe for children?	**¿Es seguro(-a) para niños?** *es segooro(-a) para neeños*
Is there a lifeguard?	**¿Hay algún salvavidas?** *eye algoon salbabeedas*
I want to rent/hire a/some …	**Quisiera alquilar…** *keeseeyera alkeelar*
deck chair	**una silla de lona** *oona seel-ya deh lona*
jet-ski	**un jet-ski [una moto acuática]** *oon yet-skee [oona moto akwateeka]*
motorboat	**una lancha de motor** *oona lancha deh motor*
skin-diving equipment	**un equipo de buceo** *oon ekeepo deh booseo*
umbrella/sunshade	**una sombrilla** *oona sombreel-ya*
surfboard	**una tabla de surf** *oona tabla deh soorf*
waterskis	**unos esquíes acuáticos** *oonos eskeeyes akwateekos*
For … hours.	**Por … horas.** *por … oras*

charreada *charreada*

The Mexican equivalent of an American rodeo. It can be seen mostly on Sunday mornings in Mexico City at the Rancho del Charro.

corrida *korreeda*

Bullfight; the **corrida** (literally "running of the bulls") will either fascinate or appall you. In some ways the spectacle resembles a ballet. There are colorful moments when the procession (**paseo**) arrives. The entry of the bull into the arena is a moment of high tension. The movement of cape and bullfighter are graceful and precise.

The **matador** and his teams of assistants goad the bull so as to assess its reactions to the cape. The **picador** weakens the bull by piercing its neck muscles with a lance. A **banderillo** then confronts the animal and thrusts three sets of barbed sticks between its shoulder blades. The crowd will be watching critically, weighing the fearlessness of bull and man, the matador's skill as he executes a series of dangerous passes, leading to the final climax of the kill.

You'll be asked whether you want a seat in the sun or shade (**sol o sombra**). Be sure to specify **sombra**, for the sun is hot. Rent a cushion (**almohadilla**) for the hard concrete stands.

jai-alai *kheye leye*

Also known as **pelota vasca** or **frontón**, this game is a popular cross between handball and racketball or squash. Players carry a kind of curved wicker basket or scoop (**cesta**), using it to catch and fling a hard, goatskin-covered ball (**pelota**) against the end wall of a court.

I'd like to see a bullfight.	**Quisiera ver una corrida.** *keeseeyera ber oona koreeda*

Skiing   Esquí

There are winter-sport resorts in Chile and Argentina, notably San Carlos de Bariloche.

I'd like to ski.	**Quisiera esquiar.** *keeseeyera eskeeyar*
Are there any ski lifts?	**¿Hay telesquí?** *eye teleskee*
I'd like to rent/hire some ...	**Quisiera alquilar un equipo de esquí...** *keeseeyera alkeelar oon ekeepo deh eskee*

Making Friends

Introductions Presentaciones

Central and South Americans are generally open and friendly and helpful.

It is considered good manners to exchange pleasantries when meeting, before getting down to conversation.

In Spanish, when referring to someone by their title, the article is required: **Este(a) es el señor/la señora/la señorita …** This is (the) Mr./Mrs./Miss … Spanish names generally consist of 3 parts; the second is the most important for formal purposes.

In Spanish, there are three forms for "you" (taking different verb forms): **tú** (singular) and **vosotros** (plural) are used when talking to relatives, close friends and children (and between young people); **usted** (singular) and **ustedes** (plural) – often abbreviated to **Vd./Vds.** – are used in all other cases. If in doubt; use **usted/ustedes**.

Hello, we haven't met.	**Hola, no nos conocemos.** *ola no nos konosemos*
My name is …	**Me llamo …** *meh l-yamo*
May I introduce …?	**Quiero presentarle a …** *keeyero presentarleh a*
Pleased to meet you.	**Mucho gusto.** *moocho goosto*
What's your name?	**¿Cómo se llama?** *komo seh l-yama*
How are you?	**¿Cómo está?** *komo esta*
Fine, thanks. And you?	**Bien, gracias. ¿Y usted?** *beeyen graseeas. y oosteth*

> – Hola, ¿cómo está usted?
> – *Muy bien, gracias. ¿Y usted?*
> – Bien, gracias.

Where are you from?
¿De dónde es usted?

Where do you come from?	**¿De dónde viene?** *de dondeh beeyeneh*
Where were you born?	**¿Dónde nació usted?** *dondeh naseeyo oosteth*
I'm from …	**Soy de…** *soy deh…*
Australia	**Australia** *aoostraleea*
Britain	**Gran Bretaña** *gran bretaña*
Canada	**Canadá** *kanada*
England	**Inglaterra** *eenglaterra*
Ireland	**Irlanda** *eerlanda*
Scotland	**Escocia** *eskoseea*
U.S.	**Los Estados Unidos** *los estados ooneedos*
Wales	**(País de) Gales** *(paees deh) gales*
Where do you live?	**¿Dónde vive usted?** *dondeh beebeh oosteth*
What part of … are you from?	**¿De qué parte de… es usted?** *de keh parteh deh … es oosteth*
Argentina	**Argentina** *arkhenteena*
Chile	**Chile** *cheeleh*
Mexico	**México** *mekheeko*
Venezuela	**Venezuela** *beneswela*
We come here every year.	**Venimos todos los años.** *veneemos todos los años*
It's my/our first visit.	**Ésta es la primera vez que vengo/venimos.** *esta es la preemera ves ke vengo/veneemos*
Have you ever been to Britain/the U.S.?	**¿Ha(n) ido alguna vez a la Gran Bretaña/ los Estados Unidos?** *a(n) eedo algoona ves a gran bretaña/los esta dos ooneedos*
Do you like it here?	**¿Le gusta este lugar?** *le goosta este loogar*
What do you think of the …?	**¿Qué opina de…?** *ke opeena deh…*
I love (the) … here.	**Me encanta el/la … de aquí.** *me enkanta el/la … deh akee.*
I don't really like the … here.	**A mí no me gusta mucho (el/la) … de aquí.** *a mee no me goosta moocho (el/la) … deh akee.*
food/people	**la comida/la gente** *la komeeda/la khenteh*

Who are you with?/Family
¿Con quién viene usted?/Familia

Who are you with?	**¿Con quién viene usted?** *kon keeyen beeyeneh oosteth*
I'm on my own.	**Vengo solo(-a).** *bengo solo(-a)*
I'm with a friend.	**Vengo con un(a) amigo(-a).** *bengo kon oon ameego(-a)*
I'm with my ...	**Vengo con ...** *bengo kon (mee/mees)*
wife	**mi esposa** *mee esposa*
husband	**mi esposo** *mee esposo*
family	**mi familia** *mee fameelya*
children	**mis niños** *mees neeños*
parents	**mis padres** *mees padres*
boyfriend/girlfriend	**mi novio/novia** *mee nobeeyo/nobeeya*
father/mother	**mi padre/madre** *mee padreh/madreh*
son/daughter	**mi hijo/hija** *mee eekho/eekha*
brother/sister	**mi hermano/hermana** *mee hermano/hermana*
uncle/aunt	**mi tío/tía** *mee teeo/teea*
What's your son's/ wife's name?	**¿Cómo se llama su hijo/esposa?** *komo se l-yama soo eekho/esposa*
Are you married?	**¿Es usted casado(-a)?** *e oosteth kasado(-a)*
I'm ...	**Soy...** *soy...*
married/single	**casado(-a)/soltero(-a)** *kasado(-a)/soltero(-a)*
divorced/separated	**divorciado(-a)/separado(-a)** *deeborseeyado(-a)/separado(-a)*
engaged	**(Estoy) comprometido(-a)** *(estoy) komprometeedo(-a)*
We live together.	**Vivimos juntos.** *beebeemos khoontos*
We've been married/ together for ... years.	**Llevamos ... años de casados/viviendo juntos.** *l-yebamos...años deh kasados/ beebeeyendo khoontos*
Do you have any children?	**¿Tienen hijos?** *teeyenen eekhos*
2 sons and a daughter	**2 hijos y una hija** *dos eekhos ee oona eekha*
How old are they?	**¿Qué edad tienen?** *keh edad teeyenen*

What do you do?
¿Qué hace usted/¿Cuál es su ocupación?

What do you do?	**¿Qué hace usted?** *keh aseh oosteth*
What are you studying?	**¿Qué está estudiando?** *keh esta estoodeeyando*
I'm studying …	**Estoy estudiando …** *estoy estoodeeyando*
sciences	**ciencias** *seeyenseeyas*
the arts	**bellas artes** *bel-yas artes*
I'm in …	**Trabajo en …** *trabakho en*
business	**administratión de empresas** *admeeneestraseeyon deh empresas*
engineering	**ingeniería** *eenkheneeyereea*
retail	**ventas al menudeo** *bentas al menoodeo*
sales	**ventas** *bentas*
Who do you work for …?	**¿Para quién trabaja?** *para keeyen trabakha*
I work for …	**Trabajo para …** *trabakho para*
I'm a/an …	**Soy (un/una) …** *soy (oon/oona)*
accountant	**un(a) contador(a)** *oon(a) kontador(a)*
housewife	**una ama de casa** *oona ama deh kasa*
student	**un(a) estudiante** *oon(a) estoodeeyanteh*
I'm retired.	**Estoy retirado(-a).** *reteerado(-a)*
I'm self-employed.	**Soy independiente.** *soy eendependeeyenteh*
I'm between jobs.	**No tengo trabajo en este momento.** *no tengo trabakho en este momento*
What are your interests/ hobbies?	**¿Cuáles son sus hobbies?** *kwales son soos khobees*
I like …	**Me gusta …** *me goosta*
music	**la música** *la moosyka*
reading	**la lectura** *la lektoora*
sport	**el deporte** *el deporteh*
Would you like to play …?	**¿Le gustaría jugar …?** *le goostareea khoogar*
cards	**cartas** *kartas*
chess	**ajedrez** *akhedres*

What weather! ¡Qué tiempo!

What a lovely day!	**¡Qué día tan hermoso!** *keh deeya tan ermoso*
What awful weather!	**¡Qué tiempo tan malo!** *keh teeyempo tan malo*
Isn't it cold/hot today!	**¡Qué frío/calor hace hoy! ¿Verdad?** *keh freeyo/kalor aseh oy. berdath*
Is it usually as warm as this?	**¿Hace normalmente este calor?** *aseh normalmente este kalor*
Do you think it's going to … tomorrow?	**¿Cree que va a … mañana?** *kreyeh keh ba a…mañana*
be a nice day	**hacer buen tiempo** *aser bwen teeyempo*
rain	**llover** *l-yober*
snow	**nevar** *nebar*
What is the weather forecast?	**¿Qué dice "El tiempo meteorológico"? [la predicción del tiempo]?** *keh deeseh "El teeyempo metereolokhiko" [la predeekseeyon del teeyempo]*
It's …	**Está …** *esta*
cloudy	**nublado** *nooblado*
rainy	**lloviendo** *l-yobeeyendo*
snowy	**nevando** *nebando*
thundery	**tronando** *tronando*
It's foggy.	**Hay niebla.** *eye neeyebla*
It was frosty last night.	**Anoche heló [hubo heladas].** *anocheh elo [oobo eladas]*
It's icy cold.	**Hace un frío helado.** *aseh oon freeyo elado*
It's windy.	**Hace viento.** *aseh beeyento*
Has the weather been like this for long?	**¿Ha estado así el tiempo últimamente?** *a estado asee el teeyempo oolteemamenteh*
What's the pollen count?	**¿Cuál es el recuento polínico?** *kwal es el rekwento poleeneeko*
high/medium/low	**alto/medio/bajo** *alto/medeeo/bakho*

Enjoying your trip?
¿Qué tal la está pasando?

¿Está de vacaciones?	Are you on vacation?
¿En qué se vino?	How did you get here?
¿Qué tal el viaje?	How was the journey?
¿Dónde se hospeda?	Where are you staying?
¿Qué tal el alojamiento?	How's the accommodations?
¿Cuánto tiempo lleva aquí?	How long have you been here?
¿Cuánto tiempo piensa quedarse aquí?	How long are you staying?

I'm here on …
a business trip

Estoy aquí … _estoy akee_
en viaje de negocios
en beeyakheh deh negoseeos

vacation/holiday

de vacaciones _de bakaseeyones_

We came by …
train/bus/plane

Vinimos en… _beeneemos en_
tren/bus/avión _tren/boos/abeeyon_

car/ferry

carro/transbordador [ferry]
karro/transbordador [ferree]

I have a rental/hire car.

He alquilado un carro. _eh alkeelado oon karro_

We're staying in …
an apartment

Nos hospedamos en … _nos ospedamos en_
un departamento _oon departamento_

a hotel/campsite

un hotel /una zona de campamento
oon otel/oona sona deh kampamento

with friends

la casa de unos amigos
la kasa deh oonos ameegos

Can you suggest …?

¿Puede sugerirme …? _pwedeh sookhereerme_

things to do

qué hacer _keh aser_

places to eat

sitios para ir a comer
seeteeyos para eer a komer

places to visit

lugares para visitar _loogares para beeseetar_

We're having a great/
awful time.

**Nos estamos divirtiendo mucho/
no nos ha ido nada bien.**
_nos estamos deebeerteeyendo moocho/
no nos a eedo nada beeyen_

Invitations   Invitaciones

Would you like to have dinner with us on …?	**¿Le gustaría cenar con nosotros el …?** _leh goostareea senar kon nosotros el_
May I invite you to lunch?	**¿Puedo invitarlo(-a) a comer [almorzar]?** _pwedo eenbeetarlo(-a) a komer [almorsar]_
Can you come for a drink this evening?	**¿Puede venir a tomar una copa esta noche?** _pwedeh beneer a tomar oona kopa esta nocheh_
We are having a party. Can you come?	**Tenemos una fiesta. ¿Puede venir?** _tenemos oona feeyesta. pwedeh beneer_
May we join you?	**¿Podemos ir con usted/ustedes?** _podemos eer kon oosteth/oostedes_
Would you like to join us?	**¿Le gustaría ir con nosotros?** _leh goostareeya eer kon nosotros_

Going out ¿Salimos?

What are your plans for …?	**¿Qué planes tiene para …?** _keh planes teeyeneh para_
today/tonight	**hoy/esta noche** _oy/esta nocheh_
tomorrow	**mañana** _mañana_
Are you free this evening?	**¿Está libre esta noche?** _esta leebreh esta nocheh_
Would you like to …?	**¿Le gustaría …?** _leh goostareeya_
go dancing	**ir a bailar** _eer a baeelar_
go for a drink/meal	**ir de copas [salir a tomar algo]/ir a cenar** _eer deh kopas [saleer a tomar algo]/eer a senar_
go for a walk	**dar un paseo** _dar oon paseyo_
go shopping	**ir de compras** _eer deh kompras_
Where would you like to go?	**¿Adónde le gustaría ir?** _adondeh leh goostareeya eer_
I'd like to go to …	**Quisiera ir a …** _keeseeyera eer a_
I'd like to see…	**Quisiera ver …** _keeseeyera behr_
Do you enjoy …?	**¿Le gusta …?** _leh goosta_
Shall we go to the movies/cinema?	**¿Vamos al cine?** _bamos al seeneh_

Accepting/Declining
Aceptar/Rehusar una invitación

That's very kind of you.

Es usted muy amable.
es oosteth mwee amableh

Great. I'd love to.

Estupendo. Me encantaría.
estoopendo. meh enkantareeya

Thank you, but I'm busy.

Gracias, pero estoy muy ocupado(-a).
graseeas pero estoy mwee okoopado(-a)

May I bring a friend?

¿Puedo llevar a un(a) amigo(-a)?
pwedo l-yebar a oon ameego(-a)

Where shall we meet?

¿Dónde nos encontramos?
dondeh nos enkontramos

I'll meet you …

Nos encontramos … *nos enkontramos*

in the bar

en el bar *en el bar*

in front of your hotel

enfrente del hotel *enfrenteh del otel*

I'll come by for you at 8.

Iré a recogerlo(-a) [Paso por usted] a las 8.
eereh a rekokherlo(-a) [paso por oosteth] a las ocho

What time shall I come?

¿A qué hora vengo? *a keh ora bengo*

How about …?

¿Qué le parece a las …?
keh leh pareseh a las

Could we make it a bit later?

¿Puede ser un poquito más tarde?
pwedeh ser oon pokeeto mas tardeh

How about another day?

¿Qué le parece otro día?
keh leh parehseh otro deeya

That will be fine.

Me parece bien. *meh pareseh beeyen*

Dining out/in Cenar fuera/en casa

Where would you like to sit?

¿Dónde quiere sentarse?
dondeh keeyereh sentarseh

Let me bring you a drink./
What would you like?

Voy a traerle una copa [algo de tomar].
¿Qué desea? *boy a trayerleh oona kopa*
[algo deh tomar]. keh deseea

Do you like …?

¿Le gusta …? *leh goosta*

What are you going to have?

¿Qué va a tomar? *keh ba a tomar*

That was a lovely meal.

Fue una cena deliciosa.
fweh oona sena deleeseeyosa

TIME ➤ 220

Getting together Encuentros

Do you mind if I …?	**¿Le molesta si …?** *leh molesta see*
sit here/smoke	**me siento aquí/fumo** *meh seeyento akee/foomo*
Can I get you a drink?	**¿Puedo ofrecerle una copa [algo de tomar]?** *pwedo ofreserleh oona kopa [algo deh tomar]*
I'd love to have some company.	**Me encantaría tener un poco de compañía.** *meh enkantareeya tener oon poko deh kompañeeya*
Why are you laughing?	**¿Por qué se ríe?** *por keh seh reeyeh*
Is my Spanish that bad?	**¿Es tan malo mi español?** *es tan malo mee español*
Shall we go somewhere quieter?	**¿Vamos a un sitio más tranquilo?** *bamos a oon seeteeo mas trankeelo*
Leave me alone, please!	**¡Déjeme tranquilo(-a), por favor!** *dekhemeh trankeelo(-a) por fabor*
You look great!	**¡Qué bien luces! [¡Te ves muy bien!]** *keh beeyen looses [teh bes mwee beeyen]*
May I kiss you?	**¿Puedo darte un beso?** *pwedo darteh oon beso*
Would you like to come back with me?	**¿Te gustaría regresar conmigo?** *teh goostareeya regresar konmeego*
I'm not ready for that.	**No estoy listo(-a) para eso.** *no estoy leesto(-a) para eso*
Thanks for the evening.	**Gracias por la velada.** *graseeas por la belada*
I'm afraid we've got to leave now.	**Lo siento, tenemos que irnos.** *lo seeyento tenemos keh eernos*
Can I see you again tomorrow?	**¿Puedo verlo(-a) mañana?** *pwedo berlo(-a) mañana*
See you soon.	**Hasta luego.** *asta lwego*
Can I have your address?	**¿Puedo anotar su dirección?** *pwedo anotar soo deereskseeyon*

126

SAFETY ➤ 65

Telephoning
Hablar por teléfono

In Mexico, international calls can be made from modern
phone booths (blue, marked **Lada** or **Larga Distancia** for
international; orange for local). Most have instructions in English. Some
take phonecards (available from stores nearby, telephone offices, and bus
and rail stations). In **casetas de teléfono** an operator will connect you and
bill you afterward according to a meter-reading.
To phone abroad from Mexico, dial 95 + area code (for U.S. and Canada);
98 + country code (for outside Americas). In Argentina, tokens (**cospeles**
or **fichas**) and cards (**tarjetas**) are used in public phones.

Can I have your telephone number?	**¿Puedo anotar su número de teléfono?** *pwedo anotar soo noomero deh telefono*
Here's my number.	**Éste es mi número.** *esteh es mee noomero*
Please call me.	**Llámeme, por favor.** *l-yamemeh por fabor*
I'll give you a call.	**Yo lo (la) llamaré.** *yo lo (la) l-yamareh*
Where's the nearest telephone booth?	**¿Dónde está el teléfono público más cercano [la cabina de teléfono]?** *dondeh esta el telefono poobleeko mas serkano [la kabeena deh telefono]*
May I use your phone?	**¿Puedo usar su teléfono?** *pwedo oosar soo telefono*
It's an emergency.	**Es una emergencia.** *es oona emerkhenseea*
I'd like to call someone in England.	**Quisiera llamar a alguien en Inglaterra.** *keeseeyera l-yamar a algeeyen en eenglaterra*
What's the area/ dialling code for …?	**¿Cuál es el código para …?** *kwal es el kodeego para*
I'd like a phone card.	**Quisiera una tarjeta de teléfono.** *keeseeyera oona tarkheta deh telefono*
What's the number for Information/ Directory Enquiries?	**¿Cuál es el número de Información?** *kwal es el noomero deh eenformaseeyon*
I'd like the number for …	**Quisiera el número de teléfono de …** *keeseeyera el noomero deh telefono deh*
I'd like to call collect/ reverse the charges.	**Quisiera llamar por cobrar [por cobro revertido].** *keeseeyera l-yamar por kobrar [por kobro reberteedo]*

Speaking on the phone Hablar por teléfono

Hello. This is …	**Aló, habla …** *alo. abla*
I'd like to speak to …	**Quisiera hablar con …** *keeseeyera ablar kon*
Extension …	**Extensión …** *extenseeyon*
Speak louder/more slowly, please.	**¿Podría hablar más alto/despacio?** *podreeya ablar mas alto/despaseeo*
Could you repeat that, please.	**¿Me lo repite, por favor?** *meh lo repeeteh por fabor*
I'm afraid he/she's not in.	**Lo siento. El/ella no se encuentra en este momento.** *lo seeyento. el/el-ya no se enkwentra en esteh momento*
You've got the wrong number.	**Lo siento. Tiene el número equivocado.** *lo seeyento. teeyeneh el noomero ekeebokado*
Just a moment, please.	**Un momento, por favor.** *oon momento por fabor*
Hold on, please.	**Espere un momento, por favor.** *espereh oon momento por fabor*
When will he/she be back?	**¿A qué hora regresará?** *a keh ora regresara*
Will you tell him/her that I called?	**¿Podría decirle que yo llamé?** *podreeya deseerleh keh yo l-yameh*
My name is …	**Mi nombre es …** *mee nombreh es*
Would you ask him/her to phone me?	**¿Podría pedirle que me llame?** *podreeya pedeerleh keh meh l-yameh*
I must go now.	**Tengo que irme.** *tengo keh eermeh*
Nice to speak to you.	**Fue un placer hablar con usted.** *fweh oon plaser ablar kon oosteth*
I'll be in touch.	**Me mantendré en contacto.** *meh mantendreh en kontakto*
Bye.	**Adiós.** *adeeyos*

Stores & Services

Stores are generally small and individual; however, large chain stores have appeared. In Mexico, for example, you will see department stores (**Palacio de Hierro**, **Sears**, **Sanborn's** and **Liverpool**) and supermarket chains (**Aurrera**, **Comercial Mexicana**, **Superama** and **Gigante**).

For souvenir shopping (see page 156) in Mexico City, go to **Mercado Artesanal Buenavista** for a huge range of goods.

Most cities and towns have at least one market; some permanent, others open just one morning a week. There is generally an opportunity to bargain over prices. Flea markets (**tianguis**) and street peddlers are also common.

ESSENTIAL

I'd like …	**Quisiera …** *keeseeyera*
Do you have …?	**¿Tiene …?** *teeyeneh*
How much is that?	**¿Cuánto cuesta eso?** *kwanto kwesta eso*
Thank you	**gracias** *graseeas*

ABIERTO	open
CERRADO	closed

Stores and services
Comercio y servicios

Where is …? ¿Dónde está …?

Where's the nearest …? **¿Dónde está … más cercano(-a)?**
dondeh esta … mas serkano(-a)

Where's there a good …? **¿Dónde hay un(a) buen(a) …?**
dondeh eye oon(a) bwen(a)

Where's the main shopping mall/centre? **¿Dónde está la principal zona de tiendas?**
dondeh esta la preenseepal sona deh teeyendas

Is it far from here? **¿Está lejos de aquí?** _esta lekhos deh akee_

How do I get there? **¿Cómo se llega allá?** _komo seh l-yega al-y_

Shops Tiendas y almacenes

antique shop	**el almacén de antigüedades** _el almasen deh antigwedades_
bakery	**la panadería** _la panadereeya_
bank	**el banco** _el banko_
bookshop	**la librería** _la leebrereeya_
butcher shop	**la carnicería** _la karneesereeya_
camera shop	**el almacén de fotografía** _el almasen deh fotografeeya_
pharmacy/chemist's	**la farmacia** _la farmaseea_
clothing store/clothes shop	**el almacén de ropa** _el almasen deh ropa_
delicatessen	**el delicatessen** _el deleekatesen_
department store	**el almacén** _el almasen_
drugstore	**la farmacia [la droguería]** _la farmaseea [la drogereeya]_
fish store/fishmonger's	**la pescadería** _la peskadereeya_
florist's	**la floristería** _la floreestereeya_
gift shop	**el almacén de regalos** _el almasen deh regalos_
greengrocer's	**la verdulería** _la berdoolereeya_
grocery store/produce store	**la tienda de abarrotes** _la teeyenda deh abarrotes_

store/health food shop	**la tienda de alimentos** **naturales** *la teeyenda deh aleementos natoorales*
jewelry/jeweler's store	**la joyería** *la khoyereeya*
market	**el mercado** *el merkado*
newsstand	**el quiosco de periódicos y revistas** *el keeyosko deh pereeyodeekos ee rebeestas*
pastry shop	**la pastelería** *la pastelereeya*
record (music) store/shop	**el almacén de discos** *el almasen deh deeskos*
shoe store/shop	**el almacén de zapatos** *el almasen deh sapatos*
souvenir shop	**el almacén de recuerdos [souvenirs]** *el almasen deh rekwerdos [soobeneers]*
sports shop	**el almacén de artículos deportivos** *el almasen deh arteekoolos deporteebos*
supermarket	**el supermercado** *el soopermerkado*
cigarette kiosk/tobacconist's	**la tabaquería** *la tabakerria*
toy and game store/shop	**la juguetería** *la khoogetereeya*
liquor store/ wine and spirit merchant's	**la vinetería [la licorería]** *la beenetereeya [la leekorereeya]*

Services Servicios

dentist	**el dentista** *el denteesta*
doctor	**el doctor** *el doktor*
dry cleaner's	**la tintorería** *la teentorereeya*
hairdresser's (ladies/men)	**el salón de belleza** *el salon deh bel-yesa*
hospital	**el hospital** *el ospeetal*
laundromat	**la lavandería** *la labandereeya*
library	**la biblioteca** *la beebleeoteka*
optician	**el oculista** *el ocooleesta*
police station	**la estación de policía** *la estaseeyon deh poleeseeya*
clinic	**la policlínica** *la poleekleeneeka*
post office	**la oficina del correo** *la ofeeseena del korreo*
travel agency	**la agencia de viajes** *la akhenseea deh beeyakhes*

Opening hours
Horarios de atención al público

When does the … open/shut?	**¿A qué hora abren/cierran …?** *a keh ora abren/seeyeran*
Are you open in the evening?	**¿Está abierto(-a) por las noches?** *esta abeeyerto(-a) por las noches*
Do you close for lunch?	**¿Cierran al mediodía?** *seeyeran al medeeodeeya*

General times for:	Opening	Closing	Lunch break	Closed
shops	10	8	none	some on Sunday
pharmacy	9	8	none	Sunday
post office	8	7	none	most on Sunday
banks	9	5	none	weekend

Where is the …	**¿Dónde está …?** *dondeh esta*
cashier/cash desk	**la caja** *la kakha*
escalator	**la escalera eléctrica** *la eskalera elektreeka*
elevator/lift	**el ascensor** *el asensor*
store guide	**la guía del almacén** *la geeya del almasen*
first floor	**la planta baja** *la planta bakha*
second floor	**el primer piso** *el preemer peeso*
Where's the … department?	**¿Dónde está el departamento [la sección] de…?** *dondeh esta el departamento [la sekseeyon] deh*

HORAS DE ATENCIÓN	business hours
CERRADO AL MEDIODÍA	closed for lunch
ABIERTO TODO EL DÍA	open all day
SALIDA	exit
SALIDA DE EMERGENCIA/ INCENDIOS	emergency/fire exit
ENTRADA	entrance
ESCALERA ELÉCTRICA	escalator
ASCENSOR	elevator/lift
ESCALERAS	stairs

Service Servicio

Can you help me? — **¿Puede atenderme?**
pwedeh atendermeh

I'm looking for ... — **Estoy buscando ...**
estoy booskando

I'm just browsing. — **Sólo estoy mirando.**
solo estoy meerando

It's my turn. — **Es mi turno.** *es mee toorno*

Do you have any ...? — **¿Tiene usted ...?** *teeyeneh oosteth*

I'd like to buy ... — **Quisiera comprar ...**
keeseeyera komprar

Could you show me ...? — **¿Podría mostrarme ...?**
podreeya mostrarmeh

How much is this/that? — **¿Cuánto cuesta esto/eso?**
kwanto kwesta esto/eso

Buenos días/Buenas tardes señora/señor.	Good morning/afternoon madam/sir.
¿Ya lo/la atendieron?	Are you being served?
¿Qué desea?	What would you like?
Voy a revisar [averiguar]	I'll just check that for you.
¿Eso es todo?	Is that everything?
¿Algo más?	Anything else?

– *¿A la orden? [¿En qué puedo servirle?]*
– *Gracias sólo estoy mirando.*
– *Está bien.*
– *¡Disculpe!*
– *¿Sí? ¿A la orden? [¿En qué puedo servirle?]*
– *¿Cuánto cuesta eso?*
– *Mmm. Voy a revisar [averiguar] ... Son 2000 pesos.*

INFORMACIÓN AL CLIENTE	customer service
REBAJA	sale

Preferences Preferencias

I want something …	**Quiero algo …** *keeyero algo*
It must be …	**Tiene que ser …** *teeyeneh keh sehr*
big/small	**grande/pequeño(-a)** *grandeh/pekeño(-a)*
cheap/expensive	**barato(-a)/caro(-a)** *barato(-a)/karo(-a)*
dark/light	**oscuro(-a)/claro(-a)** *oskooro(-a)/klaro(-a)*
light/heavy	**liviano(-a)/pesado(-a)** *leebeeyano(-a)/pesado(-a)*
oval/round/square	**ovalado(-a)/redondo(-a)/cuadrado(-a)** *obalado(-a)/redondo(-a)/kwadrado(-a)*
genuine/imitation	**original [un ejemplar auténtico]/imitación** *oreekheenal [oon ekhemplar aootenteeko]/eemeetaseeyon*
I don't want anything too expensive.	**No quiero nada demasiado caro.** *no keeyero nada demaseeyado karo*
In the region of $ …	**Alrededor de los $ …** *alrededor deh los … pesos*

¿Qué … desea?	What … would you like?
color/modelo	color/colour/shape
calidad/cantidad	quality/quantity
¿De qué clase lo/la desea?	What sort would you like?
¿Cuánto dinero piensa gastar?	What price range are you thinking of?

Do you have anything …?	**¿Tiene algo …?** *teeyeneh algo*
larger	**más grande** *mas grandeh*
better quality	**de mejor calidad** *deh mekhor kaleedath*
cheaper	**más barato** *mas barato*
smaller	**más pequeño** *mas pekeño*
Can you show me …?	**¿Podría mostrarme …?** *podreeya mostrarmeh*
that/this one	**ése(-a)/éste(-a)** *ese(-a)/este(-a)*
these/those ones	**éstos(-as)/ésos(-as)** *estos(-as)/esos(-as)*
the one in the window/ display case	**el que está en la vitrina [el aparador]/ el escaparate** *el keh esta en la beetreena [el aparador]/el eskaparateh*
some others	**otros(-as)** *otros(-as)*

COLORS ➤ 143

Conditions of purchase
Condiciones de compra

Is there a guarantee?	**¿Tiene garantía?** _teeyeneh garanteeya_
Are there any instructions with it?	**¿Trae las instrucciones?** _trayeh las eenstrookseeyones_

Out of stock Agotados(-as)

Disculpe, no nos quedan más por el momento.	I'm sorry, we haven't any.
Se nos han agotado.	We're out of stock.
¿Desea que le muestre algo diferente?	Can I show you something else?
¿Desea que se lo encarguemos?	Shall we order it for you?

Can you order it for me?	**¿Podría encargármelo?** _podreeya encargarmelo_
How long will it take?	**¿Cuánto tiempo demorará?** _kwanto teeyempo demorara_
Where else might I get …?	**¿Dónde más podría conseguir …?** _dondeh mas podreeya konsegeer_

Decisions Decisiones

That's not quite what I want.	**Eso no es exactamente lo que quiero.** _eso no es eksaktamenteh lo keh keeyero_
No, I don't like it.	**No, no me gusta.** _no no meh goosta_
That's too expensive.	**Es demasiado caro(-a).** _es demaseeyado karo(-a)_
I'd like to think about it.	**Quisiera pensarlo un poco.** _keeseeyera pensarlo oon poko_
I'll take it.	**Me lo/la llevo.** _meh lo/la l-yebo_

> – Buenos días, señora. Quiero una chaqueta.
> – ¿De qué clase la desea?
> – Grande. Y tiene que ser verde.
> – Con mucho gusto … Aquí tiene. Son 500 pesos.
> – Mmm, no es exactamente lo que estoy buscando.
> Gracias, de todas maneras.

Paying Pagar

Small businesses may not accept credit cards; however, large stores, restaurants and hotels accept major credit cards and traveler's checks/traveller's cheques—look out for the signs on the door.

Where do I pay?	**¿Dónde se paga?** _dondeh seh paga_
How much is that?	**¿Cuánto cuesta eso?** _kwanto kwesta eso_
Could you write it down, please?	**¿Podría escribírmelo, por favor?** _podreeya eskreebeermelo por fabor_
Do you accept traveler's checks/ traveller's cheques?	**¿Aceptan cheques de viajero?** _aseptan chekes deh beeyakhero_
I'll pay …	**Voy a pagar …** _boy a pagar_
by cash	**en efectivo** _en efekteebo_
by credit card	**con tarjeta de crédito** _kon tarkheta deh kredeeto_
I don't have any smaller change.	**No tengo cambio [suelto].**

¿Cómo desea pagar?	How are you paying?
Esta transacción no ha sido autorizada.	This transaction has not been approved/accepted.
Esta tarjeta no es válida [no tiene validez].	This card is not valid.
¿Tiene otro documento de identificación?	May I have further identification?
¿Tiene cambio [suelto]?	Have you got any smaller change?

Sorry, I don't have enough money.	**Disculpe, no tengo suficiente dinero.** _deeskoolpeh no tengo soofeeseeyenteh deenero_
Could I have a receipt please?	**¿Me podría dar un recibo, por favor?** _meh podreeya dar oon reseebo por fabor_
I think you've given me the wrong change.	**Creo que me ha dado mal el cambio.** _kreyo keh meh a dado mal el kambeeo_

PAGUE AQUÍ, POR FAVOR	please pay here
SE DETENDRÁ A QUIEN SE SORPRENDA ROBANDO	shoplifters will be prosecuted

Complaints Quejas [Reclamos]

This doesn't work.	**Esto está defectuoso.** _esto esta defektoooso_
Can you exchange this, please?	**¿Puede cambiarme esto, por favor?** _pwedeh kambeeyarmeh esto por fabor_
I'd like a refund.	**Quisiera que me devolvieran el dinero.** _keeseeyera keh meh debolbeeyeran el deenero_
Here's the receipt.	**Aquí está el recibo.** _akee esta el reseebo_
I don't have the receipt.	**No tengo el recibo.** _no tengo el reseebo_
I'd like to see the manager.	**Quisiera hablar con el gerente.** _keeseeyera ablar kon el kherenteh_

Repairs/Cleaning Reparaciones/Lavado

This is broken. Can you repair it?	**Esto está roto. ¿Puede arreglarlo?** _esto esta roto. pwedeh arreglarlo_
Do you have … for this?	**¿Tiene … para esto?** _teeyeneh … para esto_
a battery	**una pila** _oona peela_
replacement parts	**repuestos** _repwestos_
There's something wrong with …	**Algo anda mal con …** _algo anda mal kon_
Can you … this?	**¿Puede … esto?** _pwedeh … esto_
clean	**lavar** _labar_
press	**planchar** _planchar_
mend	**remendar** _remendar_
alter	**arreglar** _arreglar_
When will it/they be ready?	**¿Cuándo estará(n) listo(s)/-a(s)?** _kwando estara(n) leesto(s)/-a(s)_
This isn't mine.	**Esto no es mío.** _esto no es meeyo_
There's … missing.	**Falta …** _falta_

Bank/Currency exchange
Banco/Oficina de cambio

Currency exchange offices (**oficina** or **casa de cambio**) can be found in most tourist centers; they generally offer better exchange rates than hotels and banks.

Remember your passport when you want to change money.

Money can be obtained from **Bancomer** and **Banamex** ATMs/dispensers in most Mexican towns with major credit cards and cash cards.

Where's the nearest …?	**¿Dónde está … más cercano(-a)?** _dondeh esta … mas serkano(-a)_
bank	**el banco** _el banko_
currency exchange office	**la oficina de cambio** _la ofeeseena de kambeeo_

ABIERTO/CERRADO	open/closed
EMPUJE/HALE/OPRIMA	push/pull/press
CAJEROS	cashiers
TODO TIPO DE TRANSACCIONES	all transactions

Changing money Cambiar dinero

Can I exchange foreign currency here?	**¿Puedo cambiar moneda extranjera aquí?** _pwedo kambeeyar moneda ekstrankhera akee_
I'd like to change some dollars/pounds into pesos.	**Quisiera cambiar unos dólares/libras esterlinas a pesos.** _keeseeyera kambeeyar oonos dolares/leebras esterleenas a pesos_
I want to cash some traveler's checks/traveller's cheques.	**Quisiera cambiar unos cheques de viajero.** _keeseeyera kambeeyar oonos chekes deh beeakhero_
What's the exchange rate?	**¿Cuál es la tasa de cambio?** _kwal es la tasa de kambeeo_
How much commission do you charge?	**¿Cuál es la comisión?** _kwal es la komeeseeyon_
I've lost my traveler's checks/ traveller's cheques. These are the numbers.	**Se me perdieron mis cheques de viajero. Éstos son los números.** _seh meh perdeeyeron mees chekes de beeakhero. estos son los noomeros_
Could I have some smaller change?	**¿Podría darme cambio [suelto]?** _podreeya darmeh kambeeo [swelto]_

Security Seguridad

¿Me permite …?	Could I see …?
su pasaporte	your passport
un documento de identificación	some identification
su tarjeta del banco	your bank card
¿Cuál es su dirección?	What's your address?
¿Dónde se hospeda?	Where are you staying?
Llene este formulario, por favor.	Fill in this form, please.
Firme aquí, por favor.	Please sign here.

Cash machines/ATMs Cajeros automáticos

Can I withdraw money on my credit card here?

¿Puedo retirar dinero con mi tarjeta de crédito aquí? *pwedo reteerar deenero kon mee tarkheta deh kredeeto akee*

Where are the ATMs/cash machines?

¿Dónde están los cajeros automáticos? *dondeh estan los kakheros aootomateekos*

Can I use my … card in the cash machine?

¿Puedo utilizar mi tarjeta… en este cajero automático? *pwedo ooteeleesar mee tarkheta …en esteh kakhero aootomateeko*

The ATM/cash machine has eaten my card.

El cajero automático se ha quedado con mi tarjeta. *el kakhero aootomateeko seh a kedado kon mee tarkheta*

CAJERO AUTOMÁTICO	automated teller/ cash machine

Currency	100 centavos (ct.)= 1 peso ($); (Venezuela)100 céntimos = 1 bolívar (Bs)
Mexico	*Coins:* 5, 10, 20, 50 ct.; 1, 2, 5, 10, 50 pesos
	Notes: 10, 20, 50, 100, 200, 500 pesos
Argentina	*Coins:* 1, 5, 10, 25, 50 ct.
	Notes: 1, 2, 5, 10, 50, 100 pesos
Chile	*Coins:* 1, 5, 10, 50, 100 pesos (Ch$)
	Notes: 500, 1000, 5000, 10,000 pesos (Ch$)
Colombia	*Coins:* 10, 20, 50, 100, 200, 500 pesos
	Notes: 500, 1000, 5000, 10,000 pesos
Venezuela	*Coins:* , 1, 2, 5 bolívares
	Notes: 5, 10, 20, 50, 100, 500, 1000

Pharmacy Farmacia [Droguería]

Some pharmacies in major cities are open 24 hours; others offer a home delivery service. For their address and phone number, consult your hotel reception or call the information line (e.g. 04 in Mexico City).

Most pharmacies are easily recognized by their green cross and **farmacia** sign.

Where's the nearest (all-night) pharmacy?	**¿Dónde está la farmacia [droguería] de veinticuatro horas más cercana?** *dondeh esta la farmaseea [drogereeya] deh beynteekwatro oras mas serkana*
What time does the pharmacy open/close?	**¿A qué hora abren/cierran la farmacia [droguería]?** *a keh ora abren/seeyeran la farmaseea [drogereeya]*
Can you make up this prescription for me?	**¿Podría prepararme esta receta [fórmula]?** *podreeya prepararmeh esta reseta [formoola]*
Shall I wait?	**¿Tengo que esperar?** *tengo keh esperar*
I'll come back for it.	**Pasaré más tarde a recogerla.** *pasareh mas tardeh a rekokherla*

Dosage instructions Dosificación

How much should I take?	**¿Cuánto debo tomar?** *kwanto debo tomar*
How often should I take it?	**¿Cuántas veces al día debo tomarlo(-a)?** *kwantas beses al deeya debo tomarlo(-a)*
Is it suitable for children?	**¿Es apropiado(-a) [recomendable] para niños?** *es apropeeyado(-a) [rekomendableh] para neeños*

Tome ... pastillas/cucharaditas ...	Take ... tablets/... teaspoons ...
antes/después de cada comida	before/after meals
con agua	with water
pásela entera	whole
por la mañana/por la noche	in the morning/at night
durante ... días	for ... days

Asking advice Pedir consejo

What would you recommend for …?	**¿Qué me recomienda para …?** *keh meh rekomeeyenda para*
a cold	**el resfriado** *el resfreeyado*
a cough	**la tos** *la tos*
diarrhea/diarrhoea	**la diarrea** *la deearreya*
a hangover	**la cruda [la resaca/el guayabo]** *la krooda [la resaka/el gwayabo]*
hayfever	**la fiebre del heno** *la feeyebreh del eno*
insect bites	**las mordeduras de insectos** *las mordedooras deh insektos*
a sore throat	**el dolor de garganta** *el dolor deh garganta*
sunburn	**la insolación** *la eensolaseeyon*
travel sickness	**el mareo** *el mareo*
an upset stomach	**el trastorno [malestar] estomacal** *el trastorno [malestar] estomakal*
Can I get it without a prescription?	**¿Puedo conseguirlo sin receta [fórmula] médica?** *pwedo konsegeerlo seen reseta [formoola] medeeka*

Over-the-counter treatment
Medicación sin receta obligatoria

Can I have …?	**¿Puede darme … ?** *pwedeh darmeh*
antiseptic cream	**una crema antiséptica** *oona krema anteesepteeka*
aspirin	**unas aspirinas** *oonas aspeereenas*
bandage	**una venda** *oona benda*
condoms	**unos condones** *oonos kondones*
cotton/cotton wool	**un paquete de algodón** *oon paketeh deh algodon*
insect repellent	**un repelente contra insectos** *oon repelenteh kontra eensektos*
pain killers	**unos analgésicos** *oonos analkheseekos*
vitamin tablets	**unas vitaminas** *oonas beetameenas*

Toiletries   Artículos de tocador

I'd like ...	**Quisiera ...** keeseeyera
after shave	**una loción para después de la afeitada** oona loseeyon para despwes deh la afeytada
after-sun lotion	**una loción para después del sol** oona loseeyon para despwes del sol
deodorant	**un desodorante** oon desodoranteh
moisturizing cream	**crema humectante** krema oomektanteh
razor blades	**unas hojas de afeitar** oonas okhas deh afeytar
sanitary napkins/towels	**unas toallas higiénicas** oonas toal-yas eekheeyeneekas
soap	**un jabón** oon khabon
sun block	**bloqueador solar** blokeador solar
suntan cream/lotion	**crema bronceadora/loción** krema bronseadora/loseeyon
factor ...	**factor...** faktor
tampons	**unos tampones** oonos tampones
tissues	**unos kleenex ®** oonos kleeneks
toilet paper	**un rollo de papel higiénico** oon rol-yo deh papel eekheeyeneeko
toothpaste	**una pasta [crema] de dientes** oona pasta [krema] deh deeyentes

Hair care   Cuidado del cabello

comb	**el peine [la peinilla]** el peyneh [la peyneel-ya]
conditioner	**el acondicionador** el akondeeseeonador
hair mousse	**la espuma moldeadora para el cabello** la espooma moldeadora para el kabel-yo
hair spray	**la laca** la laka
shampoo	**el champú** el champoo

For the baby   Para el bebé

baby food	**comida para bebés** komeeda para bebes
baby wipes	**pañuelos húmedos para bebé** pañwelos oomedos para bebeh
diapers/nappies	**los pañales** los pañales
sterilizing solution	**la solución esterilizante** la solooseeyon estereeleesanteh

Clothing Ropa

You'll find that airport boutiques offering tax-free shopping
may have cheaper prices but less selection.

General Generalidades

I'd like …	**Quisiera …** *keeseeyera*
Do you have any …?	**¿Tiene usted …?** *teeyeneh oosteth*

ROPA PARA DAMAS	ladies' wear
ROPA PARA CABALLERO	men's wear
ROPA PARA NIÑOS	children's wear

Color Color

I'm looking for something in …	**Estoy buscando algo …** *estoy booskando algo*
beige	**beige** *beyeech*
black	**negro** *negro*
blue	**azul** *asool*
brown	**café** *kafeh*
green	**verde** *berdeh*
gray/grey	**gris** *grees*
orange	**naranja [anaranjado]** *narankha [anarankhado]*
pink	**rosado** *rosado*
purple	**morado** *morado*
red	**rojo** *rokho*
white	**blanco** *blanko*
yellow	**amarillo** *amareel-yo*
light	**claro** *klaro*
dark	**oscuro** *oskooro*
I want a lighter shade.	**Quiero un matiz más claro.** *keeyero oon matees mas klaro*
Do you have the same in …?	**¿Lo tiene también en …?** *lo teeyeneh tambeeyen en*

Clothes and accessories Ropa y accesorios

belt	**el cinturón** el seentooron
bikini	**el bikini** el beekeenee
blouse	**la blusa** la bloosa
bra	**el brassiere** el braseeyer
briefs (man's/woman's)	**calzoncillos/pantaletas** kalsonseel-yos/pantaletas
cap	**la gorra** la gorra
coat	**el abrigo** el abreego
dress	**el vestido** el besteedo
handbag	**el bolso** el bolso
hat	**el sombrero** el sombrero
jacket	**la chaqueta** la chaketa
jeans	**los jeans** los yeens
leggings	**las leggings** las legeen
panty hose/tights	**las pantimedias** las panteemedeeas
pullover	**el suéter** el sweter
raincoat	**el impermeable** el eempermeeyableh
scarf	**la bufanda** la boofanda
shirt	**la camisa** la kameesa
shorts	**los shorts** los chors
skirt	**la falda** la falda
socks	**los calcetines** los kalseteenes
stockings	**las medias** las medeeas
suit (man's/woman's)	**el traje [el vestido]/el sastre** el trakheh [el besteedo]/el sastreh
sweatshirt	**la sudadera** la soodadera
swimming trunks	**el pantalón de baño** el pantalon deh baño
swimsuit	**el traje [vestido] de baño** el trakhe [besteedo] deh baño
T-shirt	**la camiseta** la kameeseta
tie	**la corbata** la korbata
tights	**las medias pantalón** las medeeas pantalon
pants/trousers	**los pantalones** los pantalones
underpants	**los calzoncillos** los kalsonseel-yos
with long/short sleeves	**de manga larga/corta** deh manga larga/korta

Shoes Zapatos

A pair of …	**Un par de …** *oon par deh*
boots	**botas** *botas*
flip-flops	**chancletas** *chankletas*
sandals	**sandalias** *sandaleeas*
shoes	**zapatos** *sapatos*
slippers	**pantuflas** *pantooflas*
running/training shoes	**tenis** *tenees*

Walking/hiking gear Equipo de montañismo

windbreaker/cagoule	**anorak impermeable** *anorak eempermeyableh*
knapsack	**mochila** *mocheela*
walking boots	**botas de montañismo** *botas deh montañeesmo*
waterproof jacket	**chaqueta impermeable** *chakehta eempermeyableh*

Fabric Telas

I want something in …	**Quiero algo de …** *keeyero algo deh*
cotton	**algodón** *algodon*
denim	**tela vaquera** *tela bakera*
lace	**encaje** *enkakheh*
leather	**cuero** *kwero*
linen	**lino** *leeno*
wool	**lana** *lana*
Is this …?	**Esto es …?** *esto es*
pure cotton	**algodón puro** *algodon pooro*
synthetic	**sintético** *seenteteeko*
Is it hand washable/ machine washable?	**¿Esto puede lavarse a mano/en la lavadora?** *esto pwedeh labarseh a mano/en la labadora*

LAVADO A MANO SOLAMENTE	handwash only
LAVADO EN SECO SOLAMENTE	dry clean only
NO DESTEÑIBLE	colorfast
NO PLANCHAR	do not iron

Does it fit? ¿Me queda bien?

Can I try this on?	**¿Me lo puedo medir?** *me lo pwedo medeer*
Where's the fitting room?	**¿Dónde está el probador [vestier]?** *dondeh esta el probador [besteeyer]*
It fits well. I'll take it.	**Me queda bien. Me lo llevo.** *meh keda beeyen. meh lo l-yebo*
It doesn't fit.	**No me queda bien.** *no meh keda beeyen*
It's too …	**Es demasiado …** *es demaseeyado*
short/long	**corto(-a)/largo(-a)** *korto(-a)/largo(-a)*
tight/loose	**ajustado(-a)/ suelto(-a)** *akhoostado(-a)/swelto(-a)*
Do you have this in size …?	**¿Tiene este(-a) mismo(-a) … en talla …?** *teeyeneh esteh(-a) meesmo(-a) … en tal-ya*
What size is this?	**¿Qué talla es ésta?** *keh tal-ya es esta*
Could you measure me, please?	**¿Podría tomarme las medidas, por favor?** *podreeya tomarmeh las medeedas por fabor*
What size do you take?	**¿Qué talla es usted?** *keh tal-ya es oosteh*
I don't know Mexican sizes.	**No conozco las tallas mexicanas.** *no konosko las tal-yas mekheekanas*

Size Talla

	Dresses/Suits						Women's shoes			
American	8	10	12	14	16	18	6	7	8	9
British	10	12	14	16	18	20	$4^{1/2}$	$5^{1/2}$	$6^{1/2}$	$7^{1/2}$
Latin American	38	40	42	44	46	48	37	39	40	41

	Shirts				Men's shoes								
American)													
British)	15	16	17	18	6	7	8	$8^{1/2}$	9	$9^{1/2}$	10	11	
Latin American	38	41	43	46	39	41	42	42	43	44	44	45	

EXTRA GRANDE	extra large (XL)
GRANDE	large (L)
MEDIANO	medium (M)
PEQUEÑO	small (S)

1 centimeter (cm.) = 0.39 in.	1 inch = 2.54 cm.
1 meter (m.) = 39.37 in.	1 foot = 30.5 cm.
10 meters = 32.81 ft.	1 yard = 0.91 m.

Health and beauty   Salud y belleza

I'd like a …	**Quisiera …** *keeseeyera*
facial	**un tratamiento facial** *oon tratameeyento faseeyal*
manicure	**un manicure** *oon maneekooreh*
massage	**un masaje** *oon masakheh*
waxing	**una depilación con cera** *oona depeelaseeyon kon sera*

Hairdresser/Hairstylist
En la peluquería/Donde el estilista

Tipping: the hairdresser usually receives 10–15% in Mexico; 10% is normal in Argentina, Chile and Colombia; 5–10% in Venezuela.

I'd like to make an appointment for …	**Quisiera una cita para …** *keeseeyera oona seeta para*
Can you make it a bit earlier/later?	**¿Podría dármela un poco más temprano/tarde?** *podreeya darmela oon poko mas temprano/tardeh*
I'd like a …	**Quisiera …** *keeseeyera*
cut and blow-dry	**un corte y secado** *oon korteh ee sekado*
shampoo and set	**un champú y fijador** *oon champoo ee feekhador*
trim	**un recortado** *oon rekortado*
I'd like my hair …	**Quisiera que me … el pelo** *keeseeyera keh meh … el pelo*
colored/tinted	**tinture/tiña** *teentooreh/teeña*
highlighted/permed	**haga unos rayitos/una permanente** *aga oonos rayeetos/oona permanenteh*
Don't cut it too short.	**No lo quiero demasiado corto.** *no lo keeyero demaseeyado korto*
A little more off the …	**Córtelo un poco más …** *kortemelo oon poko mas*
back/front	**atrás/al frente** *atras/al frenteh*
neck/sides	**en el cuello/a los lados** *en el kwel-yo/a los lados*
top	**en la coronilla** *en la koroneel-ya*
That's fine, thanks.	**Así está bien, gracias.** *asee esta beeyen graseeas*

Household articles
Artículos para el hogar

I'd like ...	**Quisiera ...** *keeseeyera*
adapter	**un adaptador** *oon adaptador*
aluminum foil	**un rollo de papel aluminio** *oon rol-yo deh papel aloomeeneeo*
bottle opener	**un destapador** *oon destapador*
candles	**unas velas** *oonas belas*
clothes pins/pegs	**unos ganchos para colgar la ropa** *oonos ganchos para kolgar la ropa*
plastic wrap/cling film	**un rollo de plástico para envolver** *oon rol-yo deh plasteeko para enbolber*
corkscrew	**un descorchador** *oon deskorchador*
lightbulb	**un foco [un bombillo]** *oon foko [oon bombeel-yo]*
paper napkins	**unas servilletas** *oonas serbeel-yetas*
scissors	**unas tijeras** *oonas teekheras*
screwdriver	**un destornillador** *oon destornil-yador*
can opener	**un abrelatas** *oon abrelatas*

Cleaning products Artículos de aseo [limpieza]

bleach	**el blanqueador** *el blankeador*
dish cloth	**el paño [limpión]** *el paño [leempeeyon]*
dishwashing detergent	**el detergente para los platos** *el deterkhenteh para los platos*
garbage/refuse bags	**bolsas para la basura** *bolsas para la basoora*
laundry soap/washing powder	**el jabón para lavadora** *el khabon para labadora*
dishwashing/washing-up liquid	**el jabón líquido para los platos** *el khabon leekeedo para los platos*

Crockery/Cutlery Vajilla/Cubiertos

cups	**las tazas [pocillos]** *las tasas [poseel-yos]*
forks	**los tenedores** *los tenedores*
glasses/mugs	**los vasos/las tazas** *los basos/las tasas*
knives	**los cuchillos** *los koocheel-yos*
plates	**los platos** *los platos*
spoons	**las cucharas** *las koocharas*
teaspoons	**las cucharitas** *las koochareetas*

Jeweler Joyería

Could I see …?	**¿Puedo ver …?** *pwedo behr*
this/that	**esto/eso** *esto/eso*
It's in the window/ display cabinet.	**Está en la vitrina [el aparador]/ el escaparate** *esta en la beetreena [el aparador]/el eskaparateh*
I'd like …	**Quisiera …** *keeseeyera*
alarm clock/clock	**un reloj despertador/un reloj** *oon relokh despertador/oon relokh*
battery	**una pila** *oona peela*
bracelet	**una pulsera** *oona poolsera*
brooch	**un prendedor** *oon prendedor*
chain	**una cadena** *oona kadena*
earrings	**unos aretes** *oonos aretes*
necklace	**un collar** *oon kol-yar*
ring	**un anillo** *oon aneel-yo*
watch	**un reloj de pulsera** *oon relokh deh poolsera*

Materials Materiales

Is this real silver/gold?	**¿Es plata verdadera/oro verdadero?** *es plata berdadera/oro berdadero*
Is there any certification for it?	**¿Tiene algún documento que lo certifique?** *teeyeneh algoon dokoomento keh lo serteefeekeh*
Do you have anything in …?	**¿Tiene algo de …?** *teeyeneh algo deh*
copper	**cobre** *kobreh*
crystal	**cristal** *kreestal*
cut glass	**cristal tallado** *kreestal tal-yado*
diamond	**diamante** *deeamanteh*
enamel	**esmalte** *esmalteh*
gold/gold plate	**oro/chapado en oro** *oro/chapado en oro*
pearl	**perla** *perla*
pewter	**peltre** *peltreh*
platinum	**platino** *plateeno*
stainless steel	**acero inoxidable** *asero eenokseedableh*
silver plate	**plata/chapado en plata** *plata/chapado en plata*

Newsstand/Newsagent/Tobacconist
Quiosco de periódicos

Foreign newspapers can usually be found at rail stations or airports, or on newsstands in major cities.

Do you sell English-language books/newspapers?	**¿Vende usted libros/periódicos en inglés?** _bendeh oosteth leebros/pereeyodeekos en eengles_
I'd like …	**Quisiera …** _keeseeyera_
book	**un libro** _oon leebro_
candy/sweets	**un dulce** _oon doolseh_
chewing gum	**un chicle** _oon chikleh_
chocolate bar	**un chocolate [una chocolatina]** _oon chokolateh [oona chokolateena]_
cigars	**unos cigarros [unos puros]** _oonos seegarros [oonos pooros]_
package/packet of cigarettes	**una cajetilla de cigarrillos** _oona kakheteel-ya deh seegarreel-yos_
dictionary	**un diccionario** _oon deekseeonareeo_
Spanish-English	**Español/Inglés** _español/eengles_
envelopes	**unos sobres** _oonos sobres_
guidebook of …	**una guía de …** _oona geeya deh_
lighter	**un encendedor** _oon ensendedor_
magazine	**una revista** _oona rebeesta_
map of the town	**un mapa de la ciudad/del pueblo** _oon mapa deh la seeoodath/del pweblo_
road map of …	**un mapa de carreteras** _oon mapa deh karreteras_
matches	**unos fósforos** _oonos fosforos_
newspaper	**un periódico** _oon pereeyodeeko_
American	**estadounidense [de Estados Unidos]** _estado-ooneedenseh [deh los estados ooneedos]_
English	**de Inglaterra** _deh eenglaterra_
paper	**una hoja de papel** _oona okha de papel_
pen	**una pluma [un bolígrafo]** _oona plooma [oon boleegrafo]_
postcard	**una postal** _oona postal_

Photography Fotografía

I'm looking for a(n) ... camera. **Estoy buscando una cámara ...** *estoy booskando oona kamara*

automatic	**automática**	*aootomateeka*
compact	**compacta**	*kompakta*
disposable	**desechable**	*desechableh*
SLR	**de reflejo sencillo**	*deh reflekho senseel-yo*

I'd like ... **Quisiera ...** *keeseeyera*

battery	**la pila**	*la peela*
camera case	**el estuche [la funda] de la cámara**	*el estoocheh [la foonda] deh la kamara*
electronic flash	**el flash**	*el flach*
filter	**el filtro**	*el feeltro*
lens	**el objetivo**	*el obkheteebo*
lens cap	**la tapa del objetivo**	*la tapa del obkheteebo*

Film/Processing Revelado de rollos

I'd like a ... film for this camera. **Quisiera un rollo ... para esta cámara.** *keeseeyera oon rol-yo ... para esta kamara*

black and white	**en blanco y negro**	*en blanko ee negro*
color/colour	**a color**	*a kolor*
24/36 exposures	**24/36 revelaciones**	*beyntee-kwatro/treynta ee seys rebelaseeyones*

I'd like this film developed, please. **Quisiera que me revelara este rollo, por favor.** *keeseeyera keh meh rebelara esteh rol-yo por fabor*

Would you enlarge this, please? **¿Podría ampliarme esta fotografía, por favor?** *podreeya ampleeyarmeh esta fotografeeya por fabor*

How much do ... exposures cost? **¿Cuánto cuesta el revelado de ...?** *kwanto kwesta el rebelado deh ...*

When will the photos be ready? **¿Cuándo estarán listas las fotografías?** *kwando estaran leestas las fotografeeyas*

I'd like to collect my photos. Here's the receipt. **Vengo a reclamar mis fotografías. Aquí está el recibo.** *bengo a reklamar mees fotografeeyas. akee esta el reseebo*

Police Policía

Beware of pickpockets, particularly in crowded places. Report all thefts to the local police within 24 hours for your own insurance purposes.

In Mexico, a 24-hour hotline is run by **SECTUR**, to help tourists in emergencies (5) 250-01-23/51 in Mexico City, 800-9-03-92 outside.

Where's the nearest police station?	**¿Dónde está la estación de policía más cercana?** *dondeh esta la estaseeyon deh poleeseeya mas serkana*
Does anyone here speak English?	**¿Hay alguien aquí que hable inglés?** *eye algeeyen akee keh ableh eengles*
I want to report a(n) …	**Quiero informar sobre …** *keeyero eenformar sobreh*
accident/attack	**un accidente/atentado** *oon akseedenteh/atentado*
mugging/rape	**un asalto/una violación** *oon asalto/oona beeolaseeyon*
My child is missing.	**Mi hijo(-a) ha desaparecido.** *mee eekho(-a) a desapareseedo*
Someone's following me.	**Alguien me está persiguiendo.** *algeeyen meh esta perseegeeyendo*
I need an English-speaking lawyer.	**Necesito un abogado que hable inglés.** *neseseeto oon abogado keh ableh eengles*
I need to make a phone call.	**Necesito hacer una llamada telefónica.** *neseseeto aser oona l-yamada telefoneeka*
I need to contact the … Consulate.	**Necesito comunicarme con el consulado …** *neseseeto komooneekarmeh kon el konsoolado*
American/British	**norteamericano/británico** *norteamereekano/breetaneeko*

¿Puede describirlo(-la)?	Can you describe him/her?
hombre/mujer	male/female
rubio(-a)/moreno(-a)/pelirrojo(-a)	blonde/brunette/red-headed/
de cabello gris	gray/grey
de cabello largo/corto/calvo(a)	long/short hair/balding
estatura aproximada …	approximate height …
edad aproximada …	aged (approximately) …
Vestía [Llevaba puesto(-a)] …	He/She was wearing …

CLOTHES ➤ 144; COLORS ➤ 143

Lost property/Theft
Objetos perdidos/Robos

I want to report a theft/break-in.	**Quiero informar sobre un robo/asalto.** *keeyero eenformar sobre oon robo/asalto*
I've been robbed/mugged.	**Me han robado/atracado.** *meh an robado/atrakado*
I've lost my …	**Se me perdió/perdieron …** *seh meh perdeeyo/perdeeyeron*
My … has been stolen.	**Me robaron …** *meh robaron*
bicycle	**mi bicicleta** *mee beeseekleta*
camera	**mi cámara** *mee kamara*
(rental) car	**el carro que había alquilado** *el karro keh abeeya alkeelado*
credit cards	**mis tarjetas de crédito** *mees tarkhetas deh kredeeto*
handbag	**mi bolso** *mee bolso*
money	**mi dinero** *mee deenero*
passport	**mi pasaporte** *mee pasaporteh*
purse	**mi monedero** *mee monedero*
ticket	**mi boleto [tiquete]** *mee boleto [teeketeh]*
wallet	**mi billetera** *mee beeI-yetera*
watch	**mi reloj** *mi relokh*
What shall I do?	**¿Qué tengo que hacer?** *keh tengo keh aser*
I need a police form/certificate for my insurance claim.	**Necesito una certificación de la policía para la demanda de seguro.** *neseseeto oona serteefeekaseeyon deh la poleeseeya para la demanda deh segooro*

¿Qué falta?	What's missing?
¿Cuándo sucedió?	When did it happen?
¿Dónde se hospeda?	Where are you staying?
¿De dónde se lo robaron?	Where was it taken from?
¿Dónde estaba usted en ese momento?	Where were you at the time?
Vamos a conseguirle un intérprete.	We're getting an interpreter for you.
Vamos a estudiar el caso.	We'll look into the matter.
Llene esta hoja, por favor.	Please fill in this form.

Post Office El correo

Post offices are indicated by the sign **Correos y Telégrafos**.
Main offices generally operate 8 a.m.–7 p.m. The main post
office in Mexico City is open 7 a.m.–midnight, Monday–Friday;
until 8 p.m. on Saturday; and until 4 p.m. on Sunday.

Mailboxes are generally red, marked **Aéreo** for airmail items, **D.F.** (in
Mexico City) or **Local** for local mail, or **Terrestre** for surface mail.

Stamps are also sold at tobacconists, stationers, souvenir stands and from
stamp machines.

Faxes can be sent at some post offices, most hotels and some stationery shops.

General queries Información general

Where is the nearest post office?	**¿Dónde queda la oficina de correo más cercana?** _dondeh keda la ofeeseena deh korreyo mas serkana_
What time does the post office open/close?	**¿A qué hora abren/cierran el correo?** _a keh ora abren/seeyeran el korreyo_
Does it close for lunch?	**¿Cierran el correo al mediodía?** _seeyeran el korreyo al medeeodeeya_
Where's the mailbox?	**¿Dónde está el buzón?** _dondeh esta el booson_
Where's the general delivery?	**¿Dónde está la lista de correos?** _dondeh esta la leesta de korreyos_
Is there any mail for me? My name is …	**¿Hay correspondencia para mí? Me llamo …** _eye korrespondenseea para mee. meh l-yamo_

Buying stamps Comprar sellos [estampillas]

A stamp for this postcard/ letter, please.	**Un sello [estampilla] para esta postal/ carta, por favor.** _oon sel-yo [estampeel-ya] para esta postal/karta por fabor_
A … pesos stamp, please.	**Una estampilla de … pesos, por favor** _oona estampeel-ya deh … pesos por fabor_
What's the postage for a postcard/letter to …?	**¿Cuál es la tarifa de correo para una postal/carta para …?** _kwal es la tareefa deh korreyo para oona postal/karta para_

> – Hola. Quisiera enviar estas postales
>   a los Estados Unidos.
>   – _¿Cuántas?_
>   – Nueve, por favor.
> – Es un peso 50 centavos cada postal:
>   Aquí, tiene 13 pesos 50 centavos.

Sending parcels Enviar paquetes

I want to send this package/parcel by …	**Quiero enviar este paquete por …** *keeyero enbeeyar esteh paketeh por*
airmail	**correo aéreo** *korreyo ayereo*
special delivery/express	**entrega inmediata** *entrega inmedeeyata*
It contains …	**Contiene …** *konteeyeneh*

Por favor, llene la declaración de aduana.	Please fill in the customs declaration.
¿Cuál es el valor aproximado del contenido del paquete?	What is the value of the contents?
¿Qué contiene?	What's inside?

Telecommunications Telecomunicaciones

I'd like a phonecard.	**Quisiera una tarjeta de teléfono.** *keeseeyera oona tarkheta deh telefono*
50/120 units	**De cincuenta/ciento veinte unidades** *deh seenkwenta/seeyento beynteh ooneedades*
Do you have a photocopier?	**¿Tiene fotocopiadora?** *teeyeneh fotokopeeyadora*
I'd like to send a message…	**Quisiera enviar un mensaje …** *keeseeyera enbeeyar oon mensakheh*
by E-mail/fax	**por "e-mail"/fax** *por "e-mail"/fax*
What's your E-mail address?	**¿Cuál es su dirección de "e-mail"?** *kwal es soo deerekseeyon deh "e-mail"*
Can I access the Internet here?	**¿Me puede conectar con el "Internet" aquí?** *meh pwedo konektar kon el "Internet" akee*
What are the charges per hour?	**¿Cuánto se cobra por hora?** *kwanto seh kobra por ora*
How do I log on?	**¿Cómo hago la conexión?** *komo ago la konekseeyon*

SELLOS [ESTAMPILLAS]	stamps
TELEGRAMAS	telegrams
LISTA DE CORREO	general delivery/ poste restante
PRÓXIMA RECOLECCIÓN	next collection
GIRO POSTAL	money matters
PAQUETES	parcels

Souvenirs Recuerdos

Mexico and the rest of Latin America are rich in handicrafts (**artesanías**) of all kind. Shopping can be a real delight, with something new and exciting around every corner. Ceramics, silverware, papier-mâché articles, textiles and a host of other handmade or handworked local products all exude a sense of history, tradition, talent and imagination.

In Mexico, look for embroidered traditional Indian costumes, such as **huipil** (sleeveless tunic), **quechquémitl** (cape), **rebozo** (long shawl); rugs and wall hangings, yarn paintings, embroidered cloths.

Pottery: **animalitos** (small animals), **Talavera**-style plates, bowls and tiles. Mask and headdresses; gourd drinking vessels, lacquered trays, dolls; musical instruments like the maraca, tambourine, drums. Bark paintings; leatherware including sandals (**huaraches**); silver and gold jewelry; crafted tinplate; religious paintings (**retablo**). Hammocks, baskets. **Piñata** (candy-filled papier-mâché star) for children's parties and festivities.

Gifts Regalos

carpets	**tapetes [alfombras]** *tapetes [alfombras]*
copperware	**cobres** *kobres*
embroidery	**bordados** *bordados*
painted gourds	**calabazas pintadas** *kalabasas peentadas*
hand-blown glass	**vidrio soplado** *beedreeo soplado*
jewels	**joyas** *khoyas*
masks	**máscaras** *maskaras*
onyx	**ónix** *oneeks*
papier mâché	**papel maché** *papel macheh*
poncho	**jorongo [poncho]** *khorongo ["poncho"]*
pottery	**cerámica** *serameeka*
saddle	**silla de montar** *seel-ya deh montar*
sandals	**huaraches** *waraches*
shawl (woman's)	**rebozo** *reboso*
silver	**plata** *plata*
sun hat	**sombrero** *sombrero*
traditional ball game	**balero** *balero*

Music Música

I'd like a …	**Quisiera …** *keeseeyera*
cassette/compact disc	**un cassette/un compact disc** *oon kaset/oon kompak deesk*
record	**un disco** *oon deesko*
video cassette	**un video** *oon beedeo*
Who are the popular native singers/bands?	**¿Cuáles son los cantantes/las orquestas populares de la región?** *kwales son los kantantes/las orkestas popoolares deh la rekheeyon*

Toys and games Juguetes y juegos

I'd like a toy/game …	**Quisiera un juguete/juego …** *keeseeyera oon khoogeteh/khwego*
for a boy	**para un niño** *para oon neeño*
for a 5-year-old girl	**para una niña de cinco años** *para oona neeña deh seenko años*
pail and shovel/ bucket and spade	**la cubeta y la palita [el balde y la pala]** *oona koobeta ee la paleeta [el balde ee la pala]*
chess set	**un juego de ajedrez** *oon khwego deh akhedres*
doll	**una muñeca** *oona mooñeka*
electronic game	**un juego electrónico** *oon khwego elektroneeko*
teddy bear	**un oso de peluche** *oon oso deh peloocheh*

Antiques Antigüedades

It's illegal to take antiquities out of Mexico; check before purchasing.

How old is this?	**¿Cuántos años tiene esto?** *kwantos años teeneh esto*
Do you have anything of the … era?	**¿Tiene usted algo de la época …?** *teeyeneh oosteth algo deh la epoka*
Can you send it to me?	**¿Podría enviármelo?** *podreeya enbeeyarmelo*
Will I have problems with customs?	**¿Tendré problemas con la aduana?** *tendreh problemas kon la adwana*

Supermarket/Minimart
Supermercado/Minimercado
At the supermarket En el supermercado

Excuse me. Where can I find …?	**Disculpe. ¿Dónde puedo encontrar …?** *deeskoolpeh. dondeh pwedo enkontrar*
Do I pay for this here or at the checkout?	**¿Dónde pago esto, aquí o en la caja?** *dondeh pago esto akee o en la kakha*
Where are the baskets/trolleys?	**¿Dónde están los carritos/las canastas?** *dondeh estan los karreetos/las kanastas*
Is there a … here?	**¿Hay … aquí?** *eye … akee*
delicatessen	**un delicatessen [una tienda de especialidades]** *oon deleekatesen [oona teeyenda deh espeseealeedades]*
pharmacy	**una farmacia [una droguería]** *oona farmaseea [oona drogereeya]*

ALIMENTOS CONGELADOS	frozen foods
ARTÍCULOS PARA EL HOGAR	household goods
CARNE FRESCA	fresh meat
EFECTIVO SOLAMENTE	cash only
FRUTAS Y VERDURAS ENLATADAS	canned fruit/vegetables
PAN Y PASTELES [TORTAS]	bread and cakes
PESCADO FRESCO	fresh fish
POLLOS	poultry
PRODUCTOS DE LIMPIEZA	cleaning products
PRODUCTOS FRESCOS	fresh produce
PRODUCTOS LÁCTEOS	dairy products
VINOS Y LICORES	wines and spirits

Weights and measures
- **1 kilogram** or **kilo (kg.)** = **1000 grams (g.)**; **100 g.** = 3.5 oz.; **1 kg.** = 2.2 lb [1 oz. = **28.35 g.**; 1 lb. = **453.60 g.**]
- **1 liter (l.)** = 0.88 imp. quart or 1.06 U.S. quart [1 imp. quart = **1.14 l.** 1 U.S. quart = **0.951 l.** 1 imp. gallon = **4.55 l.** 1 U.S. gallon = **3.8 l.**]

Food hygiene Higiene de los alimentos

APROPIADO(A) PARA COCINAR EN MICROONDAS	microwaveable
APROPIADO(A) PARA VEGETARIANOS	suitable for vegetarians
CALIÉNTESE ANTES DE CONSUMIRSE	heat before eating
EXHÍBASE AL PÚBLICO HASTA EL ... ABIERTO	eat within ... days of opening
MANTÉNGASE EN EL REFRIGERADOR	keep refrigerated
VÉNDASE ANTES DEL ...	sell by ...

At the minimart En el súper

I'd like some of that/those.	**Quisiera un poco de eso/unos cuantos.** *keeseeyera oon poko deh eso/oonos kwantos*
This one/those	**Éste/éstos** *esteh/estos*
Over there/Here	**Por allá/por aquí** *por al-ya/por akee*
Which one/ones?	**¿Cuál/cuáles?** *kwal/kwales*
That's all, thanks.	**Eso es todo, gracias.** *eso es todo graseeas*
I'd like ...	**Quisiera ...** *keeseeyera*
a kilo of apples	**un kilo de manzanas** *oon keelo deh mansanas*
half-kilo of tomatoes	**medio kilo de tomates** *medeeo keelo deh tomates*
100 grams of cheese	**cien gramos de queso** *seeyen gramos de keso*
a liter/litre of milk	**un litro de leche** *oon leetro deh lecheh*
half-dozen eggs	**media docena de huevos** *medeea dosena deh webos*
... slices of ham	**... rebanadas de jamón** *... rebanadas deh khamon*
a piece of cake	**una rebanada [un pedazo] de pastel [torta]** *oona rebanada [oon pedaso] deh pastel [torta]*
a bottle of wine	**una botella de vino** *oona botel-ya de beeno*

> – Quisiera medio kilo de ese queso, por favor.
> – ¿De éste?
> – Sí. El queso enchilado, por favor.
> – *Con mucho gusto. ¿Eso es todo [Algo más]?*
> – También quiero cuatro
> rebanadas de jamón, por favor.
> – Aquí tiene.

Snacks/Picnic Meriendas/Picnic

butter	**la mantequilla** *la mantekeel-ya*
cheese	**el queso** *el keso*
French fries/chips	**las papas a la francesa** *las papas a la fransesa*
cookies	**los bizcochos** *los biskochos*
chips	**las papas fritas** *las papas freetas*
eggs	**los huevos** *los webos*
grapes	**las uvas** *las oobas*
ice cream	**el helado** *el elado*
instant coffee	**el café instantáneo** *el kafeh instantaneo*
loaf of bread	**el pan de molde** *el pan deh moldeh*
margarine	**la margarina** *la margareena*
milk	**la leche** *la lecheh*
rolls	**los bolillos [panecillos]** *los boleel-yos [paneseel-yos]*
sausages	**las salchichas** *las salcheechas*
six-pack of beer	**el paquete de seis latas de cerveza** *el paketeh deh seys latas de serbesa*
soft drinks/sodas	**los refrescos [las gaseosas]/las sodas** *los refreskos [las gaseosas]/las sodas*
tea bags	**las bolsas de té** *las bolsas de teh*
winebox	**la caja de vino [el cartón de vino]** *la kakha deh beeno [el karton deh beeno]*

Health

Health advice
It is advisable for tourists to drink bottled water only; be wary of foods served outdoors as hygiene standards are variable. Eat lightly until your stomach has adapted to local food (particularly tropical fruit), and avoid unwashed salads and raw seafood, or you may fall victim to Montezuma's revenge!
In mosquito-infested areas, wear loose-fitting light-colored clothing, and sleep beneath mosquito nets.

Insurance and payment (➤ 168 for phrases)
Before you leave, make sure your health insurance policy covers any illness or accident while on vacation/holiday. Mexico has no reciprocal health arrangements, so travel insurance is a must. Every Mexican town has a health center (**centro de salud**). Your nearest consulate should have a list of English-speaking doctors.

Doctor/General   Doctor/Generalidades

Where can I find a doctor/dentist?	**¿Dónde puedo encontrar un doctor/ dentista?** _dondeh pwedo enkontrar oon doktor/denteesta_
Where's there a doctor who speaks English?	**¿Dónde hay un doctor que hable inglés?** _dondeh eye oon doktor keh ableh eengles_
What are the office/ surgery/hours?	**¿Cuáles son las horas de consulta?** _kwales son las oras deh konsoolta_
Could the doctor come to see me here?	**¿Podría el doctor venir a examinarme aquí?** _podreeya el doktor beneer a eksameenarmeh akee_
Can I make an appointment for …?	**¿Me puede dar una cita para …?** _meh pwedeh dar oona seeta para_
today/tomorrow	**hoy/mañana** _oy/mañana_
as soon as possible	**cuanto antes** _kwanto antes_
It's urgent.	**Es urgente.** _es oorkhenteh_

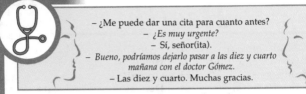

Accident and injury Accidentes y heridas

My … is hurt.	**Mi … se ha lastimado(-a).** _mee…seh a lasteemado(-a)_
My … is injured.	**Mi … está herido(-a).** _mee … esta ereedo(-a)_
husband/wife	**esposo/esposa** _esposo/esposa_
son/daughter	**hijo/hija** _eekho/eekha_
friend	**amigo(-a)** _ameego(-a)_
baby	**bebé** _bebeh_
He/She is …	**El/Ella está …** _el/el-ya esta_
unconscious	**inconsciente** _eenkonseeyenteh_
bleeding (heavily)	**sangrando (mucho)** _sangrando (moocho)_
(seriously) injured	**(gravemente) herido(-a)** _(grabementeh) ereedo(-a)_
I've got a/an …	**Tengo …** _tengo_
blister	**una ampolla** _oona ampol-ya_
boil	**un furúnculo** _oon fooroonkoolo_
bruise	**un moretón** _oon moreton_
burn	**una quemadura** _oona kemadoora_
cut	**una cortadura** _oona kortadoora_
graze	**un arañazo** _oon arañaso_
insect bite	**una mordedura de insecto** _oona mordedoora deh eensekto_
lump	**una protuberancia [una bolita]** _oona protooberanseea [oona boleeta]_
rash	**un salpullido** _oon salpool-yeedo_
sting	**una picadura** _oona peekadoora_
strained muscle	**un músculo torcido** _oon mooskoolo torseedo_
swelling	**una inflamación** _oona inflamaseeyon_
My … hurts.	**Me duele el (la) …** _me dwehleh el/la_

Symptoms Síntomas

I've been feeling ill for … days.	**He estado enfermo(-a) desde hace … días.** *eh estado enfermo(-a) desdeh aseh … deeyas*
I feel …	**Tengo …** *tengo*
dizzy/faint	**mareo** *mareyo*
feverish	**fiebre** *feeyebreh*
I've been vomiting.	**He estado vomitando.** *eh estado bomeetando*
I have diarrhea/diarrhoea.	**Tengo diarrea.** *tengo deeareya*
It hurts here.	**Me duele aquí.** *meh dweleh akee*
I have (a/an) …	**Tengo …** *tengo*
backache	**dolor de espalda** *dolor deh espalda*
cold	**un resfriado** *oon resfreeyado*
cramps	**calambres** *kalambres*
earache	**dolor de oído** *dolor deh oyeedo*
headache	**dolor de cabeza** *dolor deh kabesa*
sore throat	**dolor de garganta** *dolor deh garganta*
stiff neck	**tortícolis** *torteekolees*
stomachache	**dolor de estómago** *dolor deh estomago*
sunstroke	**una insolación** *oona eensolaseeyon*

Health conditions Estado de salud

I have arthritis.	**Tengo artritis.** *tengo artreetees*
I have asthma.	**Tengo asma.** *tengo asma*
I am …	**Soy** *soy*
deaf	**sordo(-a)** *sordo(-a)*
diabetic	**diabético(-a)** *deeabeteeko(-a)*
epileptic	**epiléptico(-a)** *epeelepteeko(-a)*
handicapped	**incapacitado(-a) [minusválido(-a)]** *eenkapaseetado(-a) [meenoosbaleedo(-a)]*
I am (… months) pregnant.	**Tengo (… meses de) embarazo.** *tengo (… meses deh) embaraso*
I have a heart condition.	**Sufro del corazón.** *soofro del korason*
I have high blood pressure.	**Tengo la presión alta.** *tengo la preseeyon alta*

163

Doctor's inquiries Preguntas del doctor

¿Cuánto tiempo hace que se siente así?	How long have you been feeling like this?
¿Es la primera vez que le sucede eso?	Is this the first time you've had this?
¿Está tomando alguna otra medicina?	Are you taking any other medicines?
¿Es alérgico(-a) a algo?	Are you allergic to anything?
¿Está vacunado(-a) contra el tétano?	Have you been vaccinated against tetanus?
¿Ha perdido el apetito?	Have you lost your appetite?

Examination Exámen médico

Voy a tomarle la temperatura/ la presión arterial.	I'll take your temperature/ blood pressure.
Súbase la manga, por favor.	Roll up your sleeve, please.
Desvístase hasta la cintura.	Please undress to the waist.
Acuéstese, por favor.	Please lie down.
Abra la boca.	Open your mouth.
Respire profundo [hondo].	Breathe deeply.
Tosa, por favor.	Cough please.
¿Dónde le duele?	Where does it hurt?
¿Le duele aquí?	Does it hurt here?

Diagnosis Diagnóstico

Quiero que le tomen una radiografía.	I want you to have an x-ray.
Quiero una muestra de sangre/ heces [materias fecales]/orina.	I want a specimen of your blood/stools/urine.
Quiero que consulte a un especialista.	I want you to see a specialist.
Quiero que vaya al hospital.	I want you to go to the hospital.
Está roto(-a)/torcido(-a)	It's broken/sprained.
Está dislocado(-a)/desgarrado(-a)	It's dislocated/torn.

Tiene ... (a/an) ...	You've got
apendicitis	appendicitis
cistitis	cystitis
gripe	flu
una fractura	fracture
gastritis	gastritis
una hernia	hernia
el/la .... inflamado(-a)	inflammation of ...
sarampión	measles
neumonía	pneumonia
ciática	sciatica
amigdalitis	tonsilitis
un tumor	tumor/tumour
una enfermedad venérea	venereal disease
Está intoxicado(-a).	You've got food poisoning.
Está infectado(-a).	It's infected.
Es contagioso(-a).	It's contagious.

Treatment Tratamiento

Le daré ...	I'll give you ...
un antiséptico	an antiseptic
un analgésico	a pain killer
Le voy a recetar [formular] ...	I'm going to prescribe ...
un tratamiento de antibióticos	a course of antibiotics
unos supositorios	some suppositories
¿Es alérgico(-a) a alguna medicina?	Are you allergic to any medicines?
Tome una píldora	Take one pill ...
cada ... horas	every ... hours
antes/después de cada comida	before/after each meal
en caso de dolor	if there is any pain
para ... días	for ... days
Consulte a un médico cuando regrese a casa.	Consult a doctor when you get home.

appendix	**el apéndice** *el apendeeseh*
arm	**el brazo** *el braso*
back	**la espalda** *la espalda*
bladder	**la vejiga** *la bekheega*
bone	**el hueso** *el weso*
breast	**el seno** *el seno*
chest	**el pecho** *el pecho*
ear	**el oído** *el oyeedo*
eye	**el ojo** *el okho*
face	**la cara** *la kara*
finger	**el dedo** *el dedo*
foot	**el pie** *el peeyeh*
gland	**la glándula/el ganglio** *la glandoola/el gangleeyo*
hand	**la mano** *la mano*
head	**la cabeza** *la kabesa*
heart	**el corazón** *el korason*
jaw	**la mandíbula** *la mandeeboola*
joint	**la articulación** *la arteekoolaseeyon*
kidney	**el riñón** *el reeñon*
knee	**la rodilla** *la rodeel-ya*
leg	**la pierna** *la peeyerna*
lip	**el labio** *el labeeo*
liver	**el hígado** *el eegado*
mouth	**la boca** *la boka*
muscle	**el músculo** *el mooskoolo*
neck	**el cuello** *el kwel-yo*
nose	**la nariz** *la narees*
rib	**la costilla** *la kosteel-ya*
shoulder	**el hombro** *el ombro*
skin	**la piel** *la peeyel*
stomach	**el estómago** *el estomago*
thigh	**el muslo** *el mooslo*
throat	**la garganta** *la garganta*
thumb	**el dedo pulgar** *el dedo poolgar*
toe	**el dedo del pie** *el dedo del peeyeh*
tongue	**la lengua** *la lengwa*
tonsils	**las amígdalas** *las ameegdalas*
vein	**la vena** *la bena*

Gynecologist El/la ginecólogo(-a)

I have …

Tengo … *tengo*

abdominal pains

**dolores abdominales
[cólicos]**
dolores abdomeenales [koleekos]

period pains

cólicos menstruales
koleekos menstrooales

a vaginal infection

una infección vaginal
oona infekseeyon bakheenal

I haven't had my period
for … months.

**Hace … meses que no tengo la regla
[la menstruación].** *aseh … meses keh no
tengo la regla [la menstrooaseeyon].*

I'm on the Pill.

Tomo la píldora. *tomo la peeldora*

Hospital En el hospital

Please notify my family.

Avísele a mi familia, por favor.
abeeseleh a mee fameeleea por fabor

I'm in pain.

Tengo mucho dolor. *tengo moocho dolor*

I can't eat/sleep.

No puedo comer/dormir.
no pwedo komer/dormeer

When will the doctor come?

¿Cuándo vendrá el doctor?
kwando bendra el doktor

Which ward is … in?

¿En qué sala está …? *en keh sala esta*

I'm visiting …

Estoy visitando … *estoy beeseetando*

Optician El/la oculista

I'm nearsighted/farsighted.

Soy miope/hipermétrope.
soy meeyopeh/eepermetropeh

I've lost …

Se me perdió … *seh meh perdeeyo*

one of my contact-lenses

uno de mis lentes de contacto
oono deh mees lentes deh kontakto

my glasses

mis gafas [anteojos]
mees gafas [anteokhos]

a lens

un lente *oon lenteh*

Could you give me
a replacement?

¿Podría darme uno(-as) nuevo(-as)?
podreeya darmeh oono(-as) nwebo(-as)

167

Dentist El dentista

I have toothache.	**Tengo dolor de muela.** *tengo dolor de mwela*
This tooth hurts.	**Me duele este diente.** *meh dweleh esteh deeyenteh*
I've lost a filling/a tooth.	**Se me cayó un empaste [una calza]/ un diente.** *seh meh kayo oon empasteh [oona kalsa]/oon deeyenteh*
Can you repair this denture?	**¿Me puede arreglar esta dentadura?** *meh pwedeh arreglar esta dentadoora*
I don't want it extracted.	**No quiero que me la saque.** *no keeyero keh meh la sakeh*

Le voy a poner una inyección/ anestesia local.	I'm going to give you an injection/a local anesthetic.
Usted necesita un empaste/ una calza.	You need a filling/crown/cap.
Voy a tener que sacarla.	I'll have to take it out.
Sólo la puedo arreglar temporalmente.	I can only fix it temporarily.
No coma nada durante … horas./Evite comer durante las próximas … horas.	Don't eat anything for … hours.

Payment and Insurance Pago y seguro

How much do I owe you?	**¿Cuánto le debo?** *kwanto leh debo*
I have insurance.	**Tengo seguro. [Estoy afiliado(-a) al seguro.]** *tengo segooro. [estoy afeeleeyado(-a) al segooro]*
Can I have a receipt for my health insurance?	**¿Podría darme un recibo para mi seguro médico?** *podreeya darmeh oon reseebo para mee segooro medeeko*
Would you fill in this health insurance form, please?	**¿Podría llenar este formulario de seguro médico, por favor?** *podreeya l-yenar este formoolareeo deh segooro medeeko por fabor*
Can I have a medical certificate?	**¿Me puede dar un certificado médico?** *meh pwedeh dar oon serteefeekado medeeko*

Dictionary
English - Spanish

To enable correct usage, most terms in this dictionary are either followed by an expression or are cross-referenced to pages where the word appears in a full phrase (numbers in blue indicate main topics).

Nouns

Nouns in Spanish are classed as either masculine (m) or feminine (f). Normally, nouns that end in a vowel add **-s** to form the plural (pl); nouns ending in a consonant add **-es**. The articles they take (a, an, the, some) depend on their gender:

masculine	**el tren**	the train	feminine	**la casa**	the house
	un tren	a train		**una casa**	a house
	los trenes	the trains		**las casas**	the houses
	unos trenes	some trains		**unas casas**	some houses

Adjectives

Adjectives agree in gender and number with the noun they are describing. In this dictionary the feminine form is shown in brackets, e.g.

pequeño(-a) small feminine form: **pequeña**

If the masculine form ends in **-e** or with a consonant, the feminine keeps in general the same form:

el muro/la casa grande the big wall/house
el mar/la flor azul the blue sea/flower

Most adjectives form their plurals in the same way as nouns:

un coche inglés - dos coches ingleses an English car/two English cars

Verbs

Verbs are generally shown in the infinitive (to say, to eat, etc.) The three main categories of regular verbs in the present tense are:

	hablar (to speak)	**comer** (to eat)	**reír** (to laugh)
	ends in **-ar**	ends in **-er**	ends in **-ir**
yo	hablo	como	río
tú	hablas	comes	ríes
usted	habla	come	ríe
él/ella	habla	come	ríe
nosotros(-as)	hablamos	comemos	reímos
vosotros(-as)	habláis	coméis	reís
ustedes	hablan	comen	ríen
ellos(-as)	hablan	comen	ríen

Negatives are generally formed by putting **no** before the verb:

Es nuevo. It's new. **No es nuevo.** It's not new.

A-Z

A

a few unos(-as) pocos(-as) 15
a little un poquito 15
a lot mucho 15
a, an un(a)
a.m. a.m.
able, to be (also ➤ **can, could**) poder
about *(approximately)* cerca de, alrededor de 28
above *(place)* arriba
abroad en el extranjero
abscess absceso m 15
accept, to aceptar 136; **do you accept…?** ¿aceptan…?
access *(n)* entrada f 100
accessories accesorios mpl
accident accidente m 152; *(road)* 92
accidentally por accidente 28
accommodation alojamiento m 123
accompany, to acompañar
accountant contador(a) m/f
ace *(cards)* as m
across al otro lado
activities actividades f
actor/actress actor m, actriz f
adaptor adaptador m 148
address dirección f 84, 93
adjoining room habitación f [cuarto m] contiguo(-a) 22
admission charge precio m de la entrada 114
adult adulto m/f 81, 100
advance, in por adelantado
aerial *(car/tv)* antena f
after *(time)* después 13; *(place)* después de 95
aftershave loción f para después de la afeitada 142
after-sun lotion loción f para después del sol 142
afternoon, in the por la tarde 221
age: what age? ¿qué edad?
aged, to be tenía… años
ago hace… 13
agree: I agree estoy de acuerdo
air conditioning aire m acondicionado 22, 25

air freshener spray m de ambiente
air mattress colchoneta f, colchón inflable m 31
air pump bomba f de aire 87
airline aerolínea f
airmail correo m aéreo 155
airplane avión m
airport aeropuerto m
airsteward/hostess auxiliar m/f de vuelo
alarm clock reloj m despertador 149
alcoholic drink bebida f alcohólica
all todo(-a), todos(-as)
all-night pharmacy farmacia f de veinticuatro horas 140
allergic, to be ser alérgico(-a) 164
allergy alergia f
allowed: is it allowed? ¿está permitido?
almost casi
alone solo(-a) 120
already ya
also también
alter, to arreglar 137
always siempre 13
am: I am soy
ambassador embajador(a)
ambulance ambulancia f 92
American *(n/adj)* estadounidense m/f 150; norteamericano(-a); ~ **football** fútbol m americano
amount cantidad f 42
amusement arcade local m de maquinitas/juegos electrónicos 113
anesthetic anestesia f
anchor, to anclar
and y
angling pesca f con caña
animal animal m 106
anorak anorak m
another otro(-a) 21; ~ **time** a otra hora/en otra ocasión
antibiotic antibiótico m
antique antigüedad f 157; ~ **shop** almacén m de antigüedades 130
antiseptic antiséptico m 165; ~ **cream** crema f antiséptica 141
any algún(a); *(negative)* ningún(a) 15
anyone else alguien más 93

anything cheaper algo más barato 21
anything else? ¿algo más?
apartment departamento [apartamento] m 28
apologize: I apologize ¡perdón!
apples manzanas f
appointment cita f 147, 161; to make an ~ pedir una cita
approximately aproximadamente
April abril 218
archery tiro con arco m
architect arquitecto m/f 104
architecture arquitectura f
are there…? ¿hay…? 17
are you…? ¿es usted…?
area área f; ~ code código m 127
Argentina Argentina 119
Argentinian (n/adj) argentino(-a)
arm brazo m 166
armband (swimming) brazalete m
around (time) cerca de [alrededor de] 13; (place) alrededor
arrange: can you arrange it? ¿puede organizarlo(-a)?
arrest, to be under estar arrestado(-a)
arrive, to llegar 68, 70, 71, 76
art arte m; ~ gallery galería f de arte 99
artery arteria f
arthritis, to have tener artritis 163
articulated truck camión m articulado
artist artista m/f 104
as soon as possible cuanto antes
ashore, to go desembarcar
ashtray cenicero m 39
ask, to: please ask her to call me back dígale que me llame, por favor
asleep, to be estar dormido(-a)
aspirin aspirina f 141
asthmatic, to be ser asmático(-a) 163
at (place) en 12; (time) a la(s) 13
at least por lo menos 23
attack (crime) atentado m 152; (medical) ataque m
attendant asistente m/f
attractive atractivo(-a)
August agosto 218
aunt tía f 120
Australia Australia 119

Australian (n/adj) australiano(-a)
authenticity autenticidad f
automatic (car) carro m automático 86
automatic camera cámara f automática 151
automobile carro m 81, 86-9
autumn otoño m 219
avalanche avalancha f
away lejos 12
awful horrible

B baby bebé m/f 39, 113, 162; ~ bottle biberón m del bebé [tetero m del bebé]; ~ food comida f para bebés 142; ~ seat asiento m para bebé; ~sitter niñera f; ~ wipes pañuelos m húmedos para bebés
back espalda f 166
backache dolor m de espalda
backpacking de mochila [con morral]
bad malo(-a) 14
baggage reclaim recogida f de equipaje
bakery panadería f 130
balance of account balance m de cuenta
ball pelota f
ballet ballet m 111
band (musical group) banda f 111, 157; orquesta f 111
bandage venda f 141
bank banco m 130, 138; ~ account cuenta f bancaria; ~ card tarjeta f del banco 139; ~ loan préstamo m bancario
bar bar m [taberna f] 112
barbecue barbacoa f [asador m]
barber barbería [peluquería] f
barge (longboat) barcaza [lancha] f
basement sótano m
basin lavamanos m
basket canasta f 158
bath towel toalla f 27
bath: to take a darse un baño
bathroom baño m 22
battery pila f 137, 149, 151; (car) batería f 88
battle site campo de batalla m 99
be, to (also ➤ am, are) ser/estar 17
beach playa f 116
beard barba f

A-Z

beautiful hermoso(-a) 14, 101
because porque 15; ~ **of** por [debido a] 15
bed cama f 21; ~ **and breakfast** habitación f con desayuno incluido 24; **I'm going to** ~ me voy a la cama [me voy a dormir]
bedding ropa f de cama
bee abeja f
beer cerveza f 40, 50
before *(time)* antes (de) 13, 221
begin, to *(also* ➤ *start)* empezar
beginning principio [comienzo] m
beige beige m 143
belt cinturón m 144
beneath debajo de
berth litera f 74, 77
best mejor m/f
better mejor 14
between entre
bib babero m
bicycle bicicleta f 75, 83, 153; ~ **hire** alquiler de bicicletas m 83; ~ **parts** 82
bidet bidet m
big grande 14, 24, 134
bikini bikini m 144
bill recibo m 32; cuenta f 42; **put it on the** ~ inclúyalo en la cuenta
binoculars binoculares mpl
bird pájaro m 106
birthday cumpleaños mpl 219
bishop *(chess)* alfil m
bite *(insect)* mordedura f
bitten: I've been bitten by a dog me mordió un perro
bitter amargo(-a) 41
black negro(-a); ~ **and white film** *(camera)* rollo en blanco y negro m 151
blanket manta f 27
bleeding hemorragia f; **to be** ~ estar sangrando 162
bless you ¡salud!
blind *(window)* persiana f 25
blister ampolla f 162
blocked, to be tapado(-a) 25; **the road is** ~ la carretera está bloqueada

blood sangre f 164; ~ **group** grupo m sanguíneo; ~ **pressure** presión f arterial 164
blouse blusa f 144
blow-dry secado m
blue azul m 143
blusher *(rouge)* rubor m
boarding card tarjeta f de embarque
boat bote m 81; ~ **trip** viaje m en barco 81
body: parts of the body partes del cuerpo 166
boil furúnculo m 162
boiler caldera f 29
Bolivia Bolivia 119
Bolivian *(n/adj)* boliviano(-a)
bone hueso m 166
book libro m 150
book, to reservar 21, 74, 81
booked up, to be estar todo reservado; no quedar nada libre 115
booking reservación f 22; *(restaurant)* 36; ~ **office** oficina f de reservaciones
bookshop/store librería f 130
boots botas f 115, 145
border *(country)* frontera f
boring aburrido(-a) 101
born: I was born in nací en
borrow: may I borrow your…? ¿me presta su…?
botanical garden jardín m botánico 99
bottle botella f 159; ~ **bank** banco m de botellas; ~ **opener** destapador m 148
bow *(ship)* proa f
bowel intestino m
box of chocolates caja f de chocolates
box office boletería [taquilla] f
boxing boxeo m
boy niño m 157
boyfriend novio m 120
bra brassiere m 144
bracelet pulsera f 149
brass latón m
Brazil Brasil 119
Brazilian *(n/adj)* brasileño(-a)
bread pan m 38
break, to romper 28
break-in asalto m 153
breakage ruptura f

breakdown *(mechanical)* averías f 88; **to have a ~** estar descompuesto/varado 88

breakfast desayuno m 26, 27

breast seno m 166

breathe, to respirar 92, 164

bridge puente m 107; *(cards)* bridge m

briefcase maletín [portafolio] m

briefs *(man's)* calzoncillos mpl, *(woman's)* pantaletas fpl 144

brilliant brillante m/f 101

bring, to traer

Britain la Gran Bretaña 119

British *(n/adj)* británico(-a)

brochure folleto m

broken roto(-a) 137; **to be ~** estar roto(-a) 25, 164

bronchitis bronquitis f

bronze bronce m

brooch prendedor m 149

brother hermano m 120

brown café m 143

browse, to mirar 133

bruise moretón m 162

brush cepillo m

bucket cubeta m [balde m] 157

build, to construir 104

building edificio m

built construido(-a) 104

bureau de change oficina f [casa f] de cambio 70, 138

burger hamburguesa f 40; **~ stand** puesto de hamburguesas m

burglary *(also ➤ theft)* robo m (de casa)

burn quemadura f; **it's burned** *(food)* está quemado(-a)

burst pipe tubo m roto

burst tire llanta f pinchada

bus autobús m 70, 78, 79; **~ route** ruta f de buses f 96; **~ station** estación f de autobuses 78; **~ stop** parada f del autobús 96; **~ terminal** para f [para dero m] 78

business class clase f ejecutiva 68

business trip viaje m de negocios 123

business, on en viaje de negocios 66

businessman/woman negociante m/f

busy, to be estar ocupado(-a) 125

but pero

butane gas gas m butano 31

butcher shop carnicería f 130

butter mantequilla f 38, 160

button botón m

buy, to comprar 67, 80

by *(time)* antes de …; **~ car** en carro 17, 94; **~ credit card** con tarjeta de crédito 17

bye! ¡adiós!

bypass carretera f de circunvalación; by-pass m

C **cabaret** cabaret m
cabin cabina f

cable car funicular m

café café m [cafetería f] 35, 40

cagoule anorak m impermeable 145

cake pastel m 40; **~ shop** pastelería f

calendar calendario m

call, to *(phone)* llamar (por teléfono) 92, 127, 128; **~ for s.o.** ir a recoger a alguien 125; **I'll call back** volveré a llamar; **call collect,** to llamar por cobro revertido 127; **call the police!** ¡llame a la policía! 92

camcorder videocámara f

camera cámara f 151, 153; **~ case** funda f [estuche m]de la cámara 151; **~ shop/store** almacén m de fotografía m 130

campbed cama plegable f 31

camper casa f móvil 30, 81; **~ site** camping m para casas móviles

camping campamento [camping] m 30; **~ equipment** equipo m de campamento 31

campsite zona de campamento 30

can I? ¿podría? 18

can I have? ¿puede traerme? 18

can you help me? ¿puede ayudarme? 18

can you recommend? ¿puede recomendarme? 97, 112

can lata f; **~ opener** abrelatas m 148

can opener abrelatas m

Canada Canadá 119

Canadian *(person/adj)* canadiense m/f

canal canal m

cancel, to

cancelar 68

cancer *(disease)* cáncer m

candles velas f 148

candy dulces mpl [caramelos] m 150

canoe canoa f

canoeing piragüismo m canotaje m

cap gorra f; *(dental)* calza f

capital city capital f

captain *(boat)* capitán m

car carro m 81, 86-9

car alarm alarma f del carro

car ferry transbordador m de carros [ferry] 81

car parts repuestos m 90-1

car rental alquiler de carros m 70, 86

car repairs reparaciones f 89

car wash servicio m de lavado de carros

car, by en carro 95

carafe jarra f 37

careful: be careful! ¡ten cuidado!

carpet *(rug)* alfombra f; *(fitted)* alfombra f fija

carrier bag bolsa f

carton caja f [cartón m]

cash efectivo m 136; **~ card** tarjeta f del cajero automático 139; **~ desk** caja f; **~ machine** *(atm, cash dispenser)* cajero m automático 139

cash, to cambiar un cheque 138

cassette cassette f 157

castle castillo m 99

casualty dept. sección f de accidentes

cat gato m

catch, to *(bus)* coger [tomar]

cathedral catedral f 99

cause, to ocasionar

cave cueva f 107

CD CD m ; **~-player** grabadora f con CD

cemetery cementerio m 99

central heating calefacción f

center of town centro m 21

ceramics cerámica f

certificate certificado m 168

certification documento m que certifique algo 149

chair silla f

change *(coins)* cambio [sencillo, suelto] m 87, 136; **keep the ~** guardar el cambio 84

change, to *(money)* cambiar 138; *(reservation)* 68; *(bus, train)* 79; *(clothes)* cambiarse; **~ lanes** cambiar de carril; **where can I change the baby?** ¿dónde puedo cambiar al bebé?

changing facilities lugar m para cambiar a los bebés 113

changing rooms vestuario m

channel *(sea)* canal m

chapel capilla f

charge precio m [tarifa *(f)*] 30, 115

charter flight vuelo m chárter

cheap barato(-a) 14, 134

cheaper más barato(-a) 21, 24, 109, 134

check, to revisar

checkbook chequera f

check guarantee card tarjeta f de garantía de cheques

check in, to presentarse [registrarse] 68

check-in desk mostrador m [ventanilla *(f)*] 69

check out, to *(hotel)* registrer m de salida/salida

checked *(patterned)* a cuadros

checkers damas chinas fpl

checkout caja f 158

cheers! ¡salud!

cheese queso m 160

chemical toilet baño portátil m

chemist farmacia [droguería] f 130, 140

chess ajedrez m 121; **~ set** juego m de ajedrez 157

chest pecho m 166

chickenpox varicela f

child niño(-a)

child's seat asiento m para niños 39

childminder niñera f

children niños m 24, 39, 66, 74, 81, 100, 113,

children's meals comida f para niños

Chile Chile

Chilean *(person/adj)* chileno(-a)

chips *(UK)* papas fpl a la francesa 160

A-Z

chips *(US)* papas fpl fritas 160

chocolate chocolate m 40; **~ bar** chocolatina f 150; **box of chocolates** caja f de chocolates

chocolate ice cream helado m de chocolate 110

christian *(adj)* cristiano(-a)

Christmas navidad f 219

church iglesia f 96, 99

cigarette cigarrillo m; **packet of ~** cajetilla f de cigarrillos 150; **~ machine** máquina f expendedora de cigarrillos

cigars cigarros [puros] m 150

cinema cine m 96, 110

circle *(balcony)* balcón m

city wall muro m de la ciudad

civil-servant miembro m/f del servicio civil

class: first class primera clase 68

clean limpio(-a) 14, 39, 41

clean, to lavar 137

cleaned: I'd like my shoes cleaned quiero que me limpie los zapatos

cleaner aseador(a) m/f 28

cleansing lotion loción f limpiadora

cliff acantilado [precipicio] m 107

clinic clínica f 131

cloakroom guardarropa m 109

clock reloj m 149

close *(near)* cerca 95

close, to cerrar 100, 132, 140

clothes ropa f 144

clothes pegs ganchos mpl para colgar la ropa 148

clothes shop *(clothing store)* almacén m de ropa 130

cloudy: it's cloudy está nublado 122

clubs *(golf)* palos mpl de golf 115

coach *(train)* coche [vagón] m 75

coast costa f

coat abrigo m 144

coathanger percha f

cockroach cucaracha f

code *(area/dialling)* código m

coffee café m 40

coffee filters papel m di filtro

coil *(contraceptive)* espiral f intrauterina

coin moneda f

cold frío(-a) 14, 41, 122; *(flu)* resfriado m 141

collapse: he's collapsed él sufrió un colapso

collect, to reclamar 151

college universidad f 121

Colombia Colombia 119

Colombian *(person/adj)* colombiano(-a)

color color m 134, 143

color film rollo m a color 151

comb peine m [peinilla f] 142

come back , to *(return)* volver; regresar 36

commission comisión f 138

communion comunión f

compact disc/disk compact disc m 157

company *(business)* compañía f

compartment *(train)* coche [vagón] m 75

compass brújula f

complaint, to make a hacer un reclamo [presentar una queja]

complaints *(hotel)* reclamos m; quejas f 41

computer computadora f

concert concierto m 111

concert hall sala f de conciertos 99, 111

concession concesión f 100

concussion, to have a tener una conmoción cerebral

conditioner acondicionador m 142

condoms condones m 141

conference conferencia f

confirm, to confirmar 22, 68

confirmation confirmación f

congratulations! ¡felicitaciones!

connection *(transport)* conexión m

conscious, to be estar consciente

constipated, to be tener estreñimiento

constipation estreñimiento m

Consulate consulado m 152

consult, to consultar 165

consultant *(medical)* especialista m/f

contact, to localizar 28

contact lens lentes de contacto m 167; **~ fluid** líquido m para lentes

contagious, to be ser contagioso(-a) 165

contain, to contener 69, 155

contemporary dance danza contemporánea f 111

A-Z

contraceptive anticonceptivo *m*
convenient conveniente
convertible *(car)* convertible
cook, to cocinar
cook cocinero(-a)
cookbook libro *m* de recetas de cocina
cookies galletas *fpl*; bizcochos *m* 160
cooking *(cuisine)* cocina *f*
copper cobre *m* 149
copy copiar
corduroy pana *f*
corkscrew descorchador *m* 148
corner esquina *f* 95
correct (➤ *also right*) bien [correcto(-a)]
cosmetics cosméticos *m*
Costa Rica Costa Rica 119
Costa Rican *(person/adj)* costarricense *m/f*
cot cuna para bebé *f* 22
cottage cabaña *f* 28
cotton algodón *m* 145
cotton wool paquete de algodón *m* 141
cough, to toser 164
cough tos *f* 141; **~ syrup** jarabe *m* para la tos
could I have...? ¿podría traerme...? 18
counter mostrador *m*
country *(nation)* país *m*
countryside campo *m*
course *(meal)* plato *m*
cousin primo(-a)
cover *(lid)* tapa *f*
cover charge consumo mínimo *m* [cover *m*] 112
craft shop tienda *f* de artesanías
cramps calambres *mpl* 163
crash: I've had a crash me estrellé
creche guardería *f* infantil
credit card tarjeta *f* de crédito 42, 136
credit card number número *m* de tarjeta de crédito 109
credit status capacidad *f* de crédito
credit, in estar en números negros
crockery loza [vajilla] *f* 29, 148
cross *(crucifix)* cruz *f*
cross, to *(road)* cruzar 95
crossing *(boat)* travesía *f*; cruce *f*

crossroad cruce *m* de carreteras 95
crowded: it's crowded hay mucha gente
crown *(dental)* corona *f* 168
cruise crucero *m*
crutches muletas *fpl*
Cuba Cuba 119
Cuban *(person/adj)* cubano(-a)
cuisine comida *f*
cup taza *f* 39
cupboard armario *m*
cups tazas *f* [pocillos *m*] 148
curlers tubos [rulos] *m*
currency moneda *f* 67, 138
currency-exchange office oficina *f* de cambio [casa *f* de cambio] 73
cushion almohadón [cojín] *m*
customs aduana *f* 67
customs declaration declaración *f* de aduana 155
cut cortadura *f* 162
cutlery cubiertos *m* 148
cycle helmet casco *m* para bicicleta
cycle path carril *m* de bicicleta
cycle route ruta *f* para tránsito de bicicletas 106
cycling ciclismo *m* 114
cyclist ciclista *m/f*
cystitis cistitis *f* 165

D **daily** diariamente
damaged, to be no funcionar 28; se dañó 71
damp *(n)* humedad *f*; *(adj)* húmedo(-a)
dance *(performance)* baile [danza] *f* 111
dancing, to go ir a bailar 124
dangerous peligroso(-a)
dark oscuro(-a) 14, 24, 134, 143
darts, to play jugar a los dardos
daughter hija *f* 120, 162
day día *m* 97
day trip viaje *m* de un día
dead muerto(-a); *(battery)* descargado(-a) 88
deaf, to be ser sordo(-a) 163
dear *(greeting)* querido(-a)
December diciembre 218
decide: we haven't decided yet no hemos decidido todavía

deck *(ship)* cubierta f
deck chair silla f de lona 116
declare, to declarar 67
deep profundo(-a)
deep-freeze congelador m
defrost, to descongelar
degrees *(temperature)* grados m
delay retraso m 70
delicate delicado(-a)
delicatessen delicatessen m [tienda f de especialidades] 130
delicious delicioso(-a) 14
deliver, to entregar
denim tela f vaquera 145
dental floss hilo m dental
dentist dentista m/f 131, 168
dentures dentadura f 168
deodorant desodorante m 142
depart, to *(train, bus)* salir
department *(in store)* departamento m [sección f]
department store almacén m 130
departure *(train)* salida f 76
departure lounge sala de embarque f
depend: it depends on depende de
deposit depósito m 24, 83, 115
describe, to describir 152
destination destino m
details detalles mpl
detergent detergente m
develop, to *(photos)* revelar 151
diabetes diabetes f
diabetic, to be ser diabético(-a) 39, 163
diagnosis diagnóstico m 164
dialling code código m 127
diamonds *(cards)* diamantes m
diapers pañales mpl 142
diarrhea diarrea f 141
dice dado m
dictionary diccionario m 150
diesel diesel 87
difficult difícil 14
dine, to cenar
dinghy bote m [barca] f
dining car coche comedor m 75, 77
dining room comedor m 26
dinner, to have cenar
dinner jacket esmoquin m
direct directo(-a) 75

direct-dial telephone teléfono dial m
direction dirección f; **in the ~ of** en dirección a 95
director *(film)* director m; *(of company)* gerente m
directory *(telephone)* directorio m
Directory Enquiries Información f 127
dirty sucio(-a) 14, 28
disabled personas fpl incapacitadas 22, 100
disco discoteca f 112
discount descuento m; **can you offer me a ~** ¿puede ofrecerme un descuento?
dish *(meal)* plato m [especialidad f]; **~ cloth** paño [limpión] m 148
dishwashing detergent detergente para los platos m 148
dislocated, to be estar dislocado(-a) 164
display cabinet escaparate m 149
display case escaparate m 134
disposable camera cámara f desechable 151
distilled water agua f destilada
district distrito m
disturb: don't disturb no interrumpir
dive, to bucear 116
diversion desvío m
divorced, to be ser divorciado(-a) 120
dizzy, to feel tener mareo
doctor doctor(a) 131, 161, 164
dog perro m
do-it-yourself almacén m de bricolaje
doll muñeca f 157
dollar dólar m 67, 138
door puerta f
dosage dosis f 140
double doble 81
double bed cama f matrimonial [doble] 21
double room habitación f doble [cuarto m doble] 21
down/downstairs abajo 12
downtown area centro m (de la ciudad) 99
dozen docena f 159, 217
draft *(wind)* corriente f de aire

A-Z

drain desaguadero [desagüe] m
drama drama m
draughts *(game)* damas chinas fpl
dress vestido m 144
drink copa f 124, 125, 126; bebida f 49
drinking water agua potable f 30
drive, to conducir [manejar] 93
driver conductor [chofer] m
driver's license licencia de conducir f
drop off, to *(someone)* dejar 83, 113
drowning: someone is drowning alguien se está ahogando
drugstore farmacia [droguería] f 130
drunk borracho(-a)
dry cleaner's tintorería [lavandería] f 131
dry cut corte m en seco
dry-clean, to lavar en seco
dual freeway autopista f
dubbed, to be tener subtítulos 110
due, to be *(payment)* vencer
dummy chupón [chupo] m
during durante
dusty que tiene polvo
duty: to pay duty pagar impuestos 67
duty-free goods mercancías fpl libres de impuestos
duty-free shop tienda f libres de impuestos 67
duvet edredón m

E

each: how much each? ¿cuánto vale cada uno?
ear oído m 166
earache dolor de oído m 163
earlier más temprano 147
early temprano 13
earrings aretes m 149
east oriente 95
Easter semana santa f 219
easy fácil 14
eat, to comer 21, 41, 167; **places ~** sitios para ir a comer; **have you eaten?** ¿Ha comido?; **we've already eaten** ya hemos comido

economical económico(-a)
economy class clase económica [de turista] 68
Ecuador Ecuador 119
Ecuadorian *(person/adj)* ecuatoriano(-a)
eight ocho 216
either... or ... o ...
elastic *(adj)* elástico(-a)
electrician electricista m/f
electric blanket cobija [manta] f eléctrica
electric fire fuego m eléctrico
electric shaver afeitadora f eléctrica
electrical store almacén m de instalaciones eléctricas
electricity electricidad f; **~ meter** medidor m eléctrico [contador eléctrico] 28
electronic flash flash m 151
eleven once 216
elevator ascensor m 26, 132
else, something algo más
embark, to *(boat)* embarcar
embassy embajada f
emergency emergencia f 127; **~ exit** salida de emergencia f; **it's an ~** es una emergencia
empty desocupado(-a) 14
end, to terminar 108
end: at the end al final
engaged, to be estar comprometido(-a) 120
engine motor m
engineer ingeniero m/f
England Inglaterra 119
English *(language)* inglés m 11, 67, 110, 150, 152, 161
English-speaking que hable inglés 98
enjoy, to gustar [disfrutar]
enlarge, to *(photos)* ampliar 151
enough suficiente 15, 42, 136
enquiry desk puesto m de información
ensuite bathroom con baño adjunto
entertainment guide guía de diversiones f
entrance fee entrada f 100
entry visa visa f de entrada al país
envelope sobre m 150
epileptic, to be ser epiléptico(-a) 140

equipment *(sports)*
  equipo deportivo m 115
error error m
escalator escalera eléctrica f 132
essential indispensable 89
estate agent agencia f de bienes raíces
estate car camioneta f
EU Unión Europea f
Eurocheque eurocheque m
evening dress traje m de noche 112
evening, in the por la noche 221
events eventos f 108
every day todos los días
every week todas las semanas 13
examination *(medical)* exámen m médico
example, for por ejemplo
except excepto
excess baggage
  exceso de equipaje m 69
exchange, to cambiar 138
exchange rate tasa de cambio f 138
excursion excursión f 97
excuse me *(apology)* disculpe [perdón]
  10; *(attention)* ¡disculpe! 10, 94
exhausted, to be
  estar muy cansado(-a) 106
exhibition exposición f
exit salida f 70; **at the ~** a la salida
expected, to be se exige
expensive caro(-a) 14, 134
expiration date fecha de vencimiento f
  109
expire, to: when does it expire? ¿cuándo
  vence?
expiry date fecha de vencimiento f 109
extension extensión f 128
extension lead extensión f
extra *(additional)* adicional 27
extracted, to be *(tooth)* sacar 168
extremely demasiado
  [extremadamente] 17
eye ojo m 166
eyeliner delineador m de ojos
eyeshadow sombra f de ojos

F **fabric** *(material)* tela f
  face cara f 166
facilities servicios m 22, 30
factor *(suntan)* factor m 142

faint, to feel
  tener mareo 163
fairground parque m de
  atracciones 113
fall *(season)* otoño m 219
fall: he's had a fall él se
  cayó
family familia f 66, 74, 120, 167
famous famoso(-a)
fan *(air)* ventilador m 25
fan: I'm a fan of soy fan [seguidora] de
far lejos; **how ~ is it?** ¿a qué distancia
  está…? 73; **is it ~?** ¿está lejos?
fare tarifa f
farsighted hipermétrope 167
farm finca f 107
fashionable, to be estar de moda
fast rápido(-a) 93
fast, to be *(clock)* estar adelantado 221
fast food comida rápida f 40;
  ~ restaurant restaurante m de comidas
  rápidas 35
fat *(food)* grasa f
father padre m 120
fault: it's my fault es mi culpa
faulty defectuoso(-a)
favorite favorito(-a)
fax *(machine)* fax m 155; **~ bureau/facili-**
  ties servicio m de fax
February febrero 218
feed, to alimentar 39
feeding bottle mamila f biberón m
feel ill, to estar enfermo(-a) 163
feel sick, to estar mareado(-a)
female mujer f 152
ferry transbordador m 81
festival festival m
feverish, to feel tener fiebre
few poco(-a) 15
fiancé(e) prometido(-a) m/f [novio(-a)]
field campo m 107
fifth quinto(-a) 217
fight *(brawl)* pelea f
fill in, to llenar
filling *(dental)* empaste m [calza f] 168;
  (in sandwich) relleno m
filling station gasolinera f
  [estación de servicio] 87
film *(camera)* rollo m 151; *(movie)* película
  f 108, 110

filter filter m 151
fine (well) bien 118; (penalty) multa f 93
finger dedo m 166
fire: There's a fire! ¡hay un incendio!
fire alarm alarma f de incendios
fire brigade bomberos m 92
fire escape escalera f de incendios
fire extinguisher extinguidor m de incendios
fireplace chimenea f
firewood leña f
first primero(-a) 68, 75, 81, 217
first class primera clase 68, 74
first floor planta baja f
first-aid kit botiquín m de primeros
fishing rod caña f de pescar
fishing, to go pescar
fishmonger's pescadería f 130
fit, to (clothes) quedar bien 146
fitting room probador [vestier] m 146
five cinco 216
fix: can you fix it? ¿puede repararlo/la?
flash (photo) flash m 151
flashlight linterna f (eléctrica)
flea pulga f
flea market mercado m de las pulgas
flight vuelo m 70; ~ **number** número m de vuelo 68; pasaje 68
flip-flops chancletas f 145
flood inundación f
floor (level) piso m 132
floor mop trapeador m
floor show espectáculo m
florist's floristería f 130
flower flor f 106
flu gripe f 165
fluent: to speak fluent Spanish hablar bien el español
fly (insect) mosca
fly, to volar
foggy: it's foggy hay niebla 122
folding chair/table silla [mesa] f plegable
follow, to seguir 95
follow, to (pursue) perseguir 152
food alimento m 39; comida f 41

food poisoning intoxicación f 165
foot pie m 166
football/soccer fútbol m 114
footpath sendero m 107
for a day para un día 86
for a week para una semana 86
for...hours por...horas 116
forecast predicción f 122
foreign extranjero(-a); ~ **currency** moneda extranjera f 138
forest selva f 107
forget, to olvidar 42
fork tenedor m 39, 41, 148; (in the road) empalme m [bifurcación f]
form formulario m 23, 153, 168
formal dress traje f de etiqueta 111
fortnight dos semanas fpl
fortunately afortunadamente 19
forty cuarenta 216
forwarding address dirección f donde remitir la correspondencia
foundation (make-up) base f
fountain fuente f 99
four cuatro 216
four-door car carro m de cuatro puertas 86
four-wheel drive tracción f a cuatro ruedas
fourth cuarto(-a) 217
foyer (hotel/theatre) vestíbulo m
frame (glasses) montura f
free (available) disponible [libre] 36, 77, 124; (of charge) libre de impuestos
freezer congelador m 29
French (language) francés m
frequently frecuentemente
fresh fresco(-a) 41
Friday viernes m 218
fridge nevera f 29
friend amigo(-a) 162
friendly amistoso(-a)
fries papas fpl a la francesa 38, 40
from de 12; (time) desde [de] 13
front door puerta f 26; ~ **key** llave f de la puerta principal
frozen congelado(-a) 134
fruit juice jugo de fruta m 40
frying pan sartén f 29
fuel (petrol) gasolina f 86

full lleno(-a) 14
full board (*A.P.*) pensión f completa 24
fun, to have divertirse
funny (*amusing/odd*) raro(-a)
furniture muebles mpl
fuse fusible m 28
fuse box caja f de fusibles 28

G gallon galón m
gamble, to jugar (juegos de azar)
game (*toy*) juego m 157
garage garaje/estacionamiento cubierto [parqueadero cubierto] m;
~ repairs taller m de mecánica
garbage can bote de la basura m [caneca f] 30
garbage can liner bolsa f de la basura
garden jardín m
gardening jardinería f
gas: I smell gas! ¡huele a gas!
gas bottle cilindro m de gas [la bombona f] 28
gas permeable lenses lentes m de gas permeable
gas station gasolinera f 87
gasoline gasolina f 87
gastritis gastritis f 165
gate (*airport*) puerta f 70
gay club club de gays m 112
general delivery lista f de correo 154
genuine original [auténtico(-a)] 134; genuino(-a)
get by: may I get by? ¿puedo pasar?
get off, to (*transport*) bajar(se) 79
get out, to (*of vehicle*) bajar(se)
get to, to llegar a 77; **how do I get to…?** ¿cómo se llega a…? 73, 94
gift regalo m 67, 156; **~ shop** almacén f de regalos 130
girl niña f 157
girlfriend novia f 120
give, to dar
glass vaso m 39, 148;
a ~ of wine una copa de vino f 39
glasses (*optical*) gafas fpl [anteojos m] 167
gliding planeo m
glossy finish (*photos*) acabado en papel brillante

glove guante m
go, to ir; **~ back** (*turn around*) regresar; **~ for a walk** dar un paseo 124;
~ out (*in evening*) salir;
~ shopping ir de compras 124; **go away!** ¡váyase!; **where does this bus go?** ¿adónde va este bus?
goggles gafas fpl de natación [gafas para deportes] f
gold oro m 149
gold plate chapado(-a) en oro 149
golf golf m 114
golf course campo de golf m 115
good bueno(-a) 14, 35; **~ afternoon** buenas tardes 10; **~ evening** buenas noches 10; **~ morning** buenos días 10; **~ night** buenas noches [hasta mañana] 10
good-bye adiós 10
got: have you got any…? ¿tiene…?
grade (*fuel*) grado m.
gram gramo m 159
grandparents abuelos mpl
grass pasto m
gratuity propina f
gray gris 143
greasy (*hair*) grasoso(-a)
green verde 143
greengrocer's verdulería [tienda] f 130
grey gris 143
grocer's/grocery store abarrotes mpl [tienda f] 129
ground floor planta f baja
group grupo m 66, 100
guarantee garantía f 135; **is it guaranteed?** ¿tiene garantía?
Guatemalan (*person/adj*) guatemalteco(-a)
guide (*tour*) guía m/f 98
guidebook guía f (turística) 150
guided tour tour m con guía 100
guitar guitarra f
gum (*mouth*) encía f
gynecologist ginecólogo(-a) 167

H hair cabello [pelo] m 147; **~ brush** cepillo m para el pelo; **~ dryer** secador m; **~ gel** gel m para el pelo; **~ mousse** espuma f

moldeadora para el cabello 142; ~ **spray** laca f 142
haircut corte m de pelo 147
hairdresser peluquero(-a) m / f 147; **hairdresser's** salón m de belleza 131
hairstylist estilista m / f 147
half, a una mitad 221
half board *(M.A.P.)* media pensión f 24
half fare medio pasaje m
half past … y media 220
hammer martillo m 31
hand mano f 166; ~ **cream** crema f de manos; ~ **luggage** equipaje m de mano 69; ~ **towel** toalla f para las manos; ~ **washable** que se puede lavar a mano 145
handbag bolso m 144, 153
handicapped, to be ser incapacitado(-a) [minusválido(-a)] 163
handicrafts artesanías f
handkerchief pañuelo m
handle manija f
hang-gliding vuelo m ala delta
hanger percha f 27
hangover cruda f [resaca f, guayabo m] 141
happen: what happened? ¿qué pasó?
happy: I'm not happy with the service no estoy satisfecho con el servicio
harbour/harbor puerto m
hard shoulder *(road)* arcén m
hardware store ferretería m
hat sombrero m 144
hatchback puerta trasera f
have, to tener
have to, to *(must)* tener que 79
head cabeza f 166
head waiter jefe m / f de meseros
headache dolor m de cabeza 163
health food shop/store tienda f de alimentos naturales 131
health insurance seguro m médico 168
hear, to oír
hearing aid audífono m
heart corazón m 166; ~ **attack** ataque m cardiaco; **I have a heart condition** sufro del corazón 163

hearts *(cards)* corazones m
heater calentador m
heating calefacción f 25
heavy pesado(-a) 14, 134
height (altitude) altura f, *(person)* estatura f, 152
helicopter helicóptero m
hello hola 10, 118
help ayuda f 94
help, to ayudar 18; **can you help me?** ¿puede ayudarme? 92
helper asistente m / f
hemorrhoids hemorroides f
her *(adj)* su(s) 16; *(pronoun)* la
here aquí 12, 17
hers suya(s); de ella 16
hi! ¡qué tal! 10
high alto(-a); ~ **tide** marea f alta
highlight, to hacer rayitos 147
highway autopista f 94
hike *(walk)* caminata 106
hiking excursionismo m
hill colina f 107
him *(pronoun)* lo
hire, to alquilar 29, 86, 115, 116
his *(pronoun)* suyo(s), de él 16; *(adj)* su(s) 16
history historia f
hitchhike, to hacer autostop
hitchhiking autostop m 83
HIV-positive, to be tener el virus del SIDA
hobby hobby m [pasatiempo m favorito] 121
hockey *(field)* hockey m
hold, to *(contain)* contener
hold on, to *(wait)* esperar un momento 128
hole *(in clothes)* agujero m
holiday, on de vacaciones 66, 123
holiday resort sitio m de veraneo
home: to go home irse a casa
homosexual *(adj)* homosexual
honeymoon, to be on estar de luna de miel
hopefully! ¡ojalá! 19
horse caballo m; ~-**racing** carreras fpl de caballos 114
horseback trip viaje m a caballo

hospital hospital m 131, 164, 167
hot muy caliente [hirviendo] 14
hot dog hot dog m
  [perro m caliente] 110
hot water agua f caliente 25; **~ bottle**
  botella f de agua caliente
hotel hotel m 21; **~ booking** reservación
  de hotel 21
hour hora f 97; **in an ~** dentro de una
  hora 84
house casa f
housewife ama f de casa 121
hovercraft hidrodeslizador m 81
how? ¿cómo? 17; **~ are you?** cómo está?
  118
how far? ¿a qué distancia? 94, 106
how long? ¿cuánto tiempo? 23, 75, 76,
  78, 88, 94 ,98, 135
how many? ¿cuántos(-as)? 15
how much is it? ¿cuánto es? ¿cuánto
  cuesta? 84, 109
how often? ¿cuántas veces al día? 140
how old? ¿cuántos años?
  [qué edad] 120
however sin embargo
hundred cien 216
hungry, to be tener hambre
hurry, to be in a estar de prisa
  [tener prisa]
hurt, to be estar herido(-a); estar
  lastimado(-a) 162; **it hurts** duele 162
husband esposo m 120, 162

I
I'd like… quisiera… 18, 36, 40
  ice hielo m 38
ice cream helado m 40, 160; **~ café**
  heladería f 35; **~ cone** cono m de helado
ice pack bolsa f de hielo
ice rink pista f de hielo
identification documento m de identifi-
  cación 136
ill, to be estar enfermo(-a)
illegal, to be ser ilegal
illness enfermedad f
imitation imitación 134
immediately inmediatamente 13
impressive impresionante
in *(place)* en 12; *(time)* dentro de 13

in-law:
  mother/father-in-law
  suegra f/suegro m
included: is… included?
  ¿está incluido(-a)…? 86,
  98
indicate, to poner las direccionales
indigestion indigestión f
indoor pool piscina f cubierta 116
inexpensive barato(-a) 35
infected, to be estar infectado(-a) 165
infection infección f 167
inflammation inflamación f 165
informal dress ropa informal f
information información f 97; **~ desk**
  oficina [ventanilla] f de información 73;
  ~ office oficina f de información 96
injection inyección f 168
injured, to be estar herido(-a) 92, 162
innocent inocente m/f
insect insecto m 25; **~ bite** mordedura f de
  insecto 141, 162; **~ repellent/spray** repe-
  lente contra insectos/atomizador m 141
inside a dentro 12
insist, to insistir
insomnia insomnio m
instead of en vez de
instructions instrucciones fpl 135
instructor instructor(a)
insulin insulina f
insurance seguro m 86, 89, 93, 168;
  ~ certificate certificado m del seguro 93;
  ~ claim demanda f de seguro 153; **~
  company** compañía f de seguros 93
interest interés m
interest rate tasa de interés f
interesting interesante 101
international internacional
**International Student
  Card** credencial m [tarjeta f] internacional de estudiante 29
interpreter intérprete m/f 93, 153
intersection intersección f
interval intervalo m [periodo]
into dentro
introduce oneself, to presentarse
invitation invitación m 124
invite, to invitar

A-Z

involved, to be estar involucrado(-a) 93
Ireland Irlanda 119
Irish *(person/adj)* irlandés(-esa)
iron *(electrical)* plancha f
iron, to *(clothes)* planchar
is there...? ¿hay...? 17
island isla f
it is esto es/está 17
Italian *(adj)* italiano(-a)
itemized bill factura f [recibo detallado (m)] 32

J **jack/knave** *(cards)* valet m, sota f
jacket chaqueta f 144
jammed, to be estar atascado(-a) 25
January enero 218
jar frasco m
jaw mandíbula f 166
jeans jeans m 144
jellyfish medusa f
jet lag: I have estoy sintiendo el desfase de horarios
jet-ski jet-ski m [moto f acuática] 116
jeweler's/jewelry store joyería f 130, 149
job: what's your job? ¿a qué se dedica?
jogging, to go trotar
joint *(body part)* articulación f 166; *(meat)* trozo m
joint passport pasaporte m conjunto 66
joke chiste m
joker *(cards)* joker m
journalist periodista m/f
journey viaje m 76, 78
jug jarra f
July julio 218
jump leads cables mpl de emergencia m
jumper suéter [saco] m
junction *(intersection)* cruce m [entronque m]
June junio 218

K **kaolin** caolín m
keep: keep the change guarde el cambio

kettle tetera f 29
key llave f 26, 27, 28, 71, 88; **~ ring** llavero m 156
kidney riñón m 166
kilo(gram) kilo m 159
kilometer kilómetro m
kind *(pleasant)* amable
kind: what kind of...? ¿qué clase de...?
king *(cards, chess)* rey m
kiosk quiosco m
kiss, to dar un beso, besar 126
kitchen paper papel m de cocina
knapsack mochila f 31, 145
knee rodilla f 166
knickers pantaletas f [pantalones m]
knife cuchillo m 39, 41, 148
knight *(chess)* caballo m
knocked down, to be ser derribado(-a)
know: I don't know no lo sé

L **label** etiqueta f
lace encaje m 145
ladder escalera f
ladies *(toilet)* baño m para damas
lake lago m 107
lamp lámpara f 29
land, to aterrizar
landlord/landlady dueño(-a) de la casa
lane carril m
language course curso m de idiomas
large *(adj)* grande 40, 110
last último(-a) 68, 75, 80, 81
last, to *(time)* durar
late *(adv.)* tarde; **late** *(delayed)* retrasado(-a) 221
later más tarde 125, 147
laugh, to reír 126
laundry lavandería f 131
laundry service servicio m de lavandería 22
lavatory baños mpl públicos
lawn césped m
lawyer abogado(-a) 152
laxative laxante m
lead-free *(petrol/gas)* sin plomo 87
leaflet folleto m
leak, to *(car)* botar; *(roof/pipe)* gotear
learn, to *(language, sport)* aprender
learner *(driver)* aprendiz(-a) m/f

least expensive el/la menos caro(-a)

leather cuero m 145

leave, to *(place)* salir 68, 70, 81, 98, 126; *(abandon)* dejar 73, 86; **leave me alone!** ¡déjeme tranquilo(-a)! 126; **are there any left?** ¿queda(n) algún(-os/-as)?

leave from, to *(transport)* salir de 78

left, on the a la izquierda 76, 95

left hand side lado m izquierdo

left-handed zurdo(-a)

left-luggage office (baggage check) depósito m de equipaje 71, 73

leg pierna f 166

legal, to be ser legal

leggings leggings f 144

lemon limón m 38

lemonade limonada f

lend: could you lend me...? ¿puede prestarme...?

length longitud f

lens objetivo m 151; lentes m 167

lesbian club club m de lesbianas

less menos 15

let: please let me know avíseme

letter carta f 154; **by ~** por escrito 22

library biblioteca f 131

lie down, to acostarse

lifebelt cinturón m salvavidas

lifeboat bote m salvavidas

lifeguard salvavidas m/f 116

lifejacket chaqueta f salvavidas

lift *(hitchhiking)* aventón m

light *(of color)* claro(-a) 14, 134, 143; *(weight)* liviano(-a) 14, 134; *(bicycle)* faro m [luz f] 83; *(cigarette)* lumbre f [encendedor m]; *(electric)* luz f 25

lightbulb foco [bombillo] m 148

lighter encendedor m 150

lighthouse faro m

lighting iluminación f [alumbrado m]

like: I'd like... quisiera... 133

like this *(similar)* como esto

limousine limosina f

line *(metro)* línea f 80; *(profession)* especialidad f 121; *(telephone)* **an outside line** una línea externa

linen lino m 145

lip labio m 166

lipsalve cacao m para los labios [manteca f de cacao]

lipstick lápiz m de labios

liqueur licor m

liquor store vinetería [licorería] f 131

litre/liter litro m 87, 159

little pequeño(-a)

live, to vivir; **~ together** vivir juntos 120

liver hígado m 166

lobby *(theatre/hotel)* sala de espera f

local de la región 35, 37

local anesthetic anestesia f local 168

local road carretera f federal [camino m vecinal]

lock chapa f, cerradura f 25; *(canal)* esclusa f

lock oneself out, to quedarse por fuera de la habitación 27

locked, to be estar cerrado(-a) con llave 26

locker casillero [lócker] m

long *(clothes)* largo(-a) 146

long *(time)* mucho tiempo; **how ~?** ¿cuánto tiempo? 164; **how much longer?** ¿cuánto tiempo más? 41

long-distance bus autocar m 78

long-distance call llamada de larga distancia f

look, to have a *(check)* revisar

look: I'm just looking sólo estoy mirando

look after: please look after my case for a minute cuídeme mi maleta un momento, por favor

look for, to buscar 18

look like, to ser 71

loose suelto(-a) 146

lose, to perder 28, 153

lost-and-found (lost property office) oficina f de objetos perdidos 73

lost, to be estar perdido(-a); **I've lost...** se me perdió

lotion loción f

lots muchos(-as)

loud, it's too está demasiado alto(-a)

love: I love you te amo

low-fat bajo en grasa

lower *(berth)* inferior 74
luck: good luck buena suerte 219
luggage *(baggage)* equipaje m 32, 67, 69, 71; ~ **allowance (baggage allowance),** cantidad de equipaje permitido f; ~ **lockers,** casilleros [lóckers] m, 71, 73; ~ **tag,** etiqueta f de equipaje; ~ **ticket,** boleto [tiquete] m de equipaje, 71; ~ **trolleys** *(carts),** carros [carritos] m de equipaje 71
lump protuberancia f 162
lumpy *(mattress)* lleno de bultos
lunch comida f [almuerzo m] 98
lung pulmón m
luxury lujo m

M

machine washable que se puede lavar en la lavadora 145
madam *(dear)* señora f
made: what is it made of ¿de qué está hecho?
magazine revista f 150
magnetic north norte m magnético
magnificent suntuoso(-a) [majestuoso(-a)] 101
maid empleado(-a) m/f 27
maiden name apellido m de soltera
mail, to llevar al correo
mail *(post)* carta f [correspondencia f] 27, 154
mailbox buzón m
main principal 130; ~ **course** plato m principal; ~ **rail station** estación f (principal) de tren 73; ~ **street** calle f principal 96
mains red f eléctrica
make *(brand)* marca f
make an appointment, to pedir una cita 161
makeup maquillaje m
male hombre m 152
mall zona f de tiendas 130, 131
man hombre m
manager gerente m [administrador(a)] 25, 41, 137

manicure manicure m 147
many muchos(-as)
map mapa m 106, 150
March marzo 218
margarine margarina f 160
market mercado m 99, 131
market day día m de mercado
married, to be ser casado(-a) 120
mascara rímel m [pestaña f]
mask *(diving)* gafas fpl de bucear
mass misa f 105
massage masaje m 147
match *(game)* partido m 114
matches fósforos m 31, 150
matinée matiné m, función de la tarde f 109
matt/mat finish *(photos)* acabado mate
matter: it doesn't matter no importa; **what's the matter?** ¿qué pasa?
mattress colchoneta f [colchón inflable] m 31
May mayo 218
may I…? ¿puedo…? 18
maybe tal vez
me me
meal comida f; cena f
mean: what does it mean? ¿qué significa eso? 11
measles sarampión m 165
measure, to tomar las medidas 146
measurement medida f
meat carne f 41
medical certificate certificado m médico 168
medicine medicina f [remedio m] 164, 165
medium *(regular)* mediano(-a) 40; *(steak)* a medio cocinar
meet, to encontrarse con 125; **pleased to meet you** mucho gusto 118
meeting place sitio m de encuentro [de reunión]
member *(of club)* miembro m 112, 115
men *(toilets)* baños mpl para caballeros
mend, to remendar
mention: don't mention it no es nada [no hay de qué] 10
menu menú m [carta f]

message recado m [razón f] 27; mensaje m
metal metal m
meter *(taxi)* taxímetro m
methylated spirits alcohol m desnaturalizado/metilado 31
Mexican *(person/adj)* mexicano(-a)
Mexican peso peso m mexicano 67
Mexico México 119
microwave *(oven)* horno m microondas
midday mediodía m
midnight medianoche f 220
migraine migraña f
mileage kilometraje m 86
milk leche f 160; **with ~** con leche 40; **~ of magnesia** leche de magnesia f
million millón m 217
mind: do you mind? ¿le molesta? 77, 126; **I've changed my mind** he cambiado de opinión
mine mío(-a) 16; **it's ~** es mío(-a)
mineral water agua f mineral 51
minibar mini-bar m 32
minibus minibús m [buseta f]
minimart súper [minimercado] m 158
minimum mínimo m
minister ministro m
minor road carretera f secundaria
minute minuto m
mirror espejo m
miss, to pasar(se); perder
missing, to be faltar 137; *(person)* estar desaparecido(-a) 152
mistake equivocación f [error m] 32, 41, 42
misunderstanding: there's been a ~ ha habido un mal entendido
mobile home casa f móvil
modern moderno(-a) 14; **~ art** arte moderno m
moisturizer *(cream)* crema f hidratante
monastery monasterio m 99
Monday lunes m 218
money dinero m 42,139, 153; **~ order** giro m postal; **~-belt** cinturón m para llevar el dinero

month mes m 218
monument monumento m
moor, to amarrar
mooring amarradero m
moped ciclomotor m; velomotor m 83
more más 15, 67; **I'd like some more** quisiera un poco más 39
morning, in the por la mañana 221
morning-after pill píldora del día siguiente
moslem *(adj)* musulmán(a)
mosquito mosquito m; **~ bite** picadura de mosquito f
mother madre f 120
motorbike motocicleta f 83
motorboat lancha de motor f 116
motorcycle motocicleta f; **~ parts** 82
motorway *(expressway)* autopista f 94
mountain montaña f 107; **~ bike** bicicleta de montaña f; **~ pass** cruce m de montaña 107; **~ range** cordillera f 107
mountaineering montañismo m
mousetrap ratonera f
moustache bigote m
mouth boca f 166
mouth ulcer llaga f en la boca
move, to trasladarse 25; *(house)* mudar; **don't move him!** ¡no lo mueva! 92
movie theater cine m 96, 110
Mr. señor m
Mrs. señora f
much mucho(-a) 15
mugged, to be ser asaltado(-a) [atracado(-a)] 153
mugging asalto m 152
mugs tazas fpl 148
multiplex cinema cinema m múltiple 110
mumps paperas f
muscle músculo m 166
museum museo m 99
music música f 111; **~ box** caja de música f
musician músico(-a)
must: I must tengo que
my mi(s) 16

N **nail polish** esmalte m

A-Z

nail scissors tijeras para uñas f
name nombre m 36, 93; **my name is me llamo** 118; **what's your name?** ¿cómo te llamas? 118
napkin (*serviette*) servilleta f 39
narrow angosto(-a) 14
national nacional m/f
national health seguro m social
nationality nacionalidad f
nature reserve reserva f natural 107
nature trail ruta f ecológica
nausea náusea f
navy blue azul m marino
near cerca 12, 84
nearby cerca de aquí; por aquí 87
nearest el/la más cercano(-a) 80, 88, 92, 130
nearsighted miope 167
necessary necesario(-a) 89
neck cuello m 166
necklace collar m 149
need: I need to... necesito 18
needle aguja f
negative (*photo*) negativo m
neighbor vecino(-a)
nephew sobrino m
nerve nervio m
never nunca 13
new nuevo(-a) 14
new year año nuevo m 219
New Zealand Nueva Zelanda 119
newspaper periódico m 150
newsstand puesto [kiosko, quiosco] m de periódicos 131
next próximo(-a) 75, 81, 87;
  ~ stop! ¡próximo paradero! 79
next to al lado de 95
Nicaragua Nicaragua 119
Nicaraguan (*person/adj*) nicaragüense
niece sobrina f
night, at de noche; por la noche 221
night porter portero m nocturno
nightclub club m nocturno 112
nightdress camisón m
nine nueve 216
no no 10
noisy ruidoso(-a) 14
non-alcoholic que no contenga alcohol

non-smoking (*adj*) no fumadores 36, 69; (*area*) sección f de no fumadores
none (*person*) nadie; (*thing*) ninguno(-a), nada 15
noon mediodía m
no one nadie 16, 92
north norte m 95
Northern Ireland Irlanda del Norte
nose nariz f 166
nosebleed hemorragia f nasal
not that one ése(-a) no 16
note billete m
notebook cuaderno m
nothing to declare nada que declarar
nothing else nada más 15
nothing for me nada para mí
notice board cartelera f de anuncios
notify, to avisar 167
November noviembre 218
now ahora 13, 84
nudist beach playa nudista f
number (*telephone*) número m 84; **sorry, wrong ~** disculpe, número equivocado
number plate número de matrícula [número de placas] m
nurse enfermera f
nursery slope pista f para principiantes
nylon nylon m

O
o'clock: it's... o'clock son las... en punto 220
observatory observatorio m
occupied ocupado(-a) 14
October octubre 218
odds (*betting*) probabilidades f 114
of de
of course por supuesto [claro que sí] 19
off-road (multipurpose) vehicle jeep m
office oficina f
often a menudo 13
oil aceite m
oil lamp lámpara f de aceite 31
okay de acuerdo [bueno] 10
old viejo(-a) 14; **~ fashioned** pasado(-a) de moda [anticuado(-a)] 14; **~ town** ciudad f vieja 96, 99
on (*day, date*) el 13; (*place*) sobre
on board (*ship*) a bordo
on foot a pie 17, 95

on the left a la izquierda 12
on the other side al otro lado 95
on the right a la derecha 12
on, to be *(showing)* presentar 108, 110
on/off switch interruptor de prender y apagar
once una vez 217
once a week una vez a la semana
one uno 216; **~ like that** uno(-a) como ése(-a) 16
one-way ticket boleto m de ida 68, 74, 79
open abierto(-a) 14; **~ to the public** abierto(-a) al público 100
open, to abrir 132, 140
open-air pool piscina f al aire libre 116
opening hours horarios m 100
opera ópera f 108, 111; **~ house** teatro m de la ópera 99, 111
operation operación f
operator *(tel.)* operador m
opposite enfrente de 12
optician oculista 131, 167
or o
orange naranja [anaranjado] m 143, *(fruit)* naranja f
orchestra orquesta f 111
order, to pedir 32, 37, 41; encargar 89
organized walk/hike caminata f 106
others otros(-as) 134
our(s) nuestro(s)(-a(s)) 16
out: he's out él no se encuentra
outdoor al aire libre
outside fuera de 12; afuera 36
oval ovalado(-a) 134
oven horno m
over por encima de; **~ there** por allá 76
overdone *(adj)* demasiado asado(-a) 41
overheated recalentado(-a)
overnight durante la noche
owe: how much do I owe you? ¿Cuánto le debo?
own: on my own solo(-a)
owner propietario(-a) m/f

P **pacifier** chupón [chupo] m
pack of cards baraja [las cartas] f

pack, to empacar 69
package paquete m
packed lunch almuerzo m [lonchera f]
packet paquete m; **~ of cigarettes** cajetilla f de cigarrillos 150
paddling pool piscina f para niños 113
padlock candado m
pail cubeta f [balde m] 157
pain, to be in tener mucho dolor 167
pain killer analgésico m 141, 165
paint, to pintar
painter pintor(a)
painting pintura f
pair of, a un par m de 217
pajamas piyama f
palace palacio m 99
palpitations palpitaciones f
Panama Panamá 119
Panamanian *(person/adj)* panameño(-a)
panorama panorama f 107
pantomime pantomima f
pants pantalones mpl 144
paper hoja f de papel; **~ napkins** servilletas f 148
paraffin parafina f 31
Paraguay Paraguay 119
Paraguayan *(person/adj)* paraguayo(-a)
paralysis parálisis f
parcel *(package)* paquete m 155
pardon? ¿perdón? 11
parents padres mpl 120
park parque m 96, 99, 107
park, to estacionar
parking estacionamiento [parqueo] m 87; **~ meter** parquímetro m 87; **~ lot** estacionamiento m 96
partner *(boyfriend/girlfriend)* compañero(-a)
parts *(components)* repuestos m 89
party *(social)* fiesta f 124
pass cruce m 107
pass through, to estar de paso 66
pass, to pasar 77
passenger pasajero m
passport pasaporte m 66, 69, 153
pastry shop/store pastelería f 131
patch, to poner un parche

A-Z

path camino m
patient paciente m
pavement, on the andén m [acera f]
pay, to pagar 42, 136; ~ a fine pagar una multa 93; ~ by credit card pagar con tarjeta de crédito
pay phone teléfono público m
paying pagar 32, 42, 136
payment pago m
peak pico m 107
pearl perla f 149
pedestrian crossing cruce m peatonal 96
pedestrian zone *(precinct)* zona f peatonal 96
pedicure pedicura f
pen pluma f [bolígrafo m] 150
pencil lápiz m
penfriend amigo(-a) por correspondencia
penicillin penicilina f
penknife navaja f
pensioner pensionado(-a) 100
people gente f, personas f 92
pepper pimienta f 38
per day por día 30, 83, 86, 87, 115
per hour por hora 87, 115
per night por noche
per week por semana 83, 86
performance función f
perhaps quizá [tal vez] 19
period periodo m; *(menstrual)* regla [menstruación] f 167; ~ pains cólicos mpl menstruales 167
perm permanente f
permit permiso m
personal stereo walkman m [radio/grabadora m con audífonos]
Peru Perú
Peruvian *(person/adj)* peruano(-a)
peso peso m 136
pet animal doméstico m
petrol gasolina f 87, 88; ~ can bidón m de gasolina; ~ station gasolinera f 87
pharmacy farmacia [droguería] f 158
phone teléfono m; ~ call llamada f telefónica 152; ~ card tarjeta f de teléfono 127, 155 (also ➤ telephone)

photo, to take a tomar una fotografía
photo: passport-sized fotografía f tamaño pasaporte 115
photocopier fotocopiadora f 155
photographer fotógrafo(-a) m/f
photography fotografía f 151
phrase frase f 11; ~ book libro m de frases 11
piano piano m
pick up, to reclamar 28, 109
picnic picnic m
picnic area zona f de picnic 107
piece rebanada f [pedazo m] 40, 159
pill: to be on the pill estar tomando anticonceptivos ; tomar la píldora f 167
pillow almohada f 27; ~ case funda f
pilot light piloto m
pink rosado 143
pint vaso m grande de cerveza
pipe *(water)* tubería f; *(smoking)* pipa f ~ cleaners limpiadores mpl de pipa; ~ tobacco tabaco m de pipa
pity: it's a pity ¡qué lástima!
place *(space)* cupo m, lugar m
place a bet, to hacer una apuesta 114
plain *(not patterned)* sin adornos
plane avión m 68
plans planes mpl 124
plant planta f
plastic bags bolsas fpl plásticas
plate plato m 39, 148
platform andén m 73, 76, 77
play, to jugar; *(music)* tocar 111
play group guardería f
playground patio de recreo [patio de juego] m 113
playing cards naipes mpl [juego m de cartas]
playwright autor m 110
pleasant agradable 14
please por favor 10
pliers alicates mpl
plug tapón m 148
plumber plomero m
p.m. p.m.
pneumonia neumonía f 165
point to, to señalar [mostrar] 11

poison veneno *m*

poisonous venenoso(-a)

police policía *f* 92, 152; **~ certificate** certificación de la policía *f* 153; **~ station** estación *f* de policía 96, 131, 152

pollen count recuento *m* polínico 122

pond laguna *m* 107

pony ride paseo en pony *m*

pop music música pop *f*

popcorn palomitas *fpl* de maíz [maíz *f* pira] 110

popular popular 157

port *(harbour)* puerto *m*

porter portero *m*; señor [maletero] *m* 71

portion porción *f* 40

possible: as soon as ~ cuanto antes

possibly posiblemente

post, to llevar al correo

post correo *m*

post office oficina *f* de correo 96, 154

postcard postal *f* 150, 154

poster afiche *m*

postman cartero *m*

pottery *(objects)* cerámica *f*, *(craft)* alfarería *f*

pound *(sterling)* libra *f* esterlina 67, 138

power cut apagón *m* [corte de corriente]

power point toma *f* de corriente

pregnant, to be estar embarazada

premium *(gas)* súper 87

prescribe, to recetar [formular] 165

prescription receta [fórmula] *f* 140, 141

present *(gift)* regalo *m*

press, to *(iron)* planchar 137

pretty bonito(-a)

priest sacerdote *m*

prison prisión [cárcel] *f*

private bathroom baño *m* privado

probably probablemente

program programa *m*

program of events programa *m* de eventos 108

prohibited: is it prohibited? ¿está prohibido?

promenade deck cubierta *f* de paseo

pronounce, to pronunciar

properly apropiadamente

Protestant protestante *m/f*

public bulding edificio *m* público 96

public holiday día *m* festivo 219

pullover suéter *m* 144

pump *(petrol/gas)* bomba *f*

puncture *(flat)* pinchada *m* 83, 88

puppet show función *f* de títeres 113

pure *(material)* puro(-a) 145

purple morado 143

purpose motivo *m*

purse monedero *m* 153

put by, to *(in shop)* guardar

put up: can you put me up for the night? ¿me puede alojar esta noche?

putting course campo de golf pequeño para entrenamiento *m*

Q **quality** calidad *f* 134
quantity cantidad *f* 134

quarantine cuarentena *f*

quarter, a un cuarto 217

quarter past *(after)* … y cuarto 220

quarter to *(before)* un cuarto para las … 220

quay muelle *m*

queen *(cards, chess)* reina *f*

question pregunta *f*

queue *(line)* cola [fila] *f*

queue, to hacer cola [fila] 112

quick rápido(-a) 14

quickly rápidamente 17

quiet tranquilo(-a) 14

quieter más tranquilo 126

R **rabbi** rabí *m*
race *(cars/horses)* carrera *f*; **~ course** *(track)* pista *f* de carreras 114

racket (tennis, squash) raqueta *f* 115

radio radio *m*

railroad ferrocarril *m*

rail station estación de tren *f* 73

A-Z

railway ferrocarril m

rain, to llover 122

raincoat impermeable m 144

rape violación f 152

rapids rápidos mpl 107

rare (*unusual*) raro(-a); (*steak*) poco hecho(-a)

rarely rara vez

rash salpullido m 162

razor máquina f de afeitar; **~ blades** hojas de afeitar [máquinas de afeitar desechables] 142

re-enter, to volver a entrar

reading (*interest*) lectura f; **~ glasses** anteojos para la lectura m

ready listo(-a) 89, 137, 151

real (*genuine*) verdadero(-a) [auténtico(-a)] 149

receipt recibo m 32, 89, 136, 137, 151

reception (*desk*) recepción f

receptionist recepcionista f

reclaim tag etiqueta f de reclamo 71

reclaim, to reclamar

reclining seat silla f reclinable

recommend, to recomendar 21, 35, 97, 141; **can you recommend** ¿qué me/nos recomienda?

record (*LP*) disco m 157; **~ (music) shop/store** almacén m de discos 131

recovery service servicio m de rescate 88

red rojo m 143; **~ wine** vino tinto m 40

reduction descuento m 68

refrigerator m [nevera f]

refund devolución f del dinero 137

refuse bags bolsas fpl para la basura 148

refuse tip vertedero [depósito] m de basuras

regards to... recuerdos [saludos] a

region región m 106

registered mail correo certificado m

registration form hoja de registro f 23

registration number/plate número m de matrícula 88, 93

regular (*gas*) normal 87; (*size of drink*) mediano(-a) 110

regulations: I didn't know the regulations yo no conocía las reglas

religion religión f

remember: I don't remember no me acuerdo

rent, to alquilar 86

rent: for rent se alquila

rental car carro m alquilado 153

repair, to reparar 89; arreglar 137, 168

repairs reparaciones f 89, 137

repeat, to repetir 94, 128; **please repeat that** repítamelo por favor 11

replacement uno(-a) nuevo(-a) 167; **~ part** repuesto m 137

report, to informar sobre 152

representative representante m/f 27

required, to be exigir(se) 112

reservation reservación f 68

reservations desk taquilla f [ventanilla f] 109

reserve, to reservar 36, 109

rest, to descansar

restaurant restaurante m 35

retired, to be estar retirado(-a) 121

return ticket boleto [tiquete] de ida y vuelta m 68, 74

return, to (*take back*) devolver 86; (*come back*) regresar 81

reverse the charges, to llamar por cobro revertido 127

revolting asqueroso(-a) 14

rheumatism reumatismo m

rib costilla f 166

right (*correct*) bien [correcto(-a)] 14; apropiado(-a)

right of way derecho a la vía m

right, on the a la derecha 76, 95; **to drive ~** conducir por la derecha

right-handed diestro(-a)

right: that's right muy bien [correcto]

ring anillo m 149

rip-off estafa f 101

river río m 107; **~ cruise** crucero m por el río 81

road carretera f 94, 95; **~ accident** accidente m de tráfico; **~ map** mapa m de carreteras 150; **~ signs** señales fpl de carreteras 96

robbed, to be ser robado(-a) 153

robbery robo m

rock climbing alpinismo m

rock concert concierto m de rock

rocks rocas f

roller blades/skates patines mpl de ruedas

romantic romántico(-a) 101

roof *(house/car)* techo m

roof-rack portaequipajes m

rook *(chess)* torre f

room habitación f [cuarto m] 21; **~ service** servicio m a la habitación 26

rope cuerda f

round *(shape)* redondo(-a) 134; *(of golf)* ronda f 115

roundabout glorieta f

round-trip ticket boleto m de ida y vuelta 68, 74

route ruta f 106

rowing remo m

rubbish bote m de la basura [caneca f] 28

rucksack mochila f

rude, to be ser grosero(-a)

rugby rugby m

ruins ruinas f 99

run into, to *(crash)* chocar 93

run out, to *(fuel)* acabarse 88

rush hour hora f pico [hora de mayor congestión]

S **safe** caja de seguridad [caja fuerte] f 27; *(not dangerous)* seguro(-a) 116; **to feel ~** sentir(se)

safety seguridad f 65; **~ pins** seguros [ganchos] m

sailboard tabla f a vela

sailboarding hacer windsurf

sailing boat barco m de vela

salad ensalada f

sales rep representante de ventas m/f

salt sal f 38, 39

Salvadorian *(person/adj)* salvadoreño(-a)

same el/la mismo(-a); **the same again** lo mismo otra vez

sand arena f

sandals sandalias fpl 145

sandwich sandwich m 40

sandy *(beach)* de arena 116

sanitary napkins toallas fpl higiénicas 142

satellite TV televisión f satélite 22

satisfied: I'm not satisfied with this no estoy satisfecho (-a) con esto

Saturday sábado m 218

sauna sauna m

sausage salchicha f 160

say: how do you say...? ¿cómo se dice...?; **what did he say?** ¿qué dijo él?

scarf bufanda f 144

scenic route ruta f pintoresca 106

scheduled flight vuelo m regular

school colegio m

scientist científico m

scissors tijeras fpl 148

scooter motoneta f

Scotland Escocia 119

Scottish *(person/adj)* escocés(a)

scouring pad estropajo m

screw tornillo m

screwdriver destornillador m 148

scrubbing brush cepillo m de fregar

sculptor escultor(a)

sea mar m 107

seafront malecón f

seasick, I feel estoy mareado(-a)

season ticket boleto [tiquete] m de temporada

seat asiento m 74, 77

second segundo(-a) 217; **~ class** segunda clase 74; **~ floor** *(U.S.)* primer m piso

secondhand de segunda mano; **~ shop** almacén m de artículos de segunda mano

secretary secretaria f

security guard guardia m de seguridad [celador]

sedative sedante m

see, to ver 24, 93; **~ someone again** ver (a alguien) de nuevo 126

self-employed, to be ser independiente 121

self-service autoservicio m 87

sell, to vender

send, to enviar 88, 155

senior citizen anciano m 74

separated, to be estar separado(-a) 120

separately *(adv)* por separado 42

September septiembre 218

serious grave

served, to be *(meal)* servirse 26

service servicio m 131; *(religious)* oficio m 105; **~ charge** gastos mpl de servicio; **is ~ included?** ¿está incluido el servicio? 42

set menu menú m del día 37

seventy setenta 217

sex *(act)* acto m sexual

shady: it's too shady hay demasiada sombra 31

shallow poco profundo(-a)

shampoo champú m 142

shape modelo f 134

share, to *(room)* compartir

sharp afilado(-a)

shaver máquina de afeitar eléctrica [afeitadora eléctrica]; **~ brush** brocha f de afeitar; **~ cream** crema f de afeitar; **~ socket** toma f [enchufe m] para máquinas de afeitar

she ella

sheet *(bedding)* sábana f 28

shelf estante m

ship barco m

shivery, to feel tener escalofríos

shock *(electric)* descarga f eléctrica

shoe zapato m 145; **~ laces** cordones [lazos] m de los zapatos; **~ polish** betún m; **~ repair** zapatería [zapatero remendón] m; **~ shop/store** almacén de zapatos m 131

shoemaker zapatero

shop tienda f 130; **~ assistant** vendedor(a) [dependiente] m/f

shopkeeper/storekeeper tendero(-a)

shopping area zona f comercial 99

shopping basket canasta f

shopping center zona f de tiendas 130, 131

shopping list lista f de compras

shopping trolley carro m del supermercado

shopping, to go ir de compras

shore *(sea/lake)* orilla f

short corto(-a) 146

shorts shorts m 144

shoulder hombro m 166

show espectáculo m

show, to mostrar 133; **can you show me?** ¿puede mostrarme? 94, 106

shower gel gel m para la ducha

shower room ducha f 26

showers duchas fpl 30

shrunk: they've shrunk se encogieron

shut cerrado(-a) 14; **when do you shut?** ¿a qué hora cierran?

shutter contraventana f

shy tímido(-a)

sick, to feel tener ganas de vomitar

sick: I'm going to be voy a vomitar

side *(of road)* lado [costado] m 95

side street calle lateral m 95

sidewalk, on the andén m

sightseeing, to go hacer un viaje de turismo

sightseeing tour recorrido m por los lugares turísticos 97

sign señal f 93, 95

signpost señalización f

silk seda f

silver plata f 149

silver plate chapado(-a) en plata 149

singer cantante m/f 157

single sencillo(-a) 81; **to be ~** ser soltero(-a) 120

single ticket boleto [tiquete] de ida m 68, 74, 79

single room habitación sencilla f [cuarto individual m] 21

sink fregadero m [lavadero m]

sister hermana f 120

sit, to sentarse 36, 77, 126; **sit down** siéntese

six seis 216

six-pack of beer paquete m de seis latas de cerveza 160

size talla f 115, 146

skating rink pista f de patinaje

ski, to esquiar

ski esquí m

ski bindings correa f del esquí

ski instructor instructor(a) m/f de esquí

ski suit traje m de esquí

ski trousers pantalones m de esquí

skin piel f 166

skin-diving equipment equipo m de buceo 116

skirt falda f 144

slalom slalom m

sleep, to dormir 167

sleeping bag saco m de dormir/sleeping 31

sleeping car coche m cama 77

sleeping pill pastilla f para dormir [somnífero m]

sleeve manga f

slice rebanada f 159

slide film diapositiva [filmina] f

slip *(undergarment)* combinación f

slippers pantuflas f 145

slot machine maquina f automática

slow lento(-a) 14; **slow down!** ¡disminuya la velocidad!

slow, to be *(clock)* estar retrasado 221

slowly lentamente 17; despacio 11, 128

small pequeño(-a) 14, 24, 40, 110, 134

small change cambio [suelto] m

smoke, to fumar 126; **I don't smoke** yo no fumo

smokers fumadores 36

smoky: it's too smoky hay demasiado humo

snack bar cafetería f 73

snacks golosinas f

sneakers zapatillas de lona f

snorkel esnórkel m

snow, to nevar 122

snowed in, to be estar encerrado por la nieve

snowplow quitanieves m

soap jabón m 142; **~ powder** jabón m en polvo

socket enchufe m

socks calcetines m [medias f] 144

sofa sofá m

sofabed sofá-cama m

soft drink *(soda)* refresco m [gaseosa f] 110

solarium solario m 22

sole *(shoes)* suela f

soluble aspirin aspirina f efervecente 141

some un poco de

someone alguien 16

something algo 16

sometimes algunas veces 13

son hijo m 120, 162

soon pronto 13; **as ~ as possible** cuanto antes 161

sore throat dolor de garganta m 141, 163

sorry! perdón 10

sort clase f 134; **a ~ of** una clase de

sound-and-light show concierto de luz y sonido m

sour ácido(-a) 41

south sur m 95

souvenir recuerdo m 98, 156; **~ shop/store** almacén m de recuerdos [souvenirs] 131

spa aguas termales fpl

space sitio m 30

spade *(shovel)* pala f

spades *(cards)* picas fpl

Spain España

Spanish *(language)* español m 11, 110, 126

Spanish *(person/adj)* español(a)

spare *(extra)* de repuesto

speak, to hablar 11, 41, 67, 128; **do you speak English?** ¿habla usted inglés? 11

special rate precio m especial 86

specialist especialista m/f 164

specimen muestra f 164

spectacles gafas f

speed, to conducir a gran velocidad 93

speed limit límite m de velocidad

spell, to deletrear 11

spend, to gastar

spin-dryer secadora f (centrífugadora)

spine columna f vertebral

sponge esponja f

spoon cuchara f 39, 41, 148

sports deportes mpl 114; **~ club** club m deportivo 115; **~ ground** campos m deportivo 96; **~ shop** almacén m de artículos deportivos 131

sprained, to be estar torcido(-a) 164

spring *(water)* manantial f; *(season)* primavera f 219

square *(shape)* cuadrado(-a) 134

squash squash m

stain mancha f

stainless steel acero m inoxidable 149

A-Z

stairs escaleras fpl
stale rancio(-a) [pasado (-a)]
stall: the engine stalls el motor se apaga
stalls (orchestra) luneta, platea f 108
stamp sello m [estampilla f] 150, 154
stamp machine máquina f expendedora de sellos [estampillas]
stand in line, to hacer cola [fila] 112
standby ticket boleto [tiquete] m de stand-by
start, to empezar 98; (car) arrancar 88
starter entrada f
statement (legal) declaración f 93
station estación f 73, 96
station wagon camioneta f
stationer's papelería f
statue estatua f 99
stay, to hospedarse 123; quedar(se) 23
steak house restaurante m especializado en carnes 35
stereo estéreo [equipo de sonido] m
stiff neck tortícolis f 163
still: I'm still waiting todavía estoy esperando
sting picadura f 162
stockings medias fpl 144
stolen, to be me robaron 71
stomach estómago m 166; ~ ache dolor m de estómago 163
stools (faeces) feces [materias fecales] fpl 164
stop (bus, metro) parada f [paradero m] 79, 80: **which stop?** ¿qué parada f [paradero m]?
stop, to parar 76, 77, 78; **please stop here** pare aquí, por favor
stop over, to pasar la noche
store tienda f 130; ~ assistant vendedor(a) [dependiente] m/f; ~ guide guía f del almacén 132
stove cocina f; estufa f 28, 29
straight ahead derecho 95
strained muscle músculo m torcido 162
strange raro(-a) 101
straw (drinking) popote m [pajita f]
stream arroyo m 107
string cuerda f
striped (patterned) a rayas

strong (potent) fuerte
stuck: the key's stuck la llave está atascada
student estudiante m/f 74, 100
study, to estudiar 121
stunning sensacional 101
stupid: that was stupid! ¡qué estupidez!
sturdy resistente
style estilo m 104
styling mousse espuma f moldeadora para el cabello
subtitled, to be tener subtítulos 110
subway pasadizo m subterráneo 96
subway metro m 80; ~ station estación f de metro 80, 96
sugar azúcar f 38, 39, 160
suggest, to sugerir 123
suit (man's) traje [vestido] m 144
suitable, to be es apropiado(-a) [recomendable] 140
summer verano m 219
sun block bloqueador m solar 142
sunbathe, to tomar el sol [asolearse]
sunburn insolación f 141
Sunday domingo m 218
sundeck (ship) cubierta f para tomar el sol
sunglasses gafas f de sol
sun lounger silla f reclinable para tomar el sol
sunshade (umbrella) sombrilla f 116
sunstroke insolación f 163
suntan cream/lotion crema/loción f bronceadora 142
superb magnífico(-a) [grandioso(-a)] 101
supermarket supermercado m 131, 158
supervision vigilancia f 113
supplement sobrecargo [recargo] m 68, 69
suppositories supositorios mpl 165
sure: are you sure? ¿está seguro(-a)?
surfboard tabla f de surf 116
surgery consultorio m
surname apellido m
suspicious sospechoso(-a)
swallow, to tragar [pasar]
sweatshirt sudadera f 144
sweet (taste) dulce
sweets (candy) dulces mpl 150
swelling inflamación f 162

swim, to nadar 116

swimming natación f 114; **~ pool** piscina f 22, 26, 116; **~ trunks** pantalón m de baño 144

swimsuit traje [vestido] m de baño 144

switch interruptor m

switch on/off, to prender/apagar

swollen, to be estar inflamado(-a)

symptoms síntomas m 163

synagogue sinagoga f

synthetic sintético(-a) 145

T **T-shirt** camiseta f 144

table mesa f 36, 134; **~ cloth** mantel m; **~ tennis** ping pong [tenis de mesa] m

tablet pastilla f 140

take, to *(carry, accept)* llevar 71, 135; *(medicine)* tomar 140, 165; *(time)* durar

take away, to para llevar 40

take pictures/photos tomar fotografías 98, 100

take someone home, to llevar (a alguien) hasta su casa

takeaway restaurante m de comidas rápidas 35

taken *(occupied)* ocupado(-a) 77

talcum powder talco m

talk, to hablar

tall alto(-a) 14

tampons tampones m 142

tan, to broncearse

tap *(faucet)* llave f [grifo m] 25

taste sabor m

taxi taxi m 70, 71, 84; **~ driver** conductor de taxi [taxista] m/f; **~ rank** parada de taxi f 96

tea té m 40; **~ bags** bolsas fpl de té 160

teacher profesor(a) m/f

team equipo m 114

teaspoon cucharita f 148

teat *(for baby)* seno [pezón] m

teenager joven de 13 a 19 años [adolescente] m/f

telephone teléfono m 22, 92, 127; **~ bill** cuenta de teléfono f; **~ booth** teléfono m público [cabina f de teléfono] 127; **~ calls** llamadas fpl telefónicas 32; **~**

directory directorio m telefónico; **~ kiosk** cabina f telefónica; **~ number** número m de teléfono 127 (also ➤ phone)

telephone, to llamar por teléfono 128

television televisión f

tell, to decir 18; **tell her/him** cuéntele a él/ella; **tell me** cuénteme (a mí); decir(me); *(warn)* avisar 79

temperature temperatura f 164

temporarily temporalmente 89

temporary temporal

ten diez 216

tendon tendón m

tennis tenis m 114; **~ ball** pelota f de tenis; **~ court** cancha f de tenis 115

tent tienda f (de campaña) 30, 31; **~ pegs** estacas fpl de la tienda 31; **~ pole** poste m de la tienda 31

terminus terminal m 78

terrible terrible 101

tetanus tétano m 164

thank you gracias 10

thanks for your help gracias por su ayuda 94

that eso(-a)

that one ése(-a) 16, 134

that's all eso es todo 133

thawing snow nieve f derretida

theater teatro m 96, 99, 110

theft robo m 153

their su(s) 16

theirs suyo(s), de ellos(as) 16

theme park parque m temático

then *(time)* luego 13

there allá 12, 17

there is/are... hay... 17

thermometer termómetro m

thermos flask termo m

these estos(-as) 134

they ellos(-as)

thick grueso(-a)

thief ladrón m

thigh muslo m 166

thin delgado(-a) [flaco(-a)]

think: I think creo 42, 77

think about it, to pensarlo 135

A-Z

third tercero(-a) 217

third party insurance seguro m contra terceros

third, a un tercio [una tercera parte] 217

thirsty: I am thirsty tengo sed

this one éste(-a) 16, 134

those esos(-as)

thousand mil 217

thread hilo m

three tres 216

throat garganta f 166

throat lozenges pastillas fpl para la garganta

thrombosis trombosis f

through a través de

thumb dedo pulgar m

Thursday jueves m 218

ticket boleto [tiquete] m 68, 69, 74, 75, 77, 79, 80, 114, 153; ~ **agency/office** venta f de boletos [tiquetes] 73

tie corbata f 144; ~ **pin** prendedor [broche] m de la corbata

tight ajustado(-a) 146

tights medias pantalón m 144

till receipt recibo de caja m

time (of day) hora f 76, 78, 220; **on** ~ a tiempo 76; **free** ~ tiempo m libre 98

timetable horario m 75

tin can lata f; ~ **opener** abrelatas m 148

tin foil papel m aluminio

tinted (glass/lens) de colores

tip propina f

tire llanta f 83

tired, to be estar cansado(-a)

tissue (paper) kleenex® m 142

to (place) hacia, a 12

to be ser

toaster tostadora f

tobacco tabaco m

tobacconist tabaquería [cigarrería] m 131

tobogganing deslizarse en tobogán

today hoy 124, 218

toe dedo del pie m 166

toilet(s) baño(s) m 25

toilet paper papel m higiénico 25, 29, 142

toiletries artículos mpl de tocador 142

tomorrow mañana 84, 124, 218

tongue lengua f

tonight esta noche 124; **for** ~ para esta noche 108

tonsillitis amigdalitis f

tonsils amígdalas fpl

too (extreme) demasiado 17, 93; (also) también

too much demasiado(-a) 15

tooth diente m [muela f] 168

toothache dolor m de muela

toothbrush cepillo m de dientes

toothpaste pasta [crema] f de dientes 142

top floor último piso m

torch antorcha f 31

torn, to be (muscle) estar desgarrado(-a) 164

totally totalmente 17

tough (food) duro(-a) 41

tour tour [recorrido] m 97; ~ **guide** guía turística m/f; ~ **operator** operador(a) de viajes 26; ~ **representative** representante m/f de viaje 27

tourist turista m/f

tourist office oficina f de turismo 97

tow rope cable m de remolque

tow, to remolcar

toward en dirección a 12

towel toalla f

toweling felpa f para toallas

tower torre f 99

town ciudad m 70; pueblo m 94; ~ **hall** casa f del ayuntamiento [consejo m municipal] 99

toy juguete m 157; ~ **and game shop/store** juguetería f 131

track senda f

tracksuit ropa f de entrenamiento

traditional tradicional

traffic tráfico m; ~ **jam** embotellamiento [trancón] m; ~ **offence/violation** infracción f de tránsito

trail camino m

trailer casa f móvil 30, 81; ~ **park** camping m para casas móviles

train tren m 75, 76, 77, 80; **train times** horarios mpl de trenes 75

training shoes tenis m 145

tram tranvía f 78, 79

translate, to traducir 11

translation traducción f
translator traductor(a)
travel, to viajar
travel agency agencia f de viajes
travel iron plancha f portátil
travel sickness mareo m 141
traveler's check cheque m
de viajero 136, 138
tray bandeja f
tree árbol m 106
tremendous tremendo(-a)
trip viaje m 97
trolley carrito m 158
trouser press prensa f para pantalones
trousers pantalones mpl 144
truck camión m
true: that's not true no es cierto
true north polo m norte magnético
try on, to medir [probar] 146
Tuesday martes m 218
tumor tumor m 165
tunnel túnel m
turn, to girar 95
turn down/up, to (volume, heat)
bajar/subir
turn off, to apagar 25
turn on, to encender 25
turning giro m 95
TV televisión f 22; ~ room sala f
de televisión
TV-listings (magazine) programación f de
televisión
tweezers pinzas f
twelve doce 216
twice dos veces 217
twin bed dos camas f 21
twist: I've twisted my ankle me he torcido el tobillo
two dos 216
two-door car carro m de dos puertas 86
type: what type? ¿qué clase? 112
typical típico 37

U

ugly feo(-a) 14, 101
UK Reino m Unido
ulcer úlcera f
umbrella sombrilla f
uncle tío m 120

unconscious, to be
estar inconsciente 92, 162
under (place) debajo
underdone (adj) poco
hecho(-a)
[cruda] 41
underground metro m 80; ~
station estación f de metro 80, 96
underpants calzoncillos m 144
underpass pasadizo m subterráneo
understand, to entender [comprender]
11; I don't understand no entiendo
[no comprendo] 11, 67
undress, to desvestirse 164
unfortunately desafortunadamente 19
uniform uniforme m
unit unidad f 155
university universidad f
unleaded gasoline gasolina f sin plomo
unlimited mileage kilometraje m
ilimitado
unlock, to abrir (con llave)
unpleasant desagradable 14
unscrew, to desatornillar
until hasta 221
upper (berth) superior 74
upset stomach trastorno [malestar] m
estomacal 141
upstairs arriba 12
up to hasta
urgent urgente 161
urine orina f 164
Uruguay Uruguay 119
Uruguayan (person/adj) uruguayo(-a)
us nosotros
U.S. los Estados Unidos 119
use, to utilizar 139
useful útil m/f

V

vacancies
habitaciones disponibles/libres 21
vacant libre [disponible] 14
vacate, to desocupar 32
vacation vacaciones f
vaccination vacunación f
vaginal infection infección f vaginal 167
valet service servicio m de planchado
valid válido(-a) 75
validate, to (ticket) convalidar

valley valle m 107
valuable valioso(-a)
value valor m 155
valve *(water)* llave f de cierre 28
VAT *(sales tax)* IVA m 24, 136;
~ **receipt** recibo m del IVA 42
vegetable store verdulería f 131
vegetables verduras f 38
vegetarian vegetariano(-a) 35, 39
vehicle vehículo m
vehicle registration document documento m de matriculación del vehículo
vein vena f
vending machine vendedora f automática
venereal disease enfermedad f venérea 165
Venezuela Venezuela 119
Venezuelan *(person/adj)* venezolano(-a)
very muy 17
vest camiseta f
veterinarian veterinario(-a) m
video video m; ~ **game** juego m de video; ~ **recorder** videograbadora f
view: with a ~ of the sea con vista al mar
viewpoint mirador m 99, 107
village aldea f 107
vineyard/winery viña f 107
visa visa f
visit visita f
visit, to visitar 167
visiting hours horas fpl de visita
visitor center/centre oficina f de información
visitors' passport pasaporte m de turista
vitamin tablets vitaminas f 141
voice voz f
volleyball voleibol 114
voltage voltaje m
vomit, to vomitar 163

W **waist** cintura f
wait, to esperar 41, 76, 89, 140;
wait! ¡un momento!
waiter! ¡mesero! m 37
waiting room sala f de espera 73
waitress! ¡mesera! f 37
wake, to *(self)* despertarse; *(someone)* despertar a alguien 27

wake-up call llamada f
Wales (País de) Gales 119
walk home, to caminar hasta la casa
walk: to go for a walk salir a dar una vuelta [un paseo]
walking caminata f; ~ **boots** botas f de montañismo 145; ~ **gear** equipo m de montañismo 145; ~ **route** zona f peatonal 106
wall pared f
wallet billetera f 42, 153
want, to desear [querer]
ward *(hospital)* sala f 167
warm *(weather)* caliente m/f 122
warm, to calentar
wash, to lavar
wash basin lavamanos m 25
washer *(for tap/faucet)* arandela f
washing: to do ~ lavar; ~ **machine** lavadora f; ~ **instructions** instrucciones de lavado f; ~ **powder** jabón para lavadora m 148
washing-up liquid polvo [jabón líquido] m para lavadora/los platos 148
wasp avispa f
watch reloj m de pulsera 149, 153; ~ **strap** pulsera [correa] f del reloj
watch TV, to ver televisión
watchmaker relojero m
water agua f 87; ~ **bottle** botella f de agua; ~ **heater** calentador m 28; ~**skis** esquíes mpl acuáticos 116
waterfall cascada [catarata] f 107
waterproof jacket chaqueta f impermeable 145
wave ola f
waxing depilación con cera f 147
way *(direction)* camino m, ruta f;
I've lost my ~ estoy perdido(-a) 94;
on the ~ en la vía 83
we nosotros(as)
weak *(coffee)* suave
weak: I feel weak me siento débil
wear, to vestir [llevar puesto(-a)] 152
weather tiempo m 122; ~ **forecast** el tiempo meteorológico [la predicción del tiempo] 122
wedding boda f
wedding ring anillo m de bodas
Wednesday miércoles m 218

week semana f 23, 97
weekend fin de semana m; **at the ~** en el fin de semana 218; **~ rate** precio m de fin de semana 86
weight: my weight is… peso…
welcome to… bienvenido(-a) a…
Welsh *(person/adj)* galés(a)
west occidental m 95
wetsuit vestido m térmico
what? qué 18
what kind/sort of…? ¿qué clase de…? 37, 106
what time? ¿a qué hora? 68, 76, 78, 81
what's the time? ¿qué hora es?
wheelchair silla f de ruedas
when? ¿cuándo? 13
where? ¿dónde? 12; **~ are you from?** ¿de dónde es usted? 119
which? ¿cuál? *(sing)*/¿cuáles? *(plur)* 16
while mientras
white blanco(-a) 143; **~ wine** vino blanco m 40
who? ¿quién? 16
whole: the whole day todo el día
whose ¿de quién? 16
why? ¿por qué? 15
wide ancho(-a) 14
wildlife fauna f
window ventana f 25, 77; *(shop)* vitrina [aparador m] 134, 149
window seat asiento m cerca a la ventana/ ventanilla m 69
windscreen/windshield parabrisas m
windsurfing windsurfing
windy: it's windy hace viento 122
wine vino m 40; **~box** caja f de vino [cartón m de vino] 160; **~ list** lista de vinos f 37
wine and spirits merchant's *(liquor store)* vinetería [licorería] f 131
winter invierno m 219
wishes: best wishes to mis/nuestros mejores deseos 219
with con 17
withdraw, to *(money)* retirar 139
without sin 17
witness testigo m 93

wood *(forest)* bosque m 107; *(material)* madera f
wool lana f 145
work, to trabajar 121; *(function)* funcionar 28, 83, 89
worry: I'm worried estoy preocupado(-a)
worse peor 14; **it's got/gotten worse** está empeorando
worth: is it worth seeing? ¿vale la pena verlo(-a)?
wound herida f
wrap up, to envolver
write: write soon! *(familiar)* ¡escribe pronto!
write down, to escribir 136
writing pad libreta de notas f
wrong *(not right)* mal 88, 136; **~ number** número equivocado 128

X Y Z

x-ray radiografía f 164
yacht yate m
year año m 218
yellow amarillo m 143
yes sí 10
yesterday ayer 218
yogurt yogur m
you usted(es) 16, 118; *(familiar)* tú
young joven
your su(s); *(familiar)* tu(s) 16
yours suyo(-a)(s) 16
youth hostel albergue m juvenil 29
zebra crossing paso m de cebra
zero cero m
zip(per) cremallera f [cierre m] 131
zoo zoológico m 113

A-Z Dictionary
Spanish - English

This Spanish-English Dictionary covers all the areas where you may need to decode written Spanish: hotels, public buildings, restaurants, shops, ticket offices and on transport. It will also help with understanding forms, maps, product labels, road signs and operating instructions (for telephones, parking meters etc.). If you can't locate the exact item, you may find key words or terms listed separately.
[Note: entries are not listed under particles: **a, al, de, del, el, la**, etc.]

A **a elegir** at your choice
a la carta a la carte
a la medida made to measure
los andenes to the platforms
a prueba de choques shockproof
abierto(-a) open
abono mensual monthly ticket
abono semanal weekly ticket
abordar to board
abordar por la puerta delantera enter by the front door
ábrase por aquí open here
abril April
abroche su cinturón de seguridad fasten your seatbelt
acantilado cliff
accesorios para automóvil car accessories/spares shop/store
accesorios para baño bathroom accessories
accesorios para cuartos bedroom accessories
aceptamos (todas las) tarjetas de crédito we accept credit cards
acrílico acrylic
actualizado(-a) updated
acueducto aqueduct
adentro indoors
admisiones admissions
aduana customs control
advertencia warning
aeropuerto airport
aerobismo aerobics
aerodeslizador hovercraft/hydrofoil
afuera outdoor

agencia de viajes travel agent
agítese bien antes de usar shake well before use
agosto August
agua para beber drinking water
al aire libre open-air, outdoor
al estilo … … style
ala delta gliding
alberca swimming pool
albergue juvenil youth hostel
algodón cotton
alimentos congelados frozen foods
alpinismo mountaineering
alquilan cuartos rooms to let
alto stop
alto voltaje high voltage
altura altitude
altura máxima … low bridge (maximum height …)
altura sobre el nivel del mar height above sea level
aluminio aluminium
ambulancia ambulance
amperes amps
ampliación enlargement service
ancho libre horizontal clearance
Año Nuevo New Year's Day
antes de las comidas/los alimentos before meals
anticipe su bajada request stop
antigüedades antiques
antojitos snacks
apague su motor turn off your engine
aquí está usted you are here
aquí termina city/town limits
arcada arcade

área de servicio service area
arena movediza quick sand
arquería archery
arte art
artículos libres de impuestos duty-free goods
artículos extraviados lost property
8 artículos o menos 8 items or less
artículos que declarar goods to declare
ascensor elevator/lift
asegurador insurance agent
asiento de ventanilla window seat
asiento en el pasillo aisle seat
asiento número seat no.
atletismo athletics
atracción turística tourist feature
auditorio auditorium
auto car
auto-cinema drive-in (movie)
auto-servicio self-service
autobús bus, coach
automóvil car
avenida avenue
avenida principal main road/principal highway
avión plane
ayuntamiento town hall
azúcar sugar

B bahía bay
bahía de carga loading bay
bahía de descanso rest area
bailar dance
bailarín(a) dancer
bajo su propio riesgo/su responsabilidad at the owner's risk
balcón balcony
baloncesto basketball
banco bank
barata bargain, sale
barco ship
barco de vapor steamer
barco ultra-rápido jetfoil
base terminus
baños restrooms/toilets/baths; washing facilities
bebidas incluidas drinks included
bebidas sin alcohol soft drinks
biblioteca library
bicicleta bicycle

bicicleta de montaña mountain bike
bienes raíces estate agent
¡bienvenidos! welcome!
bloqueador solar sunblock
boletería box office
boleto de temporada season ticket
boletos tickets
boletos agotados sold out
boletos para hoy tickets for today
boliche bowling
bomba de aire pump
bomberos fire station/brigade
bosque forest
botas de esquí ski boots
bote de vapor steamboat
botes salvavidas lifeboats
botica pharmacy
botiquín medicine box
boxeo boxing
buceo deep water diving
butacas stalls

C caballeros gentlemen (toilets)
cada ... horas every ... hours
cadena montañosa mountain range
café coffee
caja checkout; box
caja de ahorro savings bank
caja rápida express checkout
cajero automático ATM/autoteller
calcio calcium
calidad estándar quality standard
calle street
calle peatonal walkway
calle principal main/high street
callejón/calle cerrada cul-de-sac
calorías calories
camarotes cabins; sleeper (train)
camine walk
camino road; path
camino angosto narrow road
camino cerrado road closed
camino de terracería unpaved road
camino derrapante slippery road
camino en construcción road under construction
camino estrecho narrow road
camino irregular poor road surface
camión bus; coach; truck/lorry

A-Z

campo field
campo de aterrizaje airfield
campo de batalla battle site
canal canal
cancelado canceled
canoa canoe
canotaje canoeing
caña de pescar fishing rod
cañón canyon
capilla chapel
cápsulas capsules
característico typical
cargo por servicio service charge
carnaval carnival
carne meat
carnicería butcher's
carrera de galgos greyhound racing
carretera expressway/motorway/road
carretera de cuota toll road
carril lane
carril exclusivo para autobuses bus lane
carril exclusivo para ciclistas bicycle path/lane
carro car
casa house
casa de bolsa stock exchange
casa de cambio bureau de change, currency exchange office
casa de huéspedes guest house
casa de la ópera opera house
cascada waterfall
casco crash helmet
caseta de cobro toll booth
casimir cashmere
castillo castle
casualidad chance
catador de vinos winetasting
catedral cathedral
ceda el asiento a ancianos e inválidos please give up this seat to the elderly or handicapped
cementerio cemetery
centro downtown area
centro comercial shopping mall/arcade
centro deportivo y de recreación sports center/centre
cerrado closed

cereal cereal
cerrado (por hoy) day off/closed
cerrado a vehículos pesados closed to heavy vehicles
cerrado al tránsito en general closed to traffic
cerrado hasta ... closed until ...
cerrado por remodelación/reparación closed for repairs
cerrado por vacaciones closed for holiday/vacation
cerrado. regresamos a las ... closed until ...
cerveza beer
chaleco salvavidas lifejacket
charco pond
chifón chiffon
ciclismo cycling
ciclistas solamente cyclists only
ciclo de secado spin dry
cine movie theater/cinema
cine movies/cinema
cinturón de seguridad safety belt
circo circus
clasificación A universal (film classification)
clasificación B parental guidance (film classification)
clínica health clinic
club de campo country club
club de recreación sports center/centre
cobros por comisión bank charges
coche car
coche comedor buffet/dining car
cocina cookery
cocínese congelado cook from frozen
código de larga distancia area code
colina hill
comedia comedy
comedor dining room
comenzando a las ... commencing ...
comida del día menu of the day
comida saludable/sana health foods
compartimiento de (no) fumadores (non)smoking compartment
compra de divisa foreign exchange
con baño (en el cuarto) with (ensuite) bathroom
con el estómago vacío on an empty stomach

con las comidas with meals
con plomo leaded (gas/petrol)
con vista al mar with sea view
concierto pop pop concert
concurso contest
congelado frozen
conserje night porter
conservas preserves
conserve su derecha keep right
consulta externa outpatients
consulte a su médico antes de usarse/administrarse consult your doctor before use
consultorio consulting room/doctor's surgery
consúmase antes del ... best before ...
contenido de grasa fat content
contorno contour
control de pasaportes passport control
convento convent
copias e impresiones printing and copying
correo post office
corte court house
corte aquí cut here
costa coast
costurera confectioner's
cruce cross now
cruce de tren railroad/level crossing
crucero crossing; passing bay
cruceros cruises
cuadra square
cuartos vacantes/disponibles accommodations available
cuatro estrellas four-star
cubierta car deck
cubierta superior sun/upper deck
cubierto(-a) indoor
cuero leather
cueva cave
cuidad intensivo intensive care
cuidado caution
cuidado con el perro beware of the dog
cuidado con los ladrones beware pickpockets
cuide su equipaje do not leave baggage unattended
cuota toll
curva peligrosa dangerous bend
córtese aquí tear here

D damas ladies (toilets)
de ... a ... from ... to ...
de lunes a viernes weekdays only
de parte de ... sender
de temporada in season
deje rebasar yield (give way)
deje salir antes de entrar let passengers off first
deje su automóvil en primera (velocidad) leave your car in first gear
delicioso(-a) delicious
delta delta
demorado delayed
demoras posibles delays likely
dentista dentist
departamento department
departamento en renta/alquiler apartment to let
deporte sport
deportivo de recreación sports center/centre
deposite su dinero y tome su boleto insert money in machine and remove ticket
depósitos deposits
depósitos y retiros deposits and withdrawals
derrumbes falling rocks
desayunador breakfast room
desayuno breakfast
desconectado disconnected
desconéctese completamente antes de mover disconnect from mains before removing
descuentos reductions
desechable disposable
desierto desert
deslizando gliding
despacio slow
después de las comidas/los alimentos after meals
no desteñible colorfast
destino destination
desviación detour/diversion
devoluciones refund
diciembre December
dieta diet

A-Z

diócesis diocese
dique dam
dirección address
directo direct (service)
director conductor
directorio telefónico directory
discos compactos CDs
disminuya su velocidad slow down
disolver en agua dissolve in water
doblada dubbed
doble circulacion/sentido two-way traffic
domicilio particular home address
domingo Sunday
Domingo de Ramos Palm Sunday
Domingo de Pascua Easter Sunday
domingos solamente Sundays only
dos estrellas two-star
dosis para adultos adults (dose)
dosis para niños children (dose)
duchas showers
duna dune
durante ... dias for ... days

E **edificio público** public building
el próximo tour es a las... next tour at ...
el servicio no está incluido no service charge included
elevador elevator/lift
elija destino select destination/zone
embajada embassy
emergencia emergency
empieza a las ... begins at ...
empuje push
en construcción under construction/proposed
en renta for hire
en temporada in season
encienda sus luces switch on headlights
enero January
enfermería sickbay
entrada entrance, way in
entrada exclusiva de residentes access (to residents) only
entrega de equipaje baggage reclaim
entronque junction/interchange

equipaje olvidado left-luggage office
equipo de buceo scuba diving equipment
equipo de cocina kitchen equipment
equitación horse back riding
es obligatorio usar gorra de natación bathing caps must be worn
escalada en roca rock climbing
escalera eléctrica escalator
escuela school
especialidad de la casa specialty of the house
especialidades regionales local specialties
espectadores spectators
espectáculo spectacle
esquí skiing
esquí a campo traviesa cross-country skiing
esquí acuático waterskiing
esquís skis
esta máquina no da cambio this machine does not give change
esta noche this evening
estación de ambulancias ambulance station
estación de metro subway station/underground
estación de servicio service station
estación de tren rail station
estacionamiento parking lot; garage
estacionamiento exclusivo para clientes customer car park
estacionamiento gratuito free parking
estacionamiento permitido parking permitted
estacionamiento público parking lot/car park
estacionamiento subterráneo underground garage
estacione bajo su responsabilidad parking at your own risk
estadio stadium
estampillas stamps
estatua statue
estuario estuary
evento event
exclusivo para adultos under-18s not allowed
explosivo explosive

extinguidor fire extinguisher

F **fábrica** factory
fácil acceso al mar/a la playa
within easy reach of the sea
factor de protección 8
factor 8 (sunlotion)
familiar family section
farmacia pharmacy, dispensing chemist
faro lighthouse
favor de cerrar la puerta please shut
the door
favor de dejar sus bolsas aquí please
leave your bags here
favor de entrar sin alimentos
no food in the room
favor de esperar atrás de la marca/línea
please wait behind barrier/line
favor de hacer el aseo this room needs
making up
favor de mantenerse atrás de este punto
stand behind this point
**favor de mostrar sus bolsas antes de
salir** please show your bags before
leaving
favor de pagar antes de consumir
please pay for gas before
filling car
favor de pagar en el mostrador please
pay at counter
favor de pagar la tarifa exacta please
have exact change ready
favor de respetar este lugar sagrado
please respect this place of worship
favor de tocar el timbre please ring the
bell
fax público faxes sent
febrero February
fecha de nacimiento date of birth
fecha en que expira su tarjeta de crédito
credit card expiration date
feriado nacional/oficial national holiday
ferry de pasajeros passenger ferry
ficción fiction
fiesta nacional/oficial national holiday
fila row/tier
fin de reglamento de carretera end of
expressway/motorway regulation
firma signature
florería florist's

formal formal wear
fortaleza fortress
fotografía photography
frágil – vidrio fragile –
glass
freno de emergencia emergency brake
fresco fresh
frontera border crossing
fruta fruit
fuegos artificiales fireworks
fuente fountain
función nocturna evening performance
funicular drag lift
fútbol soccer/football

G **galería de arte** art gallery
galletas biscuits
ganado cattle; cattle-grid
gasolina gas/petrol
gasolinera filling station
genuino(-a) genuine
gerente manager
gimnasio fitness room
giros money orders
giros postales postal orders
glorieta (a … metros) circle (… m.
ahead)/roundabout
glutamato monosódico monosodium
glutimate
gotas drops
gratis free
grava suelta loose gravel
guardarropa/guardarropía cloakroom
guarnición de verduras
choice of vegetables
guía de la tienda/de ofertas store guide
guía telefónica directory

H **hasta terminar el tratamiento**
finish the course
**hay cuartos vacantes/
disponibles** accommodations available
hay lugares arriba seats upstairs
hay refrescos refreshments available
hecho a mano manmade
hecho en casa homemade
helicóptero helicopter
hielo icy (snow)
hipermercado supermarket

A-Z

hipódromo racecourse (for horses)
hockey sobre hielo ice hockey
hombres men (toilets)
homeópata homeopath
horario opening hours; timetable
horario de recolección times of collection
horario de verano/invierno summer/winter timetable
horas de oficina business hours
horas de visita visiting hours
hospicio hospice
hospital hospital
hoy/hoy día today

I

I.V.A. (impuesto al valor agregado) VAT/sales tax
iglesia church
impuesto incluido VAT/sales tax included
incluido en el precio included in the price
incluye inclusive
incluye una bebida includes 1 complimentary drink
incluido included
inflador pump
información information desk
información al cliente customer information
información nutricional nutritional information
informal informal wear
ingredientes ingredients
inmigración immigration control
inserte moneda insert coin
inserte tarjeta de crédito insert credit card
instrucciones de uso instructions for use
invierno winter

J

jale pull
jardín garden
jardín botánico botanical garden
jardín de iglesia churchyard
joyería jeweler's
jueves Thursday

jugos de fruta fruit juices
juguetería toyshop/store
julio July
junio June

kilómetro kilometer/kilometre

L

la bajada es por atrás exit by the rear door
lago lake
laguna pond
lana wool
lancha rowing boat
lateral secondary/minor road
lavado de coches car wash
lavandería laundry
lávese a mano hand wash only
lávese a máquina machine washable
lectura de poesía poetry reading
lencería lingerie
lenguaje language
libre for hire, vacant
libre de grasa fat-free
libre de impuestos duty-free (shop)
librería bookshop/store
límite de carga load limit
llame sin costo toll free number
llave de agua water tap
llegadas arrivals
llévese ... de regalo free gift
lo mejor del mundo world's best
lo mismo servido con ... the same served with ...
lotería lottery
lugar de nacimiento place of birth
lugar número seat no.
lugares arriba seats upstairs
lunes Monday
Lunes de Pascua Easter Monday

M

madera wood
malecón embankment/pier
maneje con cuidado drive carefully
maneje despacio drive slow
mañana tomorrow
mantenga la puerta cerrada keep gate shut
mantenga su carrril keep (get) in lane
mantenga su derecha keep to the right
mantenga su izquierda keep to the left

manténgase atrás de este punto mind the gap (metro)

manténgase en congelación keep frozen

manténgase en refrigeración keep refrigerated

manténgase en un lugar fresco keep in a cool place

manténgase fuera keep out

manténgase fuera de los jardines/del pasto keep off the grass

manténgase lejos del alcance de los niños keep out of reach of children

mar sea

marina marina

marque … para comunicarse a recepción dial … for reception

marque … para obtener línea dial … for an outside line

martes Tuesday

marzo March

mascotas pet store/shop

maternidad maternity

matiné matinée

mayo May

media pensión bed & breakfast, half board

medidor de electricidad electricity meter

mejorado(-a) improved

… menos en su próxima compra … off your next purchase

menú del día set menu

menú para turistas tourist menu

mercado market

mercancía irregular soiled goods

metro subway/underground

mientras espera while you wait

miércoles Wednesday

mimo mime

mina mine

mínimo minimum

mirador viewpoint

modista dressmaker

molino mill

molino de viento windmill

monasterio monastery

moneda extranjera foreign currency

montaña mountain

monumento monument

motel motel

moto acuática jet ski

mueblería furniture warehouse

muebles furniture

muebles de jardín garden center/centre

mujeres women (toilets)

multicinemas multiplex cinema

multipack multipack

muralla city wall

museo museum

música music

música bailable dance music

música clásica classical music

música de órgano organ music

música folklórica folk music

música viva/en vivo live music

N **nacionalidad** nationality

nada que declarar nothing to declare

natación swimming

navegación sailing

Navidad Christmas

nevada fuerte heavy snow

nieve fresca powdery snow

nivel A circle

nivel B dress circle

niñas women (bathrooms)

niños men (bathrooms)

no acampar no camping

no anclar no anchorage

no bloquee la salida do not block entrance

no correr no running

no debe ingerirse not for internal consumption

no debe ingerirse por vía oral not to be taken orally

no deje objetos de valor en su automóvil do not leave valuables in your car

no destiñe colorfast

no distraiga al conductor do not talk to the driver

no ensuciar do not litter

no esperar no waiting

no estacionar (entre… y …) no stopping (between … and …)

no estacionar sin permiso autorizado se usará grúa unauthorized vehicles will be towed away/clamped (booted) no estacionar se usará trampa wheel clamping (booting) in operation

no estacionarse no parking

no hay cambio exact fare

no hay cambios goods cannot be exchanged

no hay descuentos no discounts

no hay devoluciones no refunds

no hay entrada no entry

no hay paso no entry

no hay salida no exit

no hay vacantes/ cuartos disponibles full up

no incluye exclusive

no interrumpir do not disturb

no molestar do not disturb

no obstruir (el paso) keep clear

no pisar el pasto keep off the grass

no pise el pasto keep off the grass

no planchar do not iron

no rebase no passing/overtaking

no residentes non-residents

no retornable non-returnable

no se aceptan cheques no checks

no se aceptan tarjetas de crédito no credit cards

no se aleje de la pista no off-track skiiing

no se da cambio no change given

no se exponga al sol do not expose to sunlight

no se pega non-stick

no se recargue en la puerta do not lean against door

no sirve out of order

no tirar basura no dumping

no tocar do not touch

no tocar bocina/claxon use of horn prohibited

no tomar fotografías no photography

no usar flash/trípode no flash/tripod

nombre name

nombre de la cónyuge name of spouse

nombre de soltera maiden name

noviembre November

nuevo sistema de tráfico operando new traffic system in operation

nuevo(-a) brand new

número de afiliación al seguro social social security number

número de asiento/lugar seat number

número de cuenta credit card number

número de pasaporte passport number

número de registro de su automóvil car registration number

número de vuelo flight number

número gratuito toll free number

 O **obispo** bishop

observatorio observatory

océano ocean

octubre October

oculista optician

ocupado occupied/engaged

oferta especial special offer

oficina de información information office

oficina postal post office

operadora operator

óptica optician

oraciones prayers

oraciones vespertinas evensong

orilla del río river bank

oro gold

orquesta orchestra

orquesta sinfónica symphony orchestra

ortodoncista orthodontist

osteópata osteopath

otoño fall/autumn

P **pabellón** pavilion

padre fr. (Father)

páginas amarillas yellow pages

pague 2 y llévese 3 buy 2 get 1 free

pague aquí please pay here

pague en el parquímetro pay at the meter

palacio palace

palos de esquí ski poles/sticks

pan bread

panadería baker's/bakery

pantano marsh, swamp

papel reciclado recycled paper

papelería stationary store/stationer's

papeles de registro registration papers

paquetes parcels

para asistencia en carretera llame al ... in case of breakdown, phone/contact ...

para cabello graso/grasoso for greasy hair

para cabello normal for normal hair

para cabello seco for dry hair

para después del sol aftersun

para dos (personas) for two

para llevar take-away

para vegetarianos suitable for vegetarians/vegans

paracaídismo parachuting

parada (de autobuses) bus stop

paradas fijas stopping service

pared wall

parlamento parliament building

parque park

parque de diversiones amusement park

parque ecológico country park

parque nacional national park

parrilla barbeque

parroquia parish

partido match

pasadizo alley

pasaje flight

pasarlas enteras swallow whole

Pascua Easter

paso gorge, pass

paso a desnivel fly-over

paso cerrado (mountain) pass closed

paso de peatones pedestrian crossing

paso peatonal pedestrian crossing/precinct

paso subterráneo underground passage

pastelería baker's/bakery, cakeshop/store

pastillas pills/tablets

patinaje sobre hielo ice skating

patines skates

peatones pedestrians

pediatría pediatric ward

peligro danger

peligro de avalancha avalanche danger

peligroso dangerous

pelota de mano handball

peluquero barber

peluquería hairdresser's/stylist's

películas movie theater/cinema

pendiente pronunciada dangerous slope

pensiones pensions

pensión completa full board

permita bajar antes de subir (abordar) let passengers off first

pesca angling

pesca con autorización/permiso fishing by permit only

pescadería fish store/fishmonger's

pescado fish

pico peak

piel leather

pildoras pills/tablets

pintura fresca wet paint

piscina swimming pool

pista cerrada road closed

pista de carreras racing track

pista para esquiadores avanzados/intermedios/principiantes for advanced/intermediate/beginner skiers

plancha iron

plata silver

plataforma platform

playa beach

playa nudista nudist beach

policía police (station)

policía de caminos highway police

policía vial traffic police

poliéster polyester

pomada ointment

ponga su boleto en un lugar visible place ticket on windshield/windscreen

por... (pesos) extra extra charge/supplement

por favor conserve su boleto please retain your ticket

por favor espere su turno please wait your turn

por única ocasión/noche for 1 night only

portero night porter

portilla porthole

pósters posters

pozo well

precaución caution; drive carefully

precaución, escuela caution, school

precio por litro price per liter

A-Z

pregunte sin compromiso please ask for assistance
premier premier
preparado sobre pedido made to order
preservativos preservatives
primavera spring
primer piso second floor
primera first class
primera presentación/noche first night
privado private
probadores fitting rooms
productos lácteos dairy products
programa program
prohibida la entrada a niños menores de… años no children under …
prohibida la entrada a personas ajenas a este lugar staff only
prohibida la entrada después de iniciada la función no entry once the performance has begun
prohibida la entrada durante la misa/la ceremonia/el servicio no entry during services
prohibido … forbidden
prohibido bañarse bathing prohibited
prohibido estacionarse sin permiso autorizado unauthorized parking prohibited
prohibido hacer fogatas no fires/barbeques
prohibido jugar con pelota no ball games
prohibido nadar no swimming/bathing
prohibido pescar no fishing
próxima entrada o salida freeway/motorway entrance/exit
próximo entronque freeway/motorway junction
próxima recolección a las next collection at …
psiquiatra psychiatrist
puede hacerse en microondas microwaveable
puente bridge
puente angosto narrow bridge
puente levadizo drawbridge
puerta door, gate
puerta automática automatic door
puerta de abordar (boarding) gate

puerta de emergencia fire door
puertas automáticas automatic doors
puerto port; harbor/harbour
puesto de periódicos newspaper stand
punto de embarco embarkation point
punto de encuentro meeting point, muster station

Q queso cheese
quirófano operating theater
quiropráctico chiropractic

R rampa ramp
rancho farm
rápidos rapids
rappelear abseiling
raqueta racket/raquet
rayos X (equis) x-ray
recepción reception
reciclado de vidrio bottle bank
recital recital
referencia reference
regadera shower
regaderas públicas public showers
regalos gift shop
registro check-in counter
remo rowing
renta de coches car rental
renta de vestidos dress hire
renta de videos video rental
reparaciones repairs
reparación de calzado shoe repairs
reparación de coches car repairs
represa reservoir
reserva ecológica nature reserve
reservaciones (ticket) reservations
reservado reserved
retiros withdrawals
retornable returnable
revelado en 1 hora/4 horas/un día one-hour/4-hour/overnight developing service
revisado(-a) revised
revisión de pasaportes passport check/control
revista review
río river
rompa este vidrio en caso de emergencia break glass in case of emergency

ropa para caballeros menswear
ropa para damas ladies wear
ropa para niños(-as) children's wear
ruinas ruins
ruta bus route
ruta de transbordador/ferry ferry route
ruta de tranvía tramway

S sábado Saturday
saborizantes flavorings
sal salt
sala lounge
sala de conciertos concert hall
sala de consulta/tratamiento treatment room
sala de convenciones convention hall
sala de espera waiting room
sala de pasajeros passenger lounge
sala de T.V. television room
sala/salón de eventos conference room
sala/salón de juegos games room
salida exit, way out; gate (airport)
salida de camiones truck exit
salida de emergencia emergency exit, fire door
salidas departures
salvavidas lifeguard, lifejacket
salón de belleza hairdresser's/stylist's
sanitarios toilets/restrooms
sastre tailor
se alza el telón curtain up
se compra y vende... we buy and sell ...
se consignará a las autoridades a la persona que sea sorprendida robando shoplifting will be prosecuted
se habla inglés English spoken
se multará a la persona que se sorprenda tirando basura no littering: fine ...
se prohíbe ... ... forbidden
se prohíbe la entrada de niños sin la compañía de un adulto no unaccompanied children
se prohíbe el acceso a cubierta durante el transbordo no access to car decks during crossing
se prohíbe fumar en cubierta no smoking on car decks
se rentan cuartos rooms to let

se sancionará a la persona que se sorprenda viajando sin boleto penalty for traveling without ticket
se venden tarjetas de teléfono aquí phone cards on sale here
secador(a) de pelo hairdryer
sección de fumar smoking
sección de no fumar non-smoking
seda silk
segunda second class
segundo piso second floor
segundos seconds
seguridad security
semáforo temporal temporary traffic lights
sendero footpath
septiembre September
servicio a clientes customer service
servicio a cuartos room service
servicio incluido service included
servicio las 24 horas 24-hour service
servicio mecánico/eléctrico breakdown services
servicio nocturno night service
servicios de emergencia emergency services
si persisten las molestias, consulte a su médico if symptoms persist, consult your doctor
si rompe algo, debe pagarlo all breakages must be paid for
silencio silence
silla en cubierta deck-chair
sin azúcar sugar-free
sin grasa fat-free
sin intermedios no intervals
sin plomo unleaded
sírvase helado best served chilled
sistema de seguridad activado/en operación surveillance system in operation
sitio de taxis taxi stand/rank
solista soloist
sólo autobuses buses only
sólo carga freight only
sólo ciclistas cyclists only
sólo descarga deliveries only
sólo domingos Sundays only

sólo efectivo cash only
sólo entrada access only
sólo hombres men only
sólo mujeres women only
sólo mujeres y niños women and children only
sólo para uso externo for external use only
sólo peatones pedestrians only
sólo periódicos newspapers only
sólo personas con boleto de temporada season ticketholders only
sólo personas con permiso/autorizadas permit holders only
sólo residentes residents only
sólo tránsito local no throughway
sólo turistas tourists only
soluble dissolve in water
sombra sunshade
subtitulada subtitled
sugerencia del chef the chef suggests
supercarretera expressway/motorway
superficie helada icy road
superficie irregular uneven road surface
supermercado supermarket
suplemento supplement

T

tabaquería tobacconist's
tabla de surfeo surfboard
tabla de windsurf sailboard
tabletas tablets
taquilla box office, ticket office
tarifa rate; admission
tarifa de cambio exchange rate
tarifa exacta exact fare
tarifa por cuarto/por noche room rate
tarjeta de embarco embarkation card
tarjeta de teléfono card phone
tarjetas de teléfono de venta aquí phone cards on sale here
teatro movie theater/cinema
teatro infantil children's theater
teleférico cable car/gondola
teléfono telephone
teléfono de emergencia emergency telephone
teléfono público public telephone
telegramas telegrams
telesilla chairlift

televisión (vía satélite) en cada cuarto with (satellite) TV in every room
tenis de mesa table tennis
termina desviación end of diversion
terminal terminal, terminus
terraza terrace
tetera kettle
tienda general store
tienda de abarrotes grocery/grocer's
tienda de antigüedades antique shop/store
tienda de arte art shop/store
tienda de deportes sports shop/store
tienda de discos music shop/store
tienda de electrónica electrical shop/store
tienda de fotografía photographic shop/store
tienda de instrumentos music shop/store
tienda departamental department store
tienda duty-free duty-free shop
timbres postales stamps
tinaco water tank
tintorería dry-cleaner's
toca play
todas las transacciones all transactions
todos estos platillos acompañados de… all the above are served with …
tolerancia de peso luggage allowance
tome su boleto take ticket
toque el timbre please ring the bell
torre tower
tours guiados guided tours
tours por el río river trips
trabajos concluidos end of roadworks
tráfico en dirección opuesta traffic from the opposite direction
tráfico lento slow traffic
tráfico/tránsito en un solo sentido one-way street
tragedia tragedy
trailer trailer/caravan
tramo angosto road narrows
trampolín diving board
transbordador passenger ferry
transborde en… change at …
tránsito one way
tranvía tram

trasborde a... change
(to other metro lines)
tren local train
tren expreso express train
trolebús trolley
trolley trolley
tumba tomb
túnel tunnel
turistas non-residents
té tea
tóxico toxic

U **última entrada a las...** latest
entry at ... pm
únicamente rastrillos shavers only
unidades units
unitalla one size fits all
universidad university
uso reducido a número gratuito
emergency services/telephone
usted está aquí you are here

V **vacantes** vacancies
vajilla china
válido hasta... valid until ...
válido para las siguientes
zonas ... valid for zones ...
valle valley
vapor stream
... veces al día ... times a day
vehículos pesados heavy/slow vehicles
velador night porter
velero sailing boat
velocidad máxima maximum speed
veneno(so) poison(ous)
venta de divisa: currency sold at
venta de fin de temporada
clearance sale
venta de liquidación closing down sale
ventanilla de apuestas bookmaker's
verano summer
verdulería greengrocer's
verduras vegetables
verifique su cambio/vuelto
please check your change
vestidores changing rooms
veterinaria veterinarian
vía track

vía alternativa
alternative route
vía alternativa de auto-
buses/camiones alternative truck route
vía cerrada closed road
vía de alta velocidad high-
way/motorway
vía de tren railroad/railway
vía para ciclistas cycle track
viaje journey/trip
vidrio glass
viernes Friday
villa village/town
viñedo vineyard/winery
vino wine
vista panorámica panoramic view
vuelo número... flight number
vuelos internacionales international
flights
vuelos nacionales domestic flights

WX YZ **yate** yacht
zona de obra roadworks
zapatero cobbler's/shoemaker
zapatos shoes
zona comercial shopping area
zona de campamento campsite
zona de estacionamiento restringida
limited parking zone
zona de paisaje scenic route
zona de picnic picnic area
zona deportina sports gound
zona exclusiva para peatones
pedestrian zone/precinct
zona libre de tráfico traffic-free zone
zona residencial residential zone
zoológico zoo

Reference

Numbers

GRAMMAR

> Larger numbers are built up using the components below: e.g.
> 3.456.789 = **tres millones, cuatrocientos cincuenta y seis mil, setecientos ochenta y nueve**
>
> Note that from 31 to 99 **y** is used between tens and units, but never between hundreds and tens.

0	**cero** *sero*		20	**veinte** *beynteh*
1	**uno** *oono*		21	**veintiuno**
2	**dos** *dos*			*beyntee-oono*
3	**tres** *tres*		22	**veintidós**
4	**cuatro** *kwatro*			*beyntee-dos*
5	**cinco** *seenko*		23	**veintitrés**
6	**seis** *seys*			*beyntee-tres*
7	**siete** *seeyeteh*		24	**veinticuatro**
8	**ocho** *ocho*			*beyntee-kwatro*
9	**nueve** *nwebeh*		25	**veinticinco**
10	**diez** *deeyes*			*beyntee-seenko*
11	**once** *onseh*		26	**veintiséis**
12	**doce** *doseh*			*beyntee-seys*
13	**trece** *treseh*		27	**veintisiete**
14	**catorce** *katorseh*			*beyntee-seeyeteh*
15	**quince** *keenseh*		28	**veintiocho**
16	**dieciséis**			*beyntee-ocho*
	deeyes-ee-seys		29	**veintinueve**
17	**diecisiete**			*beyntee-nwebeh*
	deeyes-ee-seeyeteh		30	**treinta** *treynta*
18	**dieciocho**		31	**treinta y uno**
	deeyes-ee-ocho			*treynta ee oono*
19	**diecinueve**		32	**treinta y dos**
	deeyes-ee-nwebeh			*treynta ee dos*

40	**cuarenta** *kwarenta*
50	**cincuenta** *seenkwenta*
60	**sesenta** *sesenta*
70	**setenta** *setenta*
80	**ochenta** *ochenta*
90	**noventa** *nobenta*
100	**cien** *seeyen*
101	**ciento uno** *seeyento oono*
102	**ciento dos** *seeyento dos*
200	**doscientos** *doseeyentos*
500	**quinientos** *keeneeyentos*
1,000	**mil** *meel*
10,000	**diez mil** *deeyes meel*
35,750	**treinta y cinco mil setecientos cincuenta** *treynta ee seenko meel seteseeyentos seenkwenta*
1,000,000	**un millón** *oon meel-yon*
first	**primero(-a)** *preemero(-a)*
second	**segundo(-a)** *segoondo(-a)*
third	**tercero(-a)** *tersero(-a)*
fourth	**cuarto(-a)** *kwarto(-a)*
fifth	**quinto(-a)** *keento(-a)*

once	**una vez** *oona bes*
twice	**dos veces** *dos beses*
three times	**tres veces** *tres beses*
a half	**una mitad** *oona meetath*
half a(n) hour	**media hora** *medeea ora*
half a tank	**medio tanque** *medeeo tankeh*
it's half eaten	**ya está probado (-a) [tocado(-a)]** *ya esta probado (-a) [tokado(-a)]*
a quarter	**un cuarto** *oon kwarto*
a third	**un tercio [una tercera parte de]** *oon terseeo [oona tersera parteh deh]*
a pair of ...	**un par de ...** *oon par deh ...*
a dozen ...	**una docena ...** *oona dosena*
1998	**mil novecientos noventa y ocho** *meel nobeh-seeyentos nobenta y ocho*
2001	**dos mil uno** *dos meel oono*
the 1990s	**la década de los noventa** *la dekada deh los nobenta*

Days Días

Monday	**lunes** *loones*
Tuesday	**martes** *martes*
Wednesday	**miércoles** *meeyerkoles*
Thursday	**jueves** *khweves*
Friday	**viernes** *veeyernes*
Saturday	**sábado** *sabado*
Sunday	**domingo** *domeengo*

Months Meses

January	**enero** *enero*
February	**febrero** *febrero*
March	**marzo** *marso*
April	**abril** *abreel*
May	**mayo** *mayo*
June	**junio** *khooneeo*
July	**julio** *khooleeo*
August	**agosto** *agosto*
September	**septiembre** *septeeyembreh*
October	**octubre** *oktoobreh*
November	**noviembre** *nobeeyembreh*
December	**diciembre** *deeseeyembreh*

Dates Fechas

It's …	**Hoy es …** *oy es…*
July 10	**10 de julio** *deeyes deh khooleeyo*
Tuesday, March 1	**martes, primero de marzo** *martes, preemero deh marso*
yesterday/today/tomorrow	**ayer/hoy/mañana** *ayer/oy/mañana*
this/next/every	**este/el próximo/cada** *este/el prokseemo/kada*
… month/… year	**… mes/… año** *mes/año*
this/next/every week	**esta/la próxima/cada semana** *esta/la prokseema/kada semana*
last week/month	**la semana pasada/el mes pasado** *la semana pasada/el mes pasado*
at the weekend	**el fin de semana** *el feen deh semana*

Seasons Estaciones

English	Spanish	Pronunciation
spring	**la primavera**	*la preema_bera_*
summer	**el verano**	*el be_rano_*
fall/autumn	**el otoño**	*el oto_ño_*
winter	**el invierno**	*el eenbee_yerno_*
in spring	**en primavera**	*en preema_bera_*
during the summer	**durante el verano**	*doo_ranteh el be_rano_*

Greetings Saludos

English	Spanish	Pronunciation
Happy birthday!	**¡Feliz cumpleaños!**	*fe_lees_ koompley_años_*
Merry Christmas!	**¡Feliz navidad!**	*fe_lees_ nabee_dath_*
Happy New Year!	**¡Feliz año nuevo!**	*fe_lees_ año nwebo*
Happy Easter!	**¡Feliz Semana Santa!**	*fe_lees_ semana santa*
Best wishes!	**Mis/Nuestros mejores deseos**	*mees/_nwestros_ mekhores deseyos*
Congratulations!	**¡Felicitaciones!**	*feleeseetaseeyones*
Good luck!/All the best!	**¡Buena suerte! ¡Que todo salga bien!**	*bwena swerteh. keh todo salga beeyen*
Have a good trip!	**¡Buen viaje!**	*bwen beeyakheh*
Give my regards to …	**Déle mis recuerdos [saludos] a …**	*dele mees rekwerdos [saloodos] a…*

Public holidays Días festivos

National holidays observed in all Latin-American countries:

January 1	**Año Nuevo**	New Year's Day
May 1	**Día del trabajo**	Labor Day
October 12	**Día de la Raza**	Columbus Day
December 25	**Navidad**	Christmas
Moveable dates:	**Viernes Santo**	Good Friday

Others (Mexico): **Día de la Constitución** (Feb 5), **el Natalicio de Benito Juárez** (Mar 21), **Aniversario de la Batalla de Puebla** (May 5), **el Día de la Independencia** (Sept 16), **Día de todos los Santos** (1 Nov), **Día de los Muertos** (Nov 2), **el Día de la Revolución** (Nov 20), **el Día de la Virgen de Guadalupe** (Dec 12).

Time La hora

cinco para las dos
diez para las dos
un cuarto para las dos
veinte para las dos
veinticinco para las dos
la una y media
la una y cinco
la una y diez
la una y cuarto
la una y veinte
la una y veinticinco

Excuse me. Can you tell me the time?	**Disculpe. ¿Puede decirme la hora?** deeskoolpeh. pwedeh deseermeh la ora
It's five past one.	**Es la una y cinco.** es la oona ee seenko
It's …	**Son las …** son las
ten past two	**dos y diez** dos y deeyes
a quarter past three	**tres y cuarto** tres ee kwarto
twenty past four	**cuatro y veinte** kwatro ee beynteh
twenty-five past five	**cinco y veinticinco** seenko ee beyntee-seenko
half past six	**seis y media** seys ee medeea
It's …	**Faltan …** faltan
twenty-five to seven	**veinticinco para las siete** beyntee-seenko para las seeyeteh
twenty to eight	**veinte para las ocho** beynteh para las ocho
a quarter to nine	**un cuarto para las nueve** oon kwarto para las nwebeh
ten to ten	**diez para las diez** deeyes para las deeyes
five to eleven	**cinco para las once** seenko para las onseh
It's twelve o'clock (noon/midnight).	**Son las doce en punto (mediodía/ medianoche).** son las doseh en poonto (medeeo-deeya/medeea-nocheh)

at dawn	**al amanecer** *al amaneser*
in the morning	**por la mañana** *por la mañana*
during the day	**durante el día** *dooranteh el deeya*
before lunch	**antes de la comida** *antes deh la komeeda*
after lunch	**después de la comida** *despwes deh la komeeda*
in the afternoon/evening	**por la tarde** *por la tardeh*
at night	**por la noche** *por la nocheh*
I'll be ready in five minutes.	**Estaré listo(-a) en cinco minutos.** *estareh leesto(-a) en seenko meenootos*
He'll be back in a quarter of an hour.	**El volverá en un cuarto de hora.** *el volbera en oon kwarto deh ora*
She arrived half an hour ago.	**Ella llegó hace media hora.** *el-ya l-yego ase medeea ora*
The train leaves at …	**El tren sale a …** *el tren saleh a*
13:04	**la una y cuatro minutos** *la oona ee kwatro meenootos*
0:40	**doce y cuarenta** *dose ee kwarenta*
The train is 10 minutes late/early.	**El tren está retrasado/adelantado diez minutos.** *el tren esta retrasado/adelantado deeyes meenootos*
Your watch is 5 minutes fast/slow.	**Su reloj está adelantado/atrasado cinco minutos.** *soo relokh esta adelantado/ atrasado seenko meenootos*
from 9:00 a.m. to 5:00 p.m.	**de las nueve de la mañana a las cinco de la tarde** *de las nwebeh deh la mañana a las seenko deh la tardeh*
between 8:00 and 2:00	**entre las ocho y las dos** *entre las ocho y las dos*
I'll be leaving by …	**Saldré alrededor de la(s) …** *saldreh alrededor deh la(s)*
Will you be back before …?	**¿Volverá antes de la/las …?** *bolbera antes deh la/las*
We'll be here until …	**Estaremos aquí hasta la/las …** *estaremos akee asta la/las*

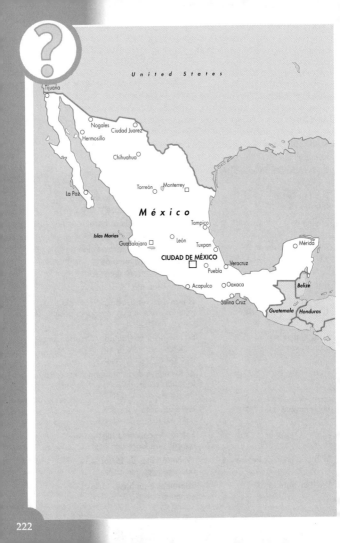

223

Quick reference Referencia rápida

Good morning.	**Buenos días.** _bwenos deeyas_
Good afternoon.	**Buenas tardes.** _bwenas tardes_
Good evening.	**Buenas tardes/noches.** _bwenas tardes/noches_

Hello.	**Hola.** _ola_
Good-bye.	**Adiós.** _adeeyos_
Excuse me (getting attention).	**Disculpe.** _deeskoolpeh_
Pardon?	**¿Perdón?** _perdon_
Sorry!	**¡Lo siento!** _lo seeyento_
Please.	**Por favor.** _por fabor_
Thank you.	**Gracias.** _graseeas_
Do you speak English?	**¿Habla usted inglés?** _abla oosteth eengles_
I don't understand.	**No entiendo.** _no enteeyendo_
Where is …?	**¿Dónde está …?** _dondeh esta_
Where are the toilets/bathrooms?	**¿Dónde están los baños?** _dondeh estan los baños_

Emergency Emergencia

Help!	**¡Socorro! [¡Ayúdenme!]** _sokorro [ayoodenmeh]_
Go away!	**¡Váyase!** _bayaseh_
Leave me alone!	**¡Déjeme tranquilo(-a)!** _dekhemeh trankeelo(-a)_
Call the police!	**¡Llamen a la policía!** _l-yamen a la poleeseeya_
Stop thief!	**¡Cojan al ladrón!** _kokhan al ladron_
Get a doctor!	**¡Traigan un doctor!** _traeegan oon doktor_
Fire!	**¡Incendio!** _eensendeeo_
I'm ill.	**Estoy enfermo(-a).** _estoy enfermo(-a)_
I'm lost.	**Estoy perdido(-a).** _estoy perdeedo(-a)_
Can you help me?	**¿Puede ayudarme?** _pwedeh ayoodarmeh_